Table of Contents

Foreword

This report on the trends now shaping future terrorism is the second report in the Proteus Trends Series. This and subsequent reports identify trends that are shaping the future and analyze their impact on specific topics. This effort is designed to assist operational and strategic analysts, planners, and decision makers across the various communities within government and the private sector in scanning the horizon and defining the future environment in order to systematically identify discrete threats and capitalize on hidden opportunities.

Dr. Marv Cetron and Mr. Owen Davies, with the assistance of their associates at Forecasting International, developed this report. Building on Forecasting International's *55 Trends*, they have identified specific implications of those trends in the area of future terrorism. Incisive commentary provided throughout by a panel of subject matter experts adds to the richness of their analysis. This report provides security officials, agencies, think tanks, and academic institutions from across government and the private sector with keen insights into key trends that will continue to influence terrorism and counter terrorism.

Proteus USA is pleased to sponsor this seminal work.

Bill Waddell
Chair, Proteus USA

Preface

This study can be viewed as a response to a call sounded by Dr. Thomas Mahnken at the Forces Transformation Chairs Meeting in February 2007. Dr. Mahnken, Deputy Assistant Secretary of Defense for Policy Planning, pointed out that the United States responds to shocks most successfully when it has already recognized and responded to the trends from which they emerge. It is less successful when those trends have gone unidentified or when no effective response to them has been mounted. One case where the trends were not recognized in time was the terrorist attacks of September 11, 2001. It thus becomes necessary, Dr. Mahnken concluded, to develop a means of identifying trends and responding to them before acute challenges emerge.

Forecasting International (FI) heartily agreed. FI is one of the world's premier futurist organizations. It specializes in the analysis of trends. To our knowledge, we were the first such organization to apply trend analysis to the problem of terrorism. We did so with considerable success.

FI began its work on terrorism in 1994, when it managed the 4th Annual Defense Worldwide Combating Terrorism Conference for the Pentagon. Its conference report, *Terror 2000: The Future Face of Terror*, accurately predicted the rise of Muslim extremism as a source of terror, the terrorists' growing taste for mass bloodletting, the use of coordinated attacks on distant targets, and even an assault on the Pentagon using a hijacked airplane (omitted at the request of the State Department). Since then, FI has often studied terrorist issues for both government and private industry.

In the current report, FI examines the future of international terrorism. In this effort, it has been assisted by more than fifty of the world's premier authorities in the fields of antiterrorism, intelligence, security, and policing. This expert panel included members of the intelligence community, specialists from the U.S. government and military, security consultants, think tank staffers, forecasters, university professors, and local police officials. Most came from the United States, but Australia, Canada, Ireland, New Zealand, Russia, and Switzerland also were represented. Several participants chose to remain anonymous, owing to their sensitive positions in government and the military. One contributor is a private citizen of whom we know nothing, save that he responded to a magazine article we had published and provided some interesting thoughts.

This typifies our approach in this work. We have tried to be inclusive, rather than exclusive. FI's own views, and those of certain experts, dominate the report, but some have been included—often in the appendices—specifically because they diverge from the mainstream and might provide useful insights or novel ideas that would not arise from more conventional sources. We have tried to omit nothing that should at least be considered. Many of the ideas presented here deserve to be seen at the highest levels of government.

Key findings from our panel of experts include:

- International terrorism will grow as veterans of the Iraq War return to their native lands, train sympathizers in the tactics of terror, and spread out across the world.

- Among the Western lands, Britain and France (owing to their large Muslim populations) and the United States will be at the greatest risk of attack, in that order. Further attacks on the scale of 9/11 are to be expected in all three countries over the range of five to ten years.

- These attacks will combine mass bloodshed and economic impact. Now that the World Trade Center is gone, Grand Central Station at rush hour would be an obvious target for Manhattan. Coordinated attacks on shopping malls, tourist attractions, casinos, schools, churches and synagogues, and sports events also are possible. For details, see Appendix A, FI's study of potential terrorist targets based on interviews with serving and retired military officers, counterterrorism specialists, futurists, and hospitality executives. (These last were included because hotels and restaurants are particularly soft targets and have proved to be among the favorite targets of terrorists around the world.) In Appendix B, noted forecaster Joseph Coates provides an alternative view and a theoretical framework for the analysis of likely targets for terrorism.

- New technologies will continue to change antiterrorism. Most will be in their early stages of development five years from now, but will advance rapidly over the following decade. These include:

    - Tiny sensors that can be scattered to detect explosives or biological warfare agents in potential target areas

    - Conversion software that allows investigators to use incompatible databases seamlessly

    - Artificial Intelligence, expert systems, and data mining software that can recognize patterns in intelligence derived from different sources and warn of a terrorist event in preparation

    - Software that can recognize suspicious activities viewed by networks of surveillance cameras

    - Facial recognition software, which already is being integrated with passive video surveillance systems to identify wanted subjects in a crowd

    - Computerized training for antiterrorism operations similar to the military's Battlefield 2 "game" simulator

- Technology is likely to change the nature of terrorism as well. Like their government adversaries, terrorists may adopt computer simulations to train recruits in tactics, strategy, and technology. However, other effects of technology are more difficult to predict. In general, as societies become increasingly dependent on high-tech for manufacturing, services, personal activities and military operations, they develop new vulnerabilities. While most terrorist attacks will be designed around old-fashioned bombs and bullets, others will be designed to exploit technological weaknesses for economic and logistical impact.

Acknowledgments

For invaluable assistance in preparing this study, we wish to thank the members of our panel of experts. Without their many contributions, this work would have been incomparably less useful.

Note: Several participants who contributed to this work have used noms de guerre or have chosen to remain anonymous because of their current, active positions in government or the military.

Our panel:

Matt Armstrong, MPD, Independent Analyst, MountainRunner blog

Cynthia E. Ayers, NSA, Visiting Professor of Information Superiority, Center for Strategic Leadership, U.S. Army War College

David A. Bray, Strategic Planning and Implementation Fellow, Centers for Disease Control and Prevention; formerly IT Chief and Informatics Strategist, Bioterrorism Program, Centers for Disease Control

Brian Bruh, CEO, Brian Bruh Associates; former director of the Defense Criminal Investigative Service and the Financial Crimes Enforcement Networkt

Dr. David W. Chobar, Associate Professor of Education, Morningside College

John C. Coale, technical director, Department of Defense; adjunct faculty, American Military University

Joseph F. Coates, Consulting Futurist

Sean S. Costigan, Director, Strategic Initiatives (International Relations and Security Network, ETH Zurich); Visiting Scholar, The New School, New York, NY

R. Kim Cragin, Associate International Policy Analyst, RAND

Lieutenant Colonel O. Shawn Cupp, U.S. Army (Ret.), Assistant Professor, U.S. Army Command and General Staff College, Department of Logistics and Resource Operations

Colonel Jonathan Czarnecki, U.S. Army (Ret.), U.S. Naval War College

Craig Fraser, Director of Management Services, Police Executive Research Forum

Peter K. Forster, Ph.D., Associate Director, International & Homeland Security Outreach Initiatives; Lecturer, Department of Political Science, Penn State University

Commander Clint Goodwin, U.S. Navy (Ret.), Associate Professor Emeritus, National Defense Intelligence College - Part-time Graduate Intelligence Program for the Reserves

Dr. William Halal, Professor of Management Science, George Washington University; President, TechCast, LLC

Gunnar Henrioulle, PO Box 9289, South Lake Tahoe, CA 96158

Donald Hodge, Deputy National Intelligence Officer for Warning, National Intelligence Council (NIC), ODNI

Bruce Hoffman, Professor, Security Studies Program, School of Foreign Service, Georgetown University

Commander Lloyd Hoffman, Jr., U.S. Navy (Ret.), Department of Political Science, West Virginia University

John Jackson, Strategist, Strategic Planning Unit, Houston Police Department

Brian Michael Jenkins, Senior Advisor, Rand Corporation; Professor, Pardee RAND Graduate School

James Kadtke, Professor, National Defense University

Lieuenant General Oleg Kalugin (Ret.), Center for Counterintelligence and Security Studies; formerly Director, Foreign Counterintelligence Directorate, KGB

John R. Kapinos, Strategic Planner, Fairfax (VA) Police Department

Arnold Keiser, President, Organization for International Cooperation

Louis Kriesberg, Maxwell Professor Emeritus of Social Conflict Studies, Maxwell School of Citizenship and Public Affairs, Syracuse University

Bruce LaDuke, founder, Integral Futuring Dialog Center

Daniel Lanotte, Senior Enterprise Architect, SI International

Dr. David R. Leffler, Executive Director, Center for Advanced Military Science at the Institute of Science, Technology and Public Policy

Dr. Thomas Mahnken, Deputy Assistant Secretary of Defense for Policy Planning, Office of the Secretary of Defense

Major Kathleen M. Meilahn, (USAFR) Analyst, U.S. Central Command. NB: The views Ms. Meilahn expresses below are strictly her own, not those of her organization.

John M. Miller, PhD, JD, Assistant Professor – Statistics, Department of Economics and International Business, College of Business Administration, Sam Houston State University

Dr. Stephen Millett, thought leader and manager of technology forecasts

Jerry Needle, Director of Research, International Association of Chiefs of Police

Dr. William Nolte, School of Public Policy, University of Maryland

E.T. Nozawa, Achtech, Ltd.

Jack Oatmon, Collection, Analysis, and Prosecution Specialist

Deborah Osborne, Analyst and Futurist

Peter Probst, Senior Partner, National Security Associates Worldwide

Angel Rabasa, Senior Political Scientist, RAND Corporation

Shane Roberts, Policy Advisor, Futures and Forecasting, Science and Technology Policy Division, Public Safety Canada

T. Irene Sanders, Executive Director, Washington Center for Complexity and Public Policy

David Shtulman, Director of Agency Endowments, United Jewish Federation Foundation

Jack Smith, Office of the National Science Advisor; Science and Technology Foresight, Ottawa, CA

Rick Smyre, President, Communities of the Future

David Pearce Snyder, Consulting Futurist and Principal Partner, The Snyder Family Enterprise

Stephen F. Steele, Ph.D., Institute for the Future, Anne Arundel Community College

Patrick D. Sullivan, Manager, Joint Capabilities Assessment, Boeing Integrated Defense Systems

Andrew T.H. Tan, Associate Professor, Social Science and International Studies, University of New South Wales

Marc A. Viola, Innovation Executive, The Vitruvian Center for Innovative Intelligence

David J. Weinstein, Senior Intelligence Officer for Warning, JCS/J2

Fulton Wilcox, Colts Neck Solutions, LLC

Peter A. Wilson, Senior Defense Research Analyst, RAND Corporation

Colonel William Wimbish, U.S. Army (Ret.), Proteus USA, U.S. Army War College

Steve A. Young, Director of Collection, Institute for the Study of Violent Groups, Sam Houston State University, Huntsville

Alan Youngs, Esq., Retired Division Chief, Lakewood Colorado Police Department

Professor Don Zettlemoyer, Justice and Safety Institute (JASI), Penn State University

Forecasting International's project staff for this work included:

Dr. Marvin J. Cetron, President, Forecasting International

Dr. Edward Cetron, Consultant

Justin Cetron, Information Technology Analyst, Forecasting International

Owen Davies, Researcher/Writer, Forecasting International

INTRODUCTION

In his introductory lecture at the Forces Transformation Chairs Meeting in February 2007, Dr. Thomas Mahnken pointed out a weakness in America's response to challenges. Dr. Mahnken, Deputy Assistant Secretary of Defense for Policy Planning, pointed out that challenges come in two forms, long-term trends and abrupt shocks. Shocks, such as the fall of the Berlin Wall, tend to be unanticipated and highly disruptive. Yet, in hindsight it is clear that most shocks are the product of long-term trends. The United States, Mahnken observed, has been most successful in responding to shocks when it has already begun to adapt to the long-term trends from which they emerged. Two examples were Pearl Harbor and the launch of Sputnik. It has responded less successfully when the trends were unrecognized or no adequate response to them had been mounted. The 9/11 terrorist attacks were such a case, Dr. Mahnken noted. Thus, it is necessary to develop some means of identifying key trends and incorporating them into our long-term planning.

This document can be seen as a response to Dr. Mahnken's call. At Forecasting International (FI), trend analysis is our stock in trade. We have often applied this skill to the needs of government. To the best of our knowledge, we were the first organization to apply the study of trends to the problem of terrorism.

For nearly half a century, Forecasting International (FI) has conducted an ongoing study of the forces changing our world. We have anticipated where those forces would lead in fields ranging from the tourist industry to the stability of nations and for clients from General Motors to the Central Intelligence Agency and the White House. On the whole, we have been reasonably successful. Not long ago, an industrial association re-examined a forecast FI had prepared for them a decade earlier. They found that of more than 100 specific predictions in the report, no fewer than 95 percent had proved to be correct.

In 1994, we turned our attention to the future of terrorism. At the request of SO/LIC, the Office of the Assistant Secretary of Defense for Special Operations and Low-Intensity Conflict, we organized and managed the 4th Annual Defense Worldwide Combating Terrorism Conference. Unlike previous conference managers, whose work had concentrated on the "state of play" in the world of terrorists and the officials charged with thwarting their schemes, FI was asked to anticipate how terrorism would change in the years ahead. Again, our work proved to be accurate, both in its broad outlines and in many details.

The common wisdom then held that terrorism was quickly becoming obsolete as rogue states learned that sponsoring terrorist attacks cost them far more than any possible benefit was worth. Sponsorship of the Lockerbie bombing had subjected Libya to an air and arms embargo, a ban on some needed oil equipment, and the loss of financial assets. Iraq, long a patron of terrorism, had finally exhausted the world's patience by invading Kuwait and had lost a precedent-setting war. With those lessons in mind, no state would be likely to sponsor future terrorist acts, and without that support, terrorism itself would dry up.

Our conference report, titled Terror 2000: The Future Face of Terror, presented a different view. It said that terrorism would grow more common, not less so. Future terrorist incidents would not be sponsored by states, but increasingly by Muslim extremists motivated by a bitter hatred of the West in general and America in particular. And it would be designed to cause bloodshed on a level never before seen, even at the cost of the terrorists' own deaths. At the time, these predictions were so far from the professional consensus that even many of the subject specialists participating in the conference rejected them. They were far better accepted by the generalist forecasters that FI had recruited to the study. In the end, they all proved to be correct.

Some specific forecasts anticipated the September 11 attack with startling accuracy. The report foresaw the execution of a second, much more successful, attack on the World Trade Towers. It predicted the success of simultaneous assaults on widely separated targets. (This capacity also was displayed in the embassy bombings of 1998.) It even foretold the deliberate crash of an airplane into the Pentagon. That last was deleted from the report at the request of the State Department, which feared that it could give terrorists a valuable idea they might not conceive on their own.

Many of the analyses and recommendations originating in *Terror 2000* were adopted with little change in later studies of terrorism. The reports of both the Commission on National Security (the Bremer Commission) in 1998 and the National Commission on Terrorism (the Rudman Commission) in 2000 relied heavily on our work. Even the 9/11 Commission used substantial portions of these three studies, including many that first appeared in the *Terror 2000* report.

Since *Terror 2000*, the future of terrorism has been a continuing interest for Forecasting International (FI). We have carried out a number of studies in this field for both private industry and government clients.

In this study, FI again has examined the future of international terrorism. This work looks at 55 important trends that FI tracks, and projects their influence on the future of terrorism. Some of the trends proved to be extremely important, others less so. Some will encourage future terrorism and permit no useful response from the target nations; these include, for example, rapid population growth in the countries of origin and the urbanization of the developing world. Other trends offer opportunities for intervention; of these, the continuing rise of technology is the most prominent.

In this work we have had the invaluable help of more than fifty of the world's most prominent and far-ranging subject specialists. Included in our panel of experts are:

- Leading experts on terrorism such as Donald Hodge, Deputy National Intelligence Officer for Warning, National Intelligence Council (NIC), ODNI; Lieutenant General Oleg Kalugin (Ret.), now of the Center for Counterintelligence and Security Studies and formerly head of the Foreign Counterintelligence Directorate of the KGB; Peter Probst, Senior Partner, National Security Associates Worldwide; and Brian Bruh, CEO of Brian Bruh Associates and former director of the Treasury Department's Financial Crimes Enforcement Network

- Active government antiterrorism specialists such as David A. Bray, Strategic Planning and Implementation Fellow at the Centers for Disease Control and Prevention (CDC) and formerly IT Chief and Informatics Strategist of CDC's bioterrorism program; Major Kathleen M. Meilahn, USAFR, CTR CENTCOM J2-PR (J5 IMA) and David J. Weinstein, Senior Intelligence Officer for Warning, JCS/J2

- Joseph F. Coates, and David Pearce Snyder,consulting futurists; William Halal, founder of TechCast; Dr. Stephen Millett, thought leader and manager of technology forecasts; T. Irene Sanders, Executive Director at the Washington Center for Complexity and Public Policy; and Rick Smyre, President of Communities of the Future; Stephen F. Steele, Ph.D., President of the Institute for the Future

- Think-tank luminaries such as Brian Michael Jenkins, Senior Advisor at the Rand Corporation and professor at the Pardee RAND Graduate School; R. Kim Cragin, Associate International Policy Analyst at RAND; and Angel Rabasa, Senior Political Scientist, RAND Corporation

- Military educators Cynthia E. Ayers, NSA Visiting Professor of Information Superiority Center for Strategic Leadership, U.S. Army War College; Lieutenant Colonel O. Shawn Cupp, USA (Ret.),

Assistant Professor with the U.S. Army Command and General Staff College, Department of Logistics and Resource Operations; Colonel Jonathan Czarnecki, USA (Ret.), Naval War College; Commander Clint Goodwin, USN (Ret.), Associate Professor Emeritus at the National Defense Intelligence College; and Professor James Kadtke of the National Defense University

- Ranking academics such as David W. Chobar, of Morningside College; Sean S. Costigan, Director of Strategic Initiatives, International Relations and Security Network, ETH Zurich, and Visiting Scholar at The New School; Peter K. Forster, Ph.D., Associate Director, International & Homeland Security Outreach Initiatives; Lecturer, Department of Political Science, Penn State University; Louis Kriesberg, Maxwell Professor Emeritus of Social Conflict Studies at the Maxwell School of Citizenship and Public Affairs, Syracuse University, and Dr. William Nolte of the University of Maryland School of Public Policy

- And policing experts John Jackson, strategist with the Houston Police Department Strategic Planning Unit; strategic planner John R. Kapinos of the Fairfax (VA) Police Department; Deborah Osborne, analyst and futurist; Alan Youngs, Esq., retired Division Chief of the Lakewood (CO) Police Department; and Professor Don Zettlemoyer of the Justice and Safety Institute (JASI) at Penn State University

These participants represent a breadth and depth of experience that have been available to few other studies of terrorism. Without exception, they devoted more of their time, attention, and expertise to this work than we would have dared to ask. Their assistance has proved to be remarkably valuable. Much of this report is built around their invaluable comments, which frequently provided insights that the FI staff could not have reached on our own. Here are just a few examples:

David Bray of CDC may have identified a workable approach to solving one of the most pressing problems of the post-9/11 era, how to provide for both protection and privacy. He writes,

> *Consider an example where public key encryption allows the masking of collected information from human eyes, but not from processing and linking to other sources of information by trusted information systems themselves. By use of encryption, this masking of collected information provides only "de-identified" information (with personal identifiers removed) to government workers (Straub and Collins, 1990; Rindfleisch, 1997). However, the trusted information systems themselves can access personal identifiers and link different sources of information.*

> *Ideally, these trusted information systems would work non-stop to sort through and identify suspicious patterns of information. Examples of suspicious patterns include an individual living in a large city purchasing a large quantity of castor beans (which can be used to make ricin toxin) with no discernable legitimate purpose, or regular records of large bank deposits from an unclear source of questionable origin. If the patterns are extremely suspicious, the information systems can present the suspicious patterns (de-identified, with personal identifiers removed) to government workers. These workers then decide whether to convene an expedited court hearing to judge if the encrypted personal identifiers associated with the information should be unlocked. Lawyers for a defense—in the absence of the unknown individual(s)—and a prosecution, present opposing sides to the best of their ability. A federal judge decides whether the de-identified pattern of activities provides sufficient cause to lift the freedom of privacy for the collected information. Should the judge rule that the de-identified pattern of information is suspicious enough to merit unlocking the protected identities, an electronic key issued by the court will permit this action. Similar to issuing a warrant, such an approach maintains*

anonymity of collected information unless a court hearing finds probable cause and temporarily removes this freedom."

From William Nolte at the University of Maryland came this observation:

[The transition from command-and-control organizational structures to information-based networks] strikes me as a top issue. Our corporate structures (public and private) reflect late 19th century efforts to deal, inter alia, with an information revolution of that time. In larger and larger companies, how did you filter information to the top while nevertheless ensuring that critical information did not get filtered out? Simple. You created layers of middle management where the prime responsibility was to sort out things that upper management didn't need to be bothered with from things upper management had to know about. As Hurricane Katrina demonstrated, we now have industrial age corporate structures trying to operate this repetitive process (scan, review, filter, transmit) in an age when the information environment is moving at Moore's Law speed, or something close thereto.

At FI, we can only agree. Government functions, including intelligence and security services, have always been built on the command-and-control model. For an age of high-tech communications and threats that often can be recognized only at late stages and from multiple data sources, transitioning to an information-based network model is an urgent necessity. This will be particularly difficult for the military.

LTC (Ret.) O. Shawn Cupp at the U.S. Army Command and General Staff College pointed out:

Agriculture is one of the easiest sectors of the U.S. economy to disrupt, and its disruption could have catastrophic consequences for the U.S. and world economies. Agriculture in the U.S. accounts for 13 percent of the current Gross Domestic Product (GDP) and provides employment for 15 percent of the population. It produces high-quality, cheap, plentiful food for domestic consumption and accounts for more than $50 billion in exports. The likelihood of terrorist acts interrupting the production, processing, and distribution of agricultural products is high.

He adds that some 70 percent of the cattle finished for slaughter in the United States are kept in an area of just 200 square miles. An outbreak of foot-and-mouth or mad cow disease would rapidly spread through this region, with devastating economic results.

Finally, Donald Hodge, Deputy National Intelligence Officer for Warning, National Intelligence Council (NIC), ODNI, provided this bracing reminder:

From a law enforcement perspective, this report is focused almost entirely on the criminal type threat. It needs to consider trends in the nation state espionage threat. The U.S. now faces more than just one or two (e.g., Russia and China) intelligence threats. Many other nation states will be targeting the U.S. for intelligence collection. Both the breadth and scope of the foreign intelligence and espionage threat to the U.S. will continue to grow. Terrorist groups will also expand their intelligence collection activities."

These and many other comments and recommendations from our panel of experts give this report a perspective that could not have been achieved without their many contributions. If this report were to accomplish nothing else, bringing the views of these diverse specialists together in one place where they can receive the attention they merit would justify our effort. However, we believe the result is more than the sum of these useful parts.

BACKGROUND

About fifteen years ago, Forecasting International condensed its decades of work into a list of trends it had found operating in the world. This list has been updated periodically. Some trends have been dropped as they matured and played themselves out, while others have been added as they arose or were recognized. The most recent total revision took place in the summer of 2007. This latest edition of FI's periodic trend report tracks 55 trends in eight major areas: economics and society; values, concerns, and lifestyles; energy; the environment; technology; the labor force and work; management; and institutions. Some of these trends examine different aspects of very wide-ranging developments, such as demographics or the changing energy picture. These may overlap to some degree, but for our purposes it is necessary that each trend stand on its own. Many of these trends can be seen in the world at large; a few are limited to the United States. Not all of them have obvious applications to terrorism and the battle against it, but many do. All 55 trends are examined in detail toward the end of this report.

For the current study, the FI staff reconsidered the trends and analyzed their probable influence on the future of terrorism. Our findings were appended to each trend, and the resulting document was sent to sixty-four respected terrorism experts and forecasters, as well as several academics with whom we had worked in the past. We also provided Web links to several of our previous writings about terrorism to ensure that the respondents would have a common background from which to work. No fewer than forty-five members of this original panel offered comments for the study. Several more candidates were suggested by the first group of experts; these additions were contacted as well, and most also chose to participate in the study.

We asked this panel of experts to examine the trends, pick out the ten that they felt would be most important to the future of terrorism, and evaluate their likely effects. Of course, we also invited them not to limit themselves to those ten but to make comments wherever they had useful observations to share. This effort was the source of the comments presented herein. Many participants also provided comments that did not deal specifically with the trends, but which clearly deserved the readers' attention. These items are included as Appendix C.

BASELINE TRENDS IN TERRORISM

At Forecasting International, we see three major changes coming in the years ahead. These trends were among the documents supplied to study participants. They will fundamentally alter both the terrorist threat to the United States and the terms on which we must fight the "war" on terror: The terrorists will continue to gain more fighters. They will gain far more destructive weapons. And they will gain the kind of legitimacy that could make them even more difficult to stop.

TERRORIST RANKS ARE GROWING

In deposing the Taliban regime in Afghanistan and depriving Al Qaeda of a safe haven there, the United States struck a major blow against the terrorist movement as it existed five years ago. Yet by failing to follow up on that success effectively, we have squandered much of the benefit that should have been gained from that first step in the counterterrorist war. And by invading Iraq, we have supplied Al Qaeda and its sympathizers with a cause around which to rally their existing forces and recruit new ones. As a result, the terrorist movement is now growing stronger, not weaker.

There is ample evidence to support this belief. Up to 30,000 foreign fighters are believed to have gravitated toward Iraq, where they are now gaining contacts and experience that will serve them well in future campaigns against the United States and its allies. In this, Iraq is now serving the function that Afghanistan provided in the 1980s. The war in Iraq is building a skilled and disciplined terrorist cadre that will fan out across the world.

Saudi Arabia even has been forced to build a major program aimed at keeping young men from going to Iraq. The Wahhid, the dominant Muslim sect in that country, is teaching that joining the *jihad* is the Muslim man's second-greatest duty, after going to Mecca. They must fight in Iraq, then come back and be available to fight for fundamentalist Islam in Saudi Arabia. Thus are terrorist cells built, independent of Al Qaeda but firmly committed to its goals and methods.

Similar developments are seen elsewhere. The Madrid railway bombings were carried out by a semi-autonomous terrorist cell based in Morocco whose members cited the invasion of Iraq as one inspiration for their efforts. In Britain, the London subway bombings in 2005 were the work of a small, independent band of British citizens inspired by Al Qaeda. In France and Australia, authorities have arrested a number of Western converts to Islam, many of whom are believed to have joined Al Qaeda or associated organizations since the invasion of Afghanistan. A report by French intelligence officials estimated that there were between 30,000 and 50,000 such converts, and by implication potential terrorists, in that country alone.

It is clear that they have considerable sympathy among Europe's Muslim population. The French riots of October and November 2005 affected at least twenty cities in that country, resulting in 2,888 arrests, and touched off lesser violence in Belgium, Denmark, Greece, the Netherlands, Spain, and even Switzerland. More such events are all but inevitable. Saudi Arabia funds an extensive network of religious schools, from New York to Pakistan. Saudi authorities have admitted that as much as 10 percent of the curriculum in those schools contains material preaching hatred of other religions, the West, and the United States. At times, those schools even have coordinated their sermons to deliver consistent anti-Western messages in far-distant locales. In a preliminary study during 2003, Dr. Borik Zadeh, of Battelle Institute, found that mosques in Ohio, London, Frankfurt, and Paris were delivering virtually identical sermons, the key message of which was an endorsement of global war against the West. In Pakistan, where Saudi Arabia's *Wahhabi* movement supports thousands of *madrassas*, the call to *jihad* is even more enthusiastic. Those schools are recruiting extremists, sending money and fighters to Iraq, and systematically building an extremist cadre that will pursue the battle against the West for generations to come. They are most dangerous in their target areas: Saudi Arabia, Australia, Europe, and to a much lesser extent the United States, which is protected by distance and the much smaller size of its Muslim population. Individuals from Europe and the Middle East are absorbing the extremist creed, going to Iraq and learning to fight, and returning to their own countries. France, Denmark, Saudi Arabia, and too many other lands now are home to revolutionaries with all the rights of citizens. Identifying these home-grown, foreign-trained terrorists will be one of the most difficult tasks for antiterrorist forces in the years ahead. Although the United States is relatively well protected against extremist fighters schooled in the Iraq War, many law enforcement officials fear that it could face a large and dangerous pool of home-grown Muslim terrorists. As the crack cocaine epidemic grew out of control in American cities during the 1980s and '90s, many young men were swept into the drug trade. They became well-armed, street-savvy, and prone to use violence and intimidation as everyday business tools. Many thousands of these street warriors ended up in prison for lengthy terms. While there, many young African-American inmates have converted to Islam. Some will lead more peaceful, positive lives as a result of this religious experience. Yet many other socially disconnected Muslim converts, very likely including the most violent, may be ripe candidates for the *jihadi* cause. Over the next decade or so, many of these prisoners will complete their terms and be paroled back into a society that offers them little future. Those who do not join terrorist cells out of belief could do so merely to gain a modest income. It is this idea, that potentially thousands of new *jihadis*, experienced with weapons and street combat and with little love for or stake in American society, could soon be out on the streets that so worries law enforcement officials. These hardened foot-soldiers could form an effective home-grown army for Al Qaeda and similar groups.

This does not guarantee that the United States soon will face a problem with native-born terrorists. However, both Britain and Australia have found that a minority of prison converts to Islam do accept the anti-Western creed and the call to *jihad*. It would not take many such recruits to cause major trouble in the years to come.

THEY WILL GAIN ACCESS TO WEAPONS OF MASS DESTRUCTION

At FI, we take it for granted that the elite among tomorrow's terrorists will have more than plastic explosives with which to make their point. They will have nuclear weapons. Dr. Abdul Qadeer Khan ensured that when he gave Pakistan what most extremists regard as an "Islamic bomb" and then spread the plans far and wide. Although American policy is to pillory Iran as a nuclear threat while ignoring the much worse threat from Pakistan, Islamabad's atomic weapons are in the hands of a fragile government surrounded by extremists. Of the two countries, Pakistan represents by far the greater opportunity for would-be nuclear terrorists. If Muslim extremists cannot lay hands on a stolen weapon from the former Soviet Union, they soon may be able to obtain them from Islamabad. Tehran remains a more distant possibility.

This is not a guarantee that terrorists will use nuclear weapons against the United States or other potential targets. The fabled "suitcase nuke" may be a terrorist's dream weapon, but it is technology that no one who would share is likely to possess. Instead, Al Qaeda or some future equivalent will receive bulky, low-yield devices that will be much harder to smuggle to their target. They may well try anyway, but it will be some time before this becomes an immediate possibility. In that interval our detection and intercept capability should improve significantly.

Other weapons of mass destruction (WMD) will be much more practical. If mushroom clouds do not appear over Manhattan or Washington DC, clouds of toxic gas or weaponized bacteria easily could. As Aum Shinrikyo, the Japanese cult that released sarin gas in the Tokyo subways in 1995, demonstrated, chemical weapons are available to essentially anyone who wants them badly enough to put in a modest effort to make them. Biological weapons suitable for military use take considerably more effort to prepare, but there are practical purposes for which all-out weaponization is not required. And even if radiological dirty bombs are not traditionally considered WMD, they could be equally disruptive if employed with skill in a major city. The discussion of possible targets and methods of attack later in this report examines several such scenarios.

THEY WILL GAIN LEGITIMACY

There is another way to obtain WMD, however, and it seems increasingly likely. Rather than begging nuclear weapons from a sympathetic government, Al Qaeda or its spinoffs may soon become the government in any of perhaps a dozen countries. Wherever secular government is weak, it might easily be replaced by a much stronger and more virulently anti-American theocracy with leaders drawn straight from the terrorist movement. Candidates for a terrorist take-over include Iran (where the job already is half-done), Iraq, Sudan, Syria, Pakistan, Afghanistan, the "Stans" of the former Soviet Union, and perhaps the Gulf states. However, our own choice for "most likely to undergo a religious revolution" is Saudi Arabia, where the royal family has supported the extremist *Wahhabi* sect for some 200 years. At FI, we will not be surprised if Osama bin Laden eventually returns to his homeland and sets up an Islamist government in Riyadh, with dire consequences for the U.S. economy and for national security.

There is precedent for the transformation from terrorist movement to legitimate government. In Russia, the Bolsheviks killed the Czar, took over the government, and established a regime that would survive for seven decades and became one of the world's most powerful nations. In Palestine, Yassir Arafat made the transition from guerilla leader to something resembling a senior statesman, only to be replaced by Hamas, which remains an active terrorist organization. On the other side of Jerusalem, the Irgun Svi, Haganah, and Stern Gang were terrorists as bloody as any Palestine has ever produced; yet they supplied Israel with Prime Ministers, senior politicians, and statesmen for more than 30 years. Bin Laden and his senior advisors can be expected to attempt to enter mainstream politics in much the same way. FI believes they could be successful.

There is ample precedent for this as well among Muslim extremist organizations. In Palestine and other parts of the Middle East, Fatah, Hamas, and Hezbollah provide the kind of social safety net that governments in the region do not. Food, clothing, education, shelter, jobs, and medical assistance all flow from these organizations, bringing them a kind of legitimacy that terrorism, however widely admired, never could. This service, combined with the corruption of the Fatah government, was the primary reason Palestinians voted Hamas into power, not the organization's intransigent rejection of Israel's existence.

This is not the last time terrorists will ascend to government leadership. At Forecasting International, we see little chance that Iraq will make a successful transition to peaceful democracy. When the United States withdraws its forces, the current unrest is likely to broaden into an all-out civil war between the Sunnis and Shiites. Although the Sunnis are heavily outnumbered, they have a near-monopoly on weapons and military experience. In the end, they will recapture control of the country, returning the Ba'ath Party to power.

There is worse to come. Within five years, and probably sooner, Al Qaeda will begin this same transition. Its practical, day-to-day contributions to the lives of ordinary citizens will provide a foundation for future political activities. Unlike any government in the Muslim world, in almost any country bin Laden already has the sympathy of a majority of the population and the allegiance of many.

Events in Pakistan following the death of Benazir Bhutto raise special concerns for that country as well. The loss of Bhutto deprived Pakistan of its most prominent advocate for democracy. Her son, Bilawal Zardari, appears committed to democracy, but he will not become a significant force in Pakistani politics—a field in which he has no experience—for at least five years. In the interim, his father, Asif Ali Zardari, will head the Pakistan People's Party. He is a divisive figure with a widespread reputation for corruption, distrusted even by many of the party faithful. This seems a poor foundation for any attempt to carry on Benazir's pro-democracy efforts.

Pakistan's tribal areas already are controlled by the Taliban and other extremist forces. The nation's military seems heavily influenced by sympathizers of radical Islam, and there is room to wonder about its intelligence service. Large majorities of the Pakistani people loathe both the United States and the Musharraf government. In this context, the possibility that the Taliban could eventually win control of Pakistan, or that the country could end up with no one effectively in charge, seems notably greater than it did while Benazir Bhutto counterbalanced radicalism with democratic populism.

If the terrorists do manage to gain control of a functional country—and at FI we are more inclined to think "when"—the nature of the game changes radically. When terrorists become the government, all terrorism is state-sponsored. The budget available to fund terrorist activities grows many-fold. The nation's laboratories and scientists become available to develop chemical, biological, and even nuclear weapons for the cause. If the country is Pakistan, nuclear devices already are available. Preventing terrorists from gaining control over those weapons is one of the most pressing necessities now facing the counterterrorist community.

Even in the absence of WMD, by gaining the status of a national government, radical Islamists will present the United States and its allies with a difficult problem. We have seen in Afghanistan the benefits that simply having a sovereign haven provides groups such as Al Qaeda. A more stable, productive nation with a government committed to violent extremism could be considerably more troublesome than Afghanistan ever was. Western leaders must develop a workable strategy to counter the rise of such a regime before the need arises, not under the pressure of immediate necessity.

LESSONS FROM THIS STUDY

That was the background against which we at Forecasting International evaluated the trends in preparation for this study: three trends, all specific to terrorism.

TEN MOST IMPORTANT TRENDS FOR THE FUTURE OF TERRORISM

Relatively few of our panelists rank-ordered the ten trends they believed would be most important for terrorism. Many simply picked out ten trends they felt deserved attention. Others provided comments for many more than ten without identifying the most significant. Some responded to only two or three trends. And of the participants who did suggest an order of importance for their selections, no two agreed with any of the others about the relative position of their choices.

Bringing order out of this chaos has required some creativity. The list below is arranged according to the average rank assigned by the participants, with some extra weight accorded to trends that were picked the most often. The first three trends in the list were reasonably clear. After that, there was less agreement. The result is not the order Forecasting International's staff would have chosen. Neither does it match the order established by any of the participants. However, we believe that it represents a rough consensus of the panelists' views as fairly as possible.

With that preface, here are the top ten most important trends for terrorism, in approximate descending order of significance. Evidence for each trend and other details are available in the next section of this report.

---

1 – THE ECONOMY OF THE DEVELOPED WORLD IS ON PATH TO GROW FOR AT LEAST THE NEXT FIVE YEARS. (TREND 1)

- The U.S. economy has been expanding continuously, though often weakly, since the fourth quarter of 2001. GDP grew by 3.2 percent in 2006, slowing to 2.6 percent in the fourth quarter of the year and just 0.7 percent in the first quarter of 2007. The consensus forecast calls for a rebound to 2.8 percent growth from the second quarter through year's end, but this depends heavily on the course of private consumption.

- Job creation and unemployment numbers are puzzling. Unemployment rates hovered around 4.5 percent in the first half of 2007, which counts as nearly full employment. About 145,000 new jobs were created each month for the first six months of 2007, according to the official data, compared with 186,000 reported in 2006.

  – Washington says it takes 140,000 new jobs each month to absorb the new workers coming into the labor market. However, a year or two ago, when the population was smaller, 150,000 new workers were said to enter the market each month. New jobs are either drawing down unemployment or leaving some new workers jobless, depending on which number you believe.

  – But that is true only if the job creation numbers are reliable. They aren't. There also is a major conflict between job surveys. For example, in April 2007, the Bureau of Labor Statistics (BLS) reported that its survey of establishments, which tallies payrolls at selected companies, found 88,000 new jobs for the month, including 25,000 in government. In contrast, the BLS household survey, which actually asks people whether they are working, reported a loss of 468,000 jobs for the month! Most economists believe the survey of establishments gives a more accurate picture of employment than the household survey, and in general we agree. Yet there are a number of "fudge factors" built into the establishment survey that may or may not be valid. At the very least, the United States needs to get a better handle on its employment situation.

- Inflation remains under control according to official reports. Both the consumer price index (CPI) and core inflation, neglecting energy and food prices, came in at 2.6 percent in 2006. In 2007, CPI has been sharply higher—up 7 percent, annualized, for the three months ending in May—thanks to spikes in the cost of energy and food. Core inflation rose by only 1.6 percent annualized for the three months ending in May. Government officials argue that core inflation is a more accurate reflection of long-term price trends because the cost of food and energy is so erratic. However, current increases in food and energy are due to long-term problems—the continuing imbalance between supply and demand of refined petroleum products and the growing diversion of corn to ethanol production. We believe CPI is now a much better measure of the economy than core inflation. If so, there may be trouble ahead for consumers.

- For the moment, those consumers do not seem to be seriously worried. In the first quarter of 2007, consumers spent 4.2 percent more than in the previous three months. Spending was off a bit in April, May, and June, but nowhere near as much as the rising CPI and monthly declines of about 0.1 percent in real household income might have suggested. Thus far, it seems consumers will continue to keep the economy growing.

- How does all this add up? At Forecasting International, we believe the growth rate will average about 2.3 percent annually through 2008—a bit more in 2007, slightly less the following year. Until the employment picture becomes much clearer, we will not be truly confident of that number. However, we see no prospect of a significant downturn in the near future.

- The world's second economic dynamo, China, continues to whir. Its GDP officially grew by 10.7 percent—adjusted for inflation—in 2006, with 10.4 percent forecast for 2007 and 2008. Thanks to China's hot export markets, the country's current-account surplus is huge, equivalent to 10.7 percent of GDP in 2007, with 9.8 percent expected in 2008.

  – In fact, China may be even wealthier than it seems. A study of its gray market in 2005, including "all illegal incomes, questionable incomes, and incomes of dubious origins," suggested the true GDP may be 24 percent larger than the official numbers. This powerhouse will keep the global economy humming even if the United States cannot.

- In Germany, Europe's biggest economy is performing well. The country's GDP grew by 3 percent in 2006, its fastest growth since 2000. Inflation is at just 1.9 percent, and real incomes are rising, if only a little. There even are signs that German consumers are beginning to spend for the first time in years. The Conference Board's leading index for Germany was up 1.6 percent for the six months ending in April, with a sharp spike at the end of that period. Economists now predict that the GDP will grow by 2.9 percent in 2007 and 2.2 percent in 2008. The German economy still has structural problems that could worsen any future downturn. Yet for the moment it seems good times should continue at least into 2010.

- The French GDP rose 2.1 percent in 2006, with growth of 2.2 percent expected in 2007 and 2008. That is the good news. Unfortunately, there is bad news as well. Unemployment is stuck above 8 percent. The Conference Board's leading indicator for France has been leveling off and actually declined slightly in May 2007. The government absorbs 50.7 percent of the GDP in taxes but spends more, giving a budget deficit of 2.4 percent. Plans to cut taxes more than spending could put the deficit over the 3 percent allowed by the European Union. In all, there is room to wonder how long France can sustain its growth beyond 2008.

- The British economy grew by 2.8 percent in 2006 and continued growing at that rate, on average, through the first half of 2007.

  - This is even better news than it sounds, as the second quarter of 2007 marks the 60th consecutive quarter of growth in Britain. Measured by GDP and inflation, the British economy has been more stable than at any other time in memory; the longest previous run of continuous growth was just nineteen quarters. Unemployment was only 5.5 percent in early 2007. Consumer spending has been strong, but was softening in early to mid-2007. Yet at mid-year, the Conference Board's leading index for the United Kingdom was growing at an annual rate of 4.5 percent. Short of a global recession, the UK's GDP seems destined to continue growing by 2.5 percent annually, or better, for the next few years.

- All this adds up to fairly good prospects for the European economy as a whole. Its aggregate GDP grew by 2.8 percent in 2006, its fastest rate in six years, with 2.7 percent growth forecast for 2007 and 2.3 percent for 2008. Modest weakness in France and Italy will be more than offset by the strength of Germany and the U.K. Europe will remain a sound trading partner for the United States and China for at least the next five years.

- Japan's GDP rose by 2.2 percent in 2006. In the fourth quarter of the year, growth hit 4.8 percent, its best showing in three years. This growth rate has slowed in 2007 but remains positive. Between November 2006 and May 2007, the Conference Board's index of leading indicators for Japan sank at a rate of 1.8 percent per year. Continued growth depends on spending by notoriously wary Japanese consumers. Nonetheless, the Organization for Economic Cooperation and Development predicts that Japan's GDP will grow by 2.4 percent in 2007 and 2.1 percent in 2008. The Japanese economy seems likely to remain healthy for at least a few years beyond 2008.

  - In the long run, Japan faces significant problems. Its population is aging, its working-age population is shrinking, and its birth rate is the lowest in the industrialized world and still declining. By 2030, the number of workers in Japan will shrink from its current 66 million to about 56 million. Over all, the country's population is expected to decline by 50 percent by 2075 and by two-thirds through 2100. At the same time, government debt equals 176 percent of GDP. This will make it extremely difficult for Tokyo to provide necessary services for tomorrow's elderly. Yet these are problems for the future. They will not affect Japan's economy during the period now under study.

- Both prices and wages should remain under control.

    - Worldwide, improved manufacturing technology will continue to boost productivity and reduce the unit cost of goods.

    - At the same time, workers who remain on the job longer will offset slow growth in the labor force and the globalization of business will keep pressure on salaries in the developed countries.

AUTHORS' COMMENT:

The data above remain as originally supplied to our expert panel. There have been a number of gloomy developments in the world economy since then. In the United States, we have had the weakest Christmas retail season in years, a collapse in the real-estate market, declining job growth, the reappearance of significant inflation, and of course the crunch in subprime mortgages, which has spread to Britain and threatens prime mortgages as well. GDP growth in 2007 came in at 2.2 percent, sliding to an anemic 0.6 percent in the fourth quarter. In Germany, inflation is up to 3.3 percent, well above the level allowed by the European central bank, and fears are rising that the strength of the euro will throttle exports. Inflation is threatening China, Australia, Eastern Europe, Russia, and the Middle East as well. In all, it seems that the economies of the United States and the world are not as healthy as they were just a few months ago.

Nonetheless, at Forecasting International we believe that the U.S. economy will continue to grow in 2008, though perhaps not as quickly as once anticipated. The global economy will remain reasonably strong as well. Our expectations for the United States would change abruptly if today's credit problems were to infect the prime mortgage market, but for the moment that continues to seem unlikely.

Assessment:

These trends have been revised many times since they were first codified in the late 1980s. Some trends have fallen out of the list as they matured or as circumstances came along to change them. Others have been added as they were recognized. This trend has remained a constant, and with each revision its effective period has been extended. To invalidate this trend would take a catastrophe on the order of the loss of Middle Eastern oil from the Western economies. No such dramatic reversal of global fortune can be foreseen.

Implications:

New growth among all these trading partners should create a "benevolent cycle," in which the health of each partner helps to ensure the continued health of the rest at least through 2012. Global growth is expected to come in at 5 percent in 2007, 4.8 percent in 2008, and 4.4 percent, on average, in the five years ending in 2013.

China has developed into an effective counterbalance for the U.S. economy. When America hits hard times, China can keep the world from following into recession. We first saw this in the post 9/11 crunch in the

United States. This should make the global economy much more stable for so long as China remains a vibrant trading nation.

Any interruptions in economic growth should be relatively short-lived.

By 2012 or so, India will expand faster than any other market in the world, with China falling into a close second place.

In the long run, the newly capitalist lands of the former Soviet Union should be among the fastest growing new markets, particularly if the oil industries of Kazakhstan and its neighbors, Kyrgyzstan and Uzbekistan, can be developed promptly.

Labor markets will remain tight, particularly in skilled fields. This calls for new creativity in recruiting, benefits, and perks, especially profit sharing. This hypercompetitive business environment demands new emphasis on rewarding speed, creativity, and innovation within the workforce.

Implications for Terrorism:

The growing gap in wealth between the rich and poor nations will further destabilize the world order, continuing to inspire potential terrorists in the developing countries to strike at the wealthy in their home countries and, in some cases, at the richer lands. The growing gap in wealth between the rich and poor within many western lands will feed discontent among the less well-off, possibly helping to inspire both random violence and native terrorists in the West. This development will increase the security-related workload of intelligence and law enforcement agencies around the world. It also will help to drive continued growth in the private security industry.

The growing gap in wealth and income between the rich and the poor also will help to inspire conversion to Islam in the West, particularly among the poor and powerless. As we have seen in England, Germany, and Australia, this can be a source of violent extremism among both immigrant and native populations.

Expert Comments:

*Note, here and throughout the report, where a respondent ranked a trend, a number in parentheses indicates that ranking.

ANONYMOUS (1): This is a trend with important, if mixed implications for terrorism. On the one hand, it will provide opportunities for young people (including migrants) who, un- or under-employed, might otherwise drift off into violence prone cults. Moreover, it will provide governments with revenues to pursue robust counter-terrorist policies, including the acquisition of needed surveillance and information processing technologies. On the other hand, such growth will exacerbate international inequalities providing motivation for terrorist actions (although inequality per se, has not been, to date, a major driver of terrorism). More significantly, growth will drive more migration, technological advance, and global warming, all of which may contribute to the problem.

ARMSTRONG: The gap itself is not the problem; the local situation is the problem. The world does not necessarily care how others are doing, but how they are doing. Local poverty and disillusionment fuel extremism and hope for a better future. Failure to address issues of security, humanitarian relief, governance, economic stabilization, and development in countries and neighborhoods creates fertile breeding grounds for extremists, terrorists, and insurgents to attack the national interests of the United States. This can be seen in inner-city development in the U.S. as well as in Iraq and elsewhere. Comparisons of the U.S. and our Western allies to "Gap" countries mean little. The response to the strategic American public diplomacy campaigns showing how great Muslims have it in the U.S. was a giant yawn, followed by "What's that got to do with me here in [pick your country: Egypt, Jordan, Palestine, Iraq, etc.]?"

KADTKE: In many regions of the world, the left-behind economies, political instability, and extremist activity will result in failed states, which will serve as breeding grounds and staging areas for further terrorist activities and recruitment. As the number of these areas increases, the UN and Western powers will not have the resources to commit globally.

KRIESBERG: One other effect of growing inequality within the United States may be worth noting. That is the impact of increased concentration of great wealth upon political decision making and policy implementation. At least some of the inadequate U.S. responses in dealing with terrorism are attributable to undue attention to the views of major political contributors, in procurement and in outsourcing.

LADUKE (3): The U.S. housing market fallout, the trade deficit, and the decline of the U.S. dollar alongside the economic advance and alliances of other developing nations is eroding the balance of power. If the U.S. economy falters and this flows into national defense, we should expect terrorist confrontations from many directions to end what is perceived (by terrorist groups and hostile nations) to be a long-standing negative imperialistic influence on our world.

MEILAHN: I disagree that the gap between rich and poor will inspire would-be terrorists in developing states to strike at the wealthy in their home states and at wealthier states. Most evidence that I have seen indicates that there are other reasons, other motivations. It is not generally the poor and/or disenfranchised that become terrorists. It is the people who are already fairly fundamental in their beliefs, who are "pushed over the edge" by U.S. consumptionism, what they perceive as poor values, "easy" women, etc.—and they feel that the U.S. influence is bad for Islam. I am doing some work on this but believe there are many other factors involved, including a desire to make up for failings or sins (when you become a martyr, all is forgiven and you go to heaven), desire to become a part of something bigger than one's self (think psychology of cults), etc.

MILLER: At the moment, this looks like a pretty shaky prediction. The concern might be that, in the face of an economic downturn, the federal government might be forced to cut back on its counter-terrorism efforts. Such curtailment would, of course, become the single most negative impact on the prevention of future attacks on civilian populations by terrorists. At this time, I would give the possibility of a federal bailout (relatively) on GWOT less than a 50-50 chance, but the rise of environmental, social, and economic pressures on the next administration may prove decisive.

OSBORNE: The demand for materials from China and India will continue to affect crime problems around the world. For example, theft of copper has increased globally due to the changing markets—theft of this and similar resources (such as water) will grow and affect crime rates and types all over the world.

SANDERS (1): See comments under "Complexity and the Future of Terrorism" in Appendix C.

SMYRE (1): As the gap widens between the economy of the developed world and the two billion plus who live on $2 per day, there will be an increased ability to recruit young terrorists who have little to no economic hope…especially as the real-time media rubs this gap into the faces of those unable to find employment.

SNYDER (8): Rising costs for food, and for oil and other basic industrial commodities due to rapid growth in global demand—plus increased energy taxes and surcharges designed to promote fuel conservation and reduce greenhouse gases—will increase long-term inflation rates in most industrial nations, especially the U.S.

Stagflationary economics and the continued dismantling of the industrial era "social contract" will sustain the widening gap between "haves" and "have-nots" in most free market economies.

So long as info-mation and globalization fail to produce a general rise in prosperity among mature industrial economies, there will be increasing political disaffection in those countries, giving rise to neo-Luddism and anarchism aimed both at multi-national corporations and central governments. Unlike international terrorists, domestic anarchists can be expected to commit increasingly sophisticated acts of cybertage in order to reduce public confidence in—and business reliance on—the Internet, thereby diminishing the technology's power as a force for transformational economic, social, and political change.

Barring a reversal of current long-term socioeconomic trends in the U.S., a populist-anarchist backlash is likely to be a greater source of overt terrorist acts in America within ten years than will international terrorism.

YOUNG: Economic expansion can only help development in the Middle East. The result may lead to an increase in the middle class, currently almost non-existent in countries readily identified with terrorism. It is likely that once the populace begins to accumulate individual wealth that support for terror will abate.

2 – MILITANT ISLAM CONTINUES TO SPREAD AND GAIN POWER. (TREND 9)

- It has been clear for years that the Muslim lands face severe problems with religious extremists dedicated to advancing their political, social, and doctrinal views by any means necessary.

- Most of the Muslim lands are overcrowded and short of resources. Many are poor, save for the oil-rich states of the Middle East. Virtually all have large populations of young men, often unemployed, who are frequently attracted to violent extremist movements.

- During its proxy war with the Soviet Union in Afghanistan, the United States massively fortified the Muslim extremist infrastructure by supplying it with money, arms, and, above all, training.

- It is making a similar mistake today. The overthrow of Saddam Hussein and the American occupation of Iraq has inspired a new generation of *jihadis*, who have been trained and battle-hardened in the growing insurgency.

- In a now-declassified National Security Estimate, the American intelligence community concluded that Al Qaeda was more powerful in 2007 than it had been before the so-called "war on terror" began—more dangerous even than it had been when it planned the attacks of September 11, 2001.

- American support for Israel has also made the United States a target for the hatred of Muslim extremists.

Assessment:

This trend may wax and wane, but it seems unlikely to disappear this side of a Muslim reformation comparable to those that transformed Christianity and Judaism.

Implications:

Virtually all of the Muslim lands face an uncertain, and possibly bleak, future of political instability and growing violence. The exceptions are the oil states, where money can still buy relative peace, at least for now.

These problems often have spilled over into the rest of the world. They will do so again.

In a 1994 terrorism study for the Department of Defense and other government clients, Forecasting International predicted that by 2020 a strong majority of the world's twenty-five or so most important Muslim lands could be in the hands of extremist religious governments. At the time, only Iran was ruled by such a regime. That forecast still appears sound.

Iraq is likely to become the next fundamentalist Muslim regime. Once American forces leave, Iran will support the establishment of a Shiite regime much like its own in Baghdad.

There is a one-in-ten chance that this will set off a general war in the Middle East, as Sunni-dominated states intercede to protect Iraqi Sunnis against Shi'a domination. However, Iraq and Saudi Arabia already are negotiating to keep this situation under control.

Any attempt to reduce the commitment of Western forces to the task of stabilizing Afghanistan will result in the restoration of the Taliban to power.

Implications for Terrorism:

The West, and particularly the United States, must expect more—and more violent—acts of terrorism for at least the next 20 years.

Europe faces a significant homegrown Muslim extremist movement, and the United States may do so in the near future. Thanks largely to waves of immigration since the 1980s, Islam is the fastest-growing religion in both regions. Extremist clerics in Europe are recruiting young Muslims to the cause of *jihad* against their adopted homes. So far, their colleagues in the United States have been much less successful. That may not always be true.

Western interests also will be vulnerable in many countries outside the Muslim core. International ties formed among Islamic militants during the anti-Soviet war in Afghanistan produced an extremist infrastructure that can support terrorist activities almost anywhere in the world. The war in Iraq is doing so even more efficiently.

This development must be taken even more seriously because, for the first time, a Muslim country—Pakistan—has nuclear weapons. Muslim extremists view this technology as an "Islamic bomb" that could be used to promote their cause. From here on out, nuclear terrorism is a realistic threat.

This risk will grow as Sudan, Iraq, and probably other countries establish fundamentalist regimes sympathetic to the cause of *jihad* against the West.

Saudi Arabia easily could be taken over by a fundamentalist regime. The Saudi rulers may well try to avoid this by providing even more support to extremists and directing their attention to the West.

The overthrow of the Taliban in Afghanistan and, especially, of Saddam Hussein in Iraq, have made future fundamentalist revolutions more likely, rather than less so, because it has strengthened the global *jihadi* movement.

This is clearly the single most important trend for terrorism.

Expert Comments:

ANONYMOUS (3): Obviously important for inspiring disaffected individuals and small groups but perhaps of diminishing significance as a driver of an organized "global guerilla" campaign. Militant Islam has failed to capture a foothold in the Maghreb or the Arab world, and may now be facing a "Thermidor-style" popular rejection due to its excesses against co-religionists in several Middle Eastern countries.

ARMSTRONG: While militant Islam does continue to spread, we must consider the Taliban's increasing reliance on foreigners as well as the rejection of Al Qaeda in parts of Iraq, both because their extremist message fails to resonate with the locals. Information drives this train, and frustration with the present condition drives recruitment. Failure to understand the Koran, the Hadith, or Islam in general permits acts otherwise abhorrent.

General Douglas Stone, chief of detainee operations in Iraq, has noted the distinction between ideologues and tag-alongs: "We are able to determine the guys that don't really give a shit about the Koran in the first place—they're using it as a discipline—those guys are beginning to fall into the category of irreconcilables, and that's helpful to me. I want to know who they are. They're like rotten eggs, you know, hiding in the Easter basket, so that's very helpful. Then it's also equally helpful to have guys who come out and say, 'I didn't know that. Now that I know that, I'm going to change my life.' And we poly[graph] them. You'd be...interesting to know, because we are trying to figure out if they are messing with us. But we are convinced that they have made a significant change. Now, you're not talking about, you know, radicals going to choir boys, but you're talking about radicals who won't use violence without a very clear understanding that they are damned if they do."

While we debate the merits of *Qutb* and its value to extremist ideology, we too often forget to ask how many extremists actually read *Qutb* in the same analytic framework as we do and aren't just spoon fed select passages from the Koran to support their violence. Also, it's worth bearing in mind that Christianity, Judaism, and Hinduism do not have the promotion and outreach campaigns for the needy and less fortunate that Islam does. We must look at what gives militant Islam its power, something we do not fully understand. The answer is more likely lie in my response to Trend 1 than in the inherent attractiveness of extremism and hate.

AYERS (1): Every success claimed (whether or not the assessment of success is an honest one) by Islamic terrorists supports their efforts to expand the scope of their activities and, in their own minds, validates the extremist agenda—to establish the global domination of Islam. In addition to the looming specter of nuclear weapons in the hands of Islamists, we now see limited support for anti-U.S., anti-Israeli terrorist operations among elements of non-Islamic rogue regimes. If, as it now appears may be the case, leaders of former or potential superpowers are added to the mix—providing assistance in the form of planning and weapons (however covertly) to increasingly dangerous state sponsors of terrorism—it might be possible for a nuclear supported and/or nuclear armed Islamist state (such as Iran) to arrange large and small-scale attacks (terrorist as well as state-to-state) around the world, simultaneously. In fact, with sufficient assistance and pre-action infiltration, it might be possible to remove the major Western powers from global connectivity long enough to create desired effects (such as the destruction of Israel followed by major and minor terrorist attacks throughout all Western countries.) Arguments over the value of multiculturalism and cultural relativism aside, calls for "demographic jihad" and attempts to indoctrinate susceptible members of immigrant populations with extremist rhetoric by organizations like Hizb ut-Tahrir (see Zeyno Baran's 2005 article "Fighting the War of Ideas" in *Foreign Affairs*, vol. 84 [6]) may increase the likelihood of pre-attack infiltration throughout Europe and the United States.

BRUH: Islamic fundmentalism is a serious law enforcement problem as well as one that affects national security. It will likely continue resulting in greater serious crime with not just economics behind the activities.

CHOBAR (3): Most local law enforcement personnel are ill informed regarding "militant Islam." Thus, places like Pakistan, England, the United States, and Canada are "harbors" for any number of Muslims who may be communicating by Internet, satellite dish, etc. There may also be significant caches of wealth being accumulated in these countries which are unknown to policing agencies but well know to terrorists.

FORSTER: I have addressed this extensively in the point on undemocratic governance. [See Appendix C.] Here I would only add that extremism is an increasing challenge as it permeates new regions and extremist movements with varying objectives coalesce. New regions of militant Islam-incited conflict include sub-Sahara Africa, particularly the Horn and Nigeria. However, the most serious threat is the increasing militancy in Western Europe's Muslim population, which lives "below the radar" until they take action. While the coalescence between the GSPC [*Groupe Salafiste pour la Prédication et le Combat*—the Salafist Group for Call and Combat—a Sunni militia that aims to overthrow the Algerian government and establish an Islamic state] and Al Qaeda is most probably the result of declining capabilities of the GSPC, these alliances often include increased radicalization of and violence by the weaker partner (e.g. GSPC). The case of the Taliban's integration of foreign fighters also has changed tactics by increasing the use of suicide bombers in Afghanistan. More strategically, the integration of foreign fighters threatens to regionalize the conflict because of regime instability in the broader area.

Two counter-terrorism issues that deserve attention involve the ultimate appeal of Islamic extremism as a "way of life" for a general population and the emergence of reform in Islam. First, the 2006 National Intelligence Estimate correctly concluded that "sharia-based extremism is neither popular nor likely to ultimately address the frustrations evident in Islamic society today." As a result, programs aimed at political modernization and economic development may defuse much of the militancy. Tied to a development strategy is the encouragement of moderate Islam among those who are tired of having their religion perverted and seek to lead an "Islamic Reformation."

JENKINS: Terrorism will continue to be a threat for the foreseeable future. The Internet has become an increasingly important venue for recruitment, exhortation, instruction, and propaganda. Terrorists are ahead of the authorities here. There will be continuing pressure on local law enforcement agencies to enhance their own intelligence capabilities. The rest of the world will be dealing with the terrorist tactics and know-how developed in Iraq for the next fifteen years. Terrorists' determination to carry out large-scale, indiscriminate violence is pushing authorities from a traditional investigations approach to preventive intervention. We do not have a well-developed corpus of law in this area.

KADTKE: While a spectrum of terrorist organizations exist globally, their total net power is overshadowed by the terror activities of militant Islamic groups, and the latter continues to expand. Moreover, these activities have caused a political awakening among Islamic groups and nations that continues to grow, and they are beginning to engage aggressively with modern public diplomacy tools such as Al Jazeera. Whether or not a clash of civilizations will occur in the future, clandestine sponsorship of militant Islamic groups will remain a major driver of these activities.

KRIESBERG: Militant Islam may be spreading to some degree. But as it overreaches and fails, it generates counter forces and resistance from other Muslims. That should be recognized. Allowing space for the highly doctrinaire to participate in governance can be part of their transformation.

Another consideration is the division within Islam between the Sunni and the Shia. The intensity of that schism could at some point become a source of support for norms of tolerance, as happened within Christianity after years of intense struggle between Catholics and Protestants.

LaDUKE (4): An obviously huge threat to the U.S. because militant Islam is seated in the midst of the interests of multiple superpower agendas, has a massive population for recruitment, and has potential to publicly or covertly gain access to advanced technology.

LANOTTE: Since the mid 19th century, there has been a distinct separation between internal law enforcement and external "instrument of foreign policy." Understanding that changing this arrangement can create a "slippery slope," it may be time to re-think the use of military assets, especially intelligence assets, to combat jihadi-like threats.

LEFFLER: Research in the Middle East, published in the peer-reviewed *Journal of Conflict Resolution,* demonstrated that a sufficiently large group of Invincible Defense Technology experts in Israel affected the war in nearby Lebanon. The Lebanon War intensity dropped 45 percent, war deaths dropped 76 percent, and quality of life improved by 0.75 standard deviation units. In Israel, crime dropped by 12 percent and quality of life improved by 1.3 standard deviation units. Areas with a low quality of life can be a breeding ground for terrorism. Based on this research, it is clear that Invincible Defense Technology is capable of greatly reducing the protracted sectarian violence in the Middle East.

MEILAHN: This is a Muslim problem that can only be fought by Muslims. The more moderate Muslims must take on this fight, and the U.S. can help them. Currently only about 2 percent are radicals; but that is still a large number. According to a Gallup analysis of polls representing 90 percent of the world's Muslim population, another 7 percent are "politically radicalized." That is, they believe the 9/11 attacks were completely justified and have an unfavorable view of the United States. And in 2006, the Pew Research Center found that 17.7 percent of Muslim respondents believed that violence against civilian targets in order to defend Islam can be justified "often" or "sometimes." At least some of the radicalized 2 percent can be re-educated about Islam and "de-radicalized," prevented from executing acts of terror. This group is the one the USG should concern itself with from a preventive standpoint.

Another point is that most of the Muslims who condoned attacks on 9/11 believe that it was justifiable because of U.S. "colonizing" and the way we are too controlling of other countries. The USG could do much with regard to its foreign policy to change its image from "occupier" to cooperative member of the world community. That would do much to decrease motivations for jihad, and keep terrorists away from our borders or our interests worldwide.

Oil states will also suffer problems (a disagreement with your list of trends) because the Shi'ia-Sunni divide will be aggravated as both militant Sunni groups (such as Al Qaeda) and militant Shi'ia groups (Hizb'Allah) influence others of like kind by their example and successes. For example, the Shi'ia in Saudi Arabia may rise up and demand their rights and representation in a mostly Sunni land. Although Iran is an "extremist" government, they are actually fairly democratic in the way they operate. Frankly, this is one government that is less concerning to me (because they have fairly good control of their state, and they are moderating politically as a somewhat post-revolutionary government—Ahmadi-Nejad's comments not withstanding—he is not the leader here, Ayatollah Khamenei is) than are other governments that are more precarious; state failure leaves the conditions ripe for extremism to grow (as along the Pakistani-Afghan border in the FATA [Federally Administered Tribal Areas of Pakistan]). Iraq is currently the center of a proxy war for influence between Saudi and Iran—the winner will be identified by what type of long term government resides there, Shi'ia or Sunni.

MILLER: Obviously, this looms large in our thinking about terrorism. I am not sure how significantly Islam's growth or even the increase in fundamentalist Muslim trained youth (in Saudi Arabia, e.g.) actually translates directly into a U.S. problem, unless we choose to make it so. There is certainly not a linear cause and effect between Muslim growth and terrorist threat to the U.S. However, there may well be a "tipping point" when the cork pops and local mid-East regimes become actively engaged in violence, and the U.S. becomes involved as an agent for the regime. The recent Iraq experience may suggest that, barring the presence of outside forces, Muslim internecine violence can be controlled, if not eliminated.

NOLTE: This is one instance in which local authorities can help to avert potential terrorism. Good policing can facilitate the process whereby an "alien" population, in this case Muslim, integrates effectively into society, rather than being further alienated from it.

PROBST: The most troubling manifestation of militant Islam is the cult of Global *jihad* that has found expression under the tutelage of Usama bin Laden and the Al Qaeda organization. Due to continued success of intelligence and security services working, al "Qaeda Central" has largely been decimated. Despite reverses, its malignant ideology has metastasized, infecting the body politic of Muslim communities worldwide. The ideology has developed a global following and a global reach. Bin Laden himself has achieved the iconic status that had previously been reserved for secular revolutionaries such as Lenin and Che Guevara. Even in the secular West and even among non-Muslims, we see efforts to "canonize" bin Laden as a freedom fighter who has defended the interests of the Muslim masses. The aim is to have the ideology of *jihad* transcend Islam and speak to the angry, oppressed, and wretched of the earth regardless of class, nationality, or religion.

RABASA: I would argue that this trend is not very cut and that, in fact, there are indications that militant Islam may have reached a high-water mark globally and may be retreating in some areas. Al-Qaeda-influenced terrorist campaigns have lost ground in Iraq, Saudi Arabia, and Indonesia. In Europe there is greater awareness on the part of political elites of the threat of radicalization of its homegrown Muslim population and steps are being taken in some countries to counter this trend.

SANDERS (4): See comments under "Complexity and the Future of Terrorism" in Appendix C.

TAN: The startling failures of U.S. grand strategy after 9/11, particularly its disastrous strategy in Iraq, have been counter-productive to the global war on terrorism. From relative stability, albeit under Saddam's dictatorial hand, Iraq has slid into chaos and has become the training ground for the global *jihad* much as Afghanistan had become the training ground from which Al Qaeda emerged. However, the jihadists in Iraq are honing their skills in combating the world's technologically most advanced armed forces and are learning to perfect techniques in IEDs, sabotage, sniping, kidnappings, assassinations, urban warfare, etc. Once dispersed throughout the world, these jihadists will re-constitute a post-Al Qaeda network that will be much more competent, effective, and deadly. Unfortunately, their first targets will be likely Muslim governments and allies of the U.S.A. throughout the Middle East. Can these regimes meet the emerging challenge of the post-Iraq militants? Will the radicalization being spawned in Iraq today seep through its borders to destabilize the entire Middle East? The question today is not how to win Iraq. The questions are: What can the U.S.A. and the West do to meet and contain the growing threat from radical Islam? How can we contain Iranian Shi'ite fundamentalism from threatening the stability of the entire Middle East?

YOUNG: As long as the conditions for Islamic extremism exist worldwide, terror activities will not subside over the short term. These conditions include but are not limited to political and economic conditions in the extremists' home countries such as corrupt leadership; lack of general, non-religious, education opportunities; support for anti-Western religious teachings; and high unemployment amongst Muslim youth. Should these conditions be addressed by a new type of Muslim leader then extremists will always have a recruiting base.

---

3 – THE WORLD'S POPULATION IS ON COURSE TO REACH 9.2 BILLION BY 2050. (TREND 2)

- Average annual growth worldwide peaked at 2.19 percent in 1963 and has fallen steadily since. The U.S. Census Bureau's International Data Base projects that annual growth will fall below 1 percent in 2016 and below 0.5 percent by 2047.

- The greatest fertility is found in those countries least able to support their existing populations: the largest population increases projected between 2000 and 2050 include the Palestinian Territory (217 percent), Niger (205 percent), Yemen (168 percent), Angola (162 percent), the Democratic Republic of Congo (161 percent), and Uganda (133 percent).

  - The Muslim world is especially fertile, with fertility rates of 7.5 in Afghanistan, 6.0 in Yemen, and 4.9 in Iraq.

  - Of the 2.7 billion extra people in the world in 2050, about 40 percent will live in sub-Saharan Africa and 30 percent in the Muslim world.

- Even these estimates may be much too low. According to the Center for Strategic and International Studies (CSIS), most official projections underestimate both fertility and future gains in longevity. They also assume that life expectancy will grow more slowly in the future, which seems unlikely.

- In contrast to the developing world, many industrialized countries will see fertility rates below the replacement level and hence significant declines in populations, excluding the effects of immigration. This means the population of the developed nations will fall from 14 percent of the total world population in 2000 to only 10 percent in 2050.

- By 2015, the workforce in Japan and much of Europe will be shrinking by 1 percent per year. By the 2030s, it will contract by 1.5 percent annually.

Assessment:

Demographic trends such as this are among the most easily recognized and difficult to derail. Barring a global plague or nuclear war—wildcard possibilities that cannot be predicted with any validity—there is little chance that the population forecast for 2050 will err on the high side.

Implications:

Rapid population growth in the United States compared with its industrialized competitors will reinforce American domination of the global economy, as the European Union falls to third place behind the United States and China.

To meet human nutritional needs over the next forty years, global agriculture will have to supply as much food as has been produced during all of human history.

Unless fertility in the developed lands climbs dramatically, either would-be retirees will have to remain on the job, or the industrialized nations will have to encourage even more immigration from the developing world. The third alternative is a sharp economic contraction and lower living standards.

A fourth alternative is the widespread automation of service jobs as well as manufacturing, to accomplish the work needed to support accustomed living standards. However, this requires development of a means other than wages to distribute wealth and to provide both a living income and a fulfilling occupation for workers and would-be workers displaced by machines and software.

Barring enactment of strict immigration controls, rapid migration will continue from the Southern Hemisphere to the North, and especially from former colonies to Europe. A growing percentage of job applicants in the United States and Europe will be recent immigrants from developing countries.

Implications for Terrorism:

Growing American prosperity relative to other countries with rapidly growing populations and overburdened economies will continue to make the United States a target for terrorism.

As one aspect of poverty, shortages of food, could help to inspire extremism unless the industrialized nations make a determined, visible effort to provide for the world's poor.

In the long run, American restrictions on immigration from Latin America could inspire extremism among both documented and undocumented aliens, conceivably resulting in a modest amount of terrorist activity. However, this will have little support among Hispanics, whether legal residents or not. There is little prospect that a Latin extremist movement could ally itself with Muslim extremists.

Expert Comments:

CHOBAR (8): With significant global population growth, there will be additional problems of hunger, poverty, poor health, and illness—especially in light of the numerous hurricanes, flooding and other global warming issues facing our planet. These will lead to serious policing issues, as people struggle to survive. If terrorists appeal to children, people and teenagers who are hungry and living in poverty, by filling their basic needs, especially children of the growing population will go over to terrorism and the glory it brings them fighting against those who have affluence and wealth.

CZARNECKI: This is one of three baseline trends that forecast a near-perfect social storm for increased societal violence, much of it expressed as terrorism. Although UN reports indicate a slowing of world population growth, this will not be a uniform slowing. Some places, especially those that can least afford and adapt to population growth, will exhibit massive growth without the resources/information to sustain that growth. The competition for the scarce resources that are available will be great and extreme. Those who find their position(s) hopeless or near-hopeless can be expected to lash out at those whom they perceive have taken their survival from them. Wherever this kind of growth-resources mismatch occurs, expect violence of the most terrible kind.

JENKINS: High levels of immigration will exacerbate ethnic tensions and provoke powerful reactions against both legal and illegal immigration. The major issue for police will be the role of local police in enforcing national policies against illegal immigration. Pressure from local citizens and Washington will push police to play a greater role in reducing illegal immigrant populations with possible adverse effects on community relations and law enforcement.

LaDUKE (7): Increased population density and megacities, largely emerging in developing nations, will be juxtaposed against advances in technology that could be applied to terrorism and destructive force. Attacks will potentially be more devastating.

MILLER: Alas, this one is more likely to be exceeded than undershot. I would put this rapidly increasing pool of potential terrorism adherents as one of the most critical in terms of its importance as a driver of future terrorism. I don't see any way to seriously affect global population growth, but it is the primary reason that the GWOT is a "long war" much like the "war" on crime.

SANDERS (2): See comments under "Complexity and the Future of Terrorism" in Appendix C.

SMYRE (2): It is expected that 80 percent of the growth in population from now to 2050 will be in poverty. This will increase the potential for more terrorism in more places unless the developed world begins to see the importance of helping the impoverished of the world improve their quality of life. This will become as important as any foreign policy initiative and will challenge the conservative philosophies of much of the U.S. population.

SNYDER (1): With 1 billion people born between 1975 and 1995, the Third-World Baby Boom will increase the labor supply of most developing countries faster than the local economies create jobs. This will curtail economic opportunity for an entire generation of young people in Africa, the Middle East, South Asia, and Latin America, and give rise to a growing population of unemployed.

STEELE: Disproportionate segments of the world's population growth in the developing world will produce a widening gap between developed and developing worlds. This produces environments of anomie and alienation as a breeding ground for terrorist ideology.

YOUNG: Much of the increase in the world's population will reside within the world's poorer countries. Lack of status and resources has been a favorite motivation for terror recruiters, and it is a situation that melds easily with question one.

---

4 – TECHNOLOGY INCREASINGLY DOMINATES BOTH THE ECONOMY AND SOCIETY. (TREND 28)

- New technologies are surpassing the previous state of the art in all fields, and technological obsolescence is accelerating.

- For most users, computers have become part of the environment rather than just tools used for specific tasks.

  – With wireless modems, portable computers give us access to networked data wherever we go.

  – Internet-equipped cell phones are even more convenient for access to e-mail and some Websites.

- Robots are taking over more and more jobs that are routine, remote, or risky, such as repairing undersea cables and nuclear power stations.

– Flexible, general-service personal robots will appear in the home by 2015, expanding on the capabilities of devices such as robotic vacuum cleaners and lawn mowers.

• By 2015, artificial intelligence (AI), data mining, and virtual reality will help most companies and government agencies to assimilate data and solve problems beyond the range of today's computers.

– AI applications include robotics, machine vision, voice recognition, speech synthesis, electronic data processing, health and human services, administration, and airline pilot assistance.

• Superconductors operating at economically viable temperatures will be in commercial use soon after 2015.

Assessment:

Technologically related changes in society and business seen over the last 20 years are just the beginning of a trend that will accelerate at least through this century.

Implications:

New technologies should continue to improve the efficiency of many industries, helping to keep costs under control.

However, this increased productivity has retarded United States job creation since at least 2002. Other developed countries are likely to feel the same effect in the future.

Technology made international outsourcing possible. It will continue to promote outsourcing to the benefit of the recipient countries, but to cause painful job losses in the donor lands.

New technologies often require a higher level of education and training to use them effectively. They also provide many new opportunities to create businesses and jobs.

Automation will continue to cut the cost of many services and products, making it possible to reduce prices while still improving profits. This will be critical to business survival as the Internet continues to push the price of many products to the commodity level.

New technology also will make it easier for industry to minimize and capture its effluent. This will be a crucial ability in the environmentally conscious future.

In 1999, a team at the technology organization Battelle compiled a list of the ten most strategic technological trends for the next 20 years. The list is available at the Battelle website at http://www.battelle.org/SPOTLIGHT/tech_forecast/technology2020.aspx. Key technologies for 2020, as forecast by Battelle:

– Gene-based medical care, from custom-tailored pharmaceuticals to cloned organs for transplantation

– High-powered energy packages such as advanced batteries, cheap fuel cells, and micro-generators

– "Green integrated technology" to eliminate manufacturing waste and make products completely recyclable

– Omnipresent computing with computers built into consumer products, clothing, and even implanted under the skin

– Nanomachines measured in atoms rather than millimeters that do everything from heating and cleaning our homes to curing cancer

– Personalized public transportation that integrates out cars into a coordinated transport network, automatically picking the fastest routes and bypassing traffic jams

– Designer foods and crops genetically engineered to resist disease and pests and be highly nutritious

– Intelligent goods and appliances such as telephones with built-in directories and food packaging that tells your stove how to cook the contents

– Worldwide inexpensive and safe water from advanced filtering, desalination, and perhaps even extraction from the air

– Super senses that use implants to give us better hearing, long-distance vision, or the ability to see in the dark

Implications for Terrorism:

Networks of video cameras are just the first of many high-tech tools that will affect antiterrorist operations in the years ahead.

To prevent or interrupt terrorist attacks, nanotech sensors capable of detecting explosives, chemical, and biological weapons will be scattered around prime targets, such as major public gatherings, relaying the location of any possible threat to the local command center. This is a likely prospect for 2015 and beyond.

Intelligence analysts, already overwhelmed by the amount of data collected each day, will face a growing torrent of data in the years ahead. As surveillance spreads through society, this will be a problem for police agencies as well. Until automated systems become available to help monitor incoming data, much of the information collected by cameras and other tools will be used more to provide evidence for prosecutions than to prevent or interrupt terrorist actions.

To assist them, engineers will develop automated systems to help "mesh" information from incompatible data stores, recognize patterns in the data, develop rigorous hypotheses, perform collaborative analyses, and "capture" the skills of the most capable analysts so that others can benefit from them, even when the analysts themselves are not available. Eventually, these systems will spread from the intelligence community to law enforcement. These techniques may offer the best chance of giving security agencies a clear advantage over their adversaries.

The recent decision by an American court to block data mining by the Department of Homeland Security (DHS) is a significant loss to security efforts in this country. While similar military projects continue, the DHS shares data with the regional Fusion Centers responsible for much of the work carried out at the local level. Loss of this resource will make their efforts notably less effective.

Expert Comments:

ANONYMOUS (7): This will continue to provide almost endless possibilities for those with even modest technological skills to disrupt the integrated workings of the economy and society. Given the fact that engineers and technologists are often attracted to terrorist causes (e.g., the 9/11 plotters) it is only a matter of time before existing technology is once again turned against society in a major way. Industry and governments will need to work together to find palliative strategies (switching to less toxic chemicals, moving LNG terminals to less populated areas), but this will be neither cheap nor easy.

ARMSTRONG: The increasing availability of information has significant consequences on peace and conflict and the utility of terrorism. The direct kinetic effects of bullets, bombs, and terrorism in general are secondary to their influence on the public opinion of foes, allies, and neutrals. Global information and transportation systems create two-way access to dynamic and global Diasporas based on "imagined communities" that are subjected to campaigns of strategic influence by the enemy while the United States sits idly by. Because the asymmetry in information operations decreases the fungibility of hard power assets, we must look at the biggest value of the "D" in WMD not as destruction but as disruption through the multiplicative effect of perceptions driven by the act, not the immediate effect of the act. We must look at technology not only as a tactical tool, but as one of operational and strategic consequence. The enemy does.

AYERS (5): a) Virtual worlds (e.g., Second Life), which are providing new opportunities for individual and commercial growth, can be used by terrorists to further their efforts in perpetrating kinetic and non-kinetic attacks. They supply extremists with flexible, and perhaps safer, venues for training *jihadis* ideologically, methodologically, and sociologically without requiring physical presence or large amounts of physical space. They may also, in the near future, provide terrorists with new ways of performing intelligence collection, information operations, and information warfare. If we are to credibly counteract the potential for terrorists to utilize virtual worlds for nefarious purposes, the intelligence community, law enforcement entities, and policy makers need to begin preparing for this eventuality sooner, rather than later.

b) Learning agents coupled with robotics will not only transform the manner in which intelligence is obtained and processed—they will transform the way in which intelligence data is viewed and acted upon by collectors, analysts, law enforcement practitioners, managers, and decision makers. Increasingly, all will be able to verbally question systems that seem much more like cognitive assistants (or super-intelligent coworkers) than the static technology we are now used to. Output will be visual (similar to our reporting systems of today) and/or auditory. These robotically supported cognitive assistants will be linked to databases worldwide as well as other learning agents of varying types and will be able to dynamically process monumental amounts of information while considering data that might normally be weeded out or inaccessible to humans or manually driven systems (e.g., those engaged in the current processes of research, analysis, and reporting.) While not all intelligence questions will be answerable instantaneously by the robotic/cognitive agents, time that humans would normally spend sifting through a substantial number of reports could be spent dissecting questions that need more attention, and reviewing agent responses. Intelligence reporting as it exists currently will increasingly become obsolete. Human expertise can be kept indefinitely, and detailed information about thinking processes could be made immediately available to those who question research methodology. (This comment is a projection based on research performed by George Mason University Learning Agent Center personnel.) Unfortunately, the period between the attainment of "massive systemic overload" and the achievement of dependable capabilities developed to alleviate overload (such as the aforementioned robotically supported cognitive assistants) will be extremely difficult, if not chaotic. It is unlikely that significant progress will be realized without having to go through a great deal of anguish in the meantime.

BRAY (1): Recall the major events of the last five years—Inadequate response to Hurricane Katrina in 2005, faulty intelligence prior to the second Iraqi war in 2003, incorrect estimates of the Al-Qaeda threat prior to the 9/11 attacks. These failures all occurred because our system of government could not appropriately link the knowledge it had across multiple departments to take action. Repeat investigations by the U.S. Government Accountability Office all report the same theme: More than sufficient information existed to mitigate these events, but the information was in a highly distributed and fragmented form across multiple departments and the White House.

Granted, the role of government is a large and onerous one. No other system exists with such a broad scope of duties to serve and protect us as citizens. For every government failure, multiple successes occur without making headlines. When our system of government works well, we all take it for granted. Government agencies confront a difficult task of determining truth from fiction, with limited (or potentially biased) sources of knowledge available.

I can attest to these difficulties. Starting the in autumn of 2000, I accepted a role with the Bioterrorism Preparedness and Response Program at the Centers for Disease Control and Prevention (CDC)—first as a fellow, later as IT Chief of the Bioterrorism Program. At 9 AM on the morning of 11 September 2001, I was to give a presentation to various government officials on how improvements in the information technology infrastructure of public health laboratories could aid national response to a bioterrorism event. The meeting never started. Instead, members of my program at the CDC were sent to an off-site command area when American Airlines Flight 11 hit the World Trade Center at 8:46AM.

The events that followed—to include the anthrax events of 2001, West Nile Virus, Severe Acute Respiratory Syndrome, monkeypox, and other disease outbreaks—all demonstrated to me that our government faces significant obstacles in effectively "connecting the dots" of knowledge held in the minds of numerous individuals working for different organizational units. Not only is the challenge to discern truth from fiction, but also to put all the pieces of knowledge together to form a complete picture. In this age of knowledge-overload, no one individual harbors sufficient knowledge to either mitigate negative outcomes or capitalize on positive opportunities. Knowledge exchanges in these government agencies must transcend physical group proximity, social networks, and the institutions themselves.

There is a significant correlation between globalization efforts and increasing knowledge velocity, volume, volatility, and veracity concerns. Human societies, economies, and civil infrastructures are increasingly interdependent and complex. Instead of attempting the traditional "top-down" approach to management, my research espouses a "bottom-up" approach to cultivating individual insights. Recall the events of 9/11 and Hurricane Katrina: no one individual harbored sufficient knowledge to mitigate these events. Such realities will occur with increasing frequency for employees of either government agencies or private entities. To assemble the entire puzzle, knowledge exchanges must occur among multiple individuals in different organizational units and institutions without prompting from the "top," but instead must be motivated at the grassroots by collaboration-fostering incentives, values, and trust-relationships; such an idea embodies innovative "knowledge ecosystems."

Bruh: Two can play the game. I believe that while new technology will be essential to effective law enforcement it will be a mixed blessing, and not just because of frauds and other crimes perpetrated through the Internet. More and more individual criminals, criminal organizations, and governments engaged in criminality will be using technology to commit serious crime in the U.S. and elsewhere. Some such crimes will occur in and or originate from the U.S., and even more will be initiated elsewhere. The technology will include the use of sophisticated cameras, electronic and wireless listening devices, and weapons, among a host of other technologies. Greed will still be at the root of most crime, but terrorism will be the world's greatest threat for as far as anyone can now see due to the many ways that large numbers of humans can be destroyed rather quickly by many who want to do such a thing.

Chobar (4): Just like it is said, "As soon as the U.S. releases new currencies, the counterfeiters already are equal to the task of printing money," sophisticated technology enables terrorists and terrorism to be ahead of policing agencies. Money often is no stumbling block. Thus, with wealthy individuals supporting terrorism, the very latest in technology can almost instantaneously be in the hands of terrorists. This can cover every new technological device from A to Z; satellite cell phones to ground-to-air missiles, to laser technology, to the most hideous war weapons—capable of killing hundreds and thousands of people at one time.

Costigan (4): Yes, and with far-ranging negative and positive consequences. If terrorist attacks continue in the United States, technology may be sought out as the first resort to discover terrorists. False-positives will also increase, and privacy will continue to wane. Costs of systems will be borne primarily by the government, while private industry attempts to continue to maximize the bottom line. Security for corporations will continue to be dominated by profit margins, and so high-tech solutions will not be preferred options.

CZARNECKI: What this really means is that information increasingly dominates. Information can be compiled through computing and/or genetics, at least as far as technology forecasting can see. Who will benefit? The rich? At who's expense, since information, like energy, can neither be created nor destroyed, just converted? The poor? Information-related technologies expand to suppress the violent inklings of the poor; Orwell's *1984* gets an updating in the name of security and public safety. Because of this, Trend 28 decreases the likelihood of terrorism—but at the cost of individual privacy and civil rights.

JENKINS: See Trend 5.

LANOTTE: "…to assist them, engineers will develop automated systems to help 'mesh' information from incompatible data stores, recognize patterns in the data, develop rigorous hypotheses, perform collaborative analyses, and 'capture' the skills of the most capable analysts so that others can benefit from them, even when the analysts themselves are not available." This is indeed a lofty goal. I can only assume that, along with this prediction, true artificial intelligence (AI) technology is imbedded in the prediction. Along with the introduction and use of AI in criminal cases, will be the requirement to make the evidence admissible in court.

NOZAWA: In the United States fundamental scientific advances have been few since 1992. Administration policy put advanced scientific projects on hold, and agencies such as DARPA [Defense Advanced Research Projects Agency] and AF Lab resorted to developing widgets. New discoveries were ignored. DARPA's attempt to regroup under the present Administration and "reach for the far shore" appears to have failed. The situation is unchanged today.

The United States is far behind Japan in the development of robots using advanced multiple-valued logic. The U.S. wasted its time in internecine wars arguing about whether fuzzy logic and other non-probabilistic logics were real or not. During the same period, China surpassed Japan and developed the largest cadre of fuzzy logicians.

Artificial intelligence as defined in the 1980s was dead by 1991. It had been built around a collapsed objective scientific philosophy. Only robotics and vision survived and continued. DARPA in 2007 is unable to make real headway since no new fundamental knowledge has been discovered by DARPA to overcome the disaster of the 1980s. Scientific semeiotics provides the answers needed, but DARPA and others have lacked the talent necessary to recognize the value of Scientific Semeiotic…they don't know that they don't know.

Airline Pilots Assistance and similar systems lack systems design methodologies to develop the envisioned technologies. Again, Scientific Semeiotic provides the necessary system design processes to develop these advanced systems.

Technologically related changes have been on hold for most of the last twenty years. The end of Cold War, the Peace Dividend, and the artificial stoppage of scientific advancement has resulted in the downward trend with nothing to stop it unless a fundamental change in scientific philosophy is made.

If the terrorists (Jihadist) see what is developing in systems design and intelligence analysis, then they will merely need to be patient and let us destroy ourselves through neglect, incompetence and the absence of critical thinking.

OSBORNE: There are not enough trained, skilled, and knowledgeable law enforcers who can tackle problems based in current technology—identity theft, white collar crimes, and cybercrime. Emerging technologies are likely to bring further challenges, which justice and security agencies will [be] ill-equipped to face. However, sometime in the next 20 years, more sophisticated technologies will become much easier to use with relatively little training. These tools will be widely adopted and will transform intelligence and policing.

SNYDER (7): IT applications will continue to eliminate mountains of paperwork—and paperworkers—de-staffing back-office operations and curtailing commodity white-collar employment in the industrialized world.

STEELE: The reliance of microchip technology in about everything would render major systems inoperable if coordinated EMP [Electromagnetic Pulse] bombs were detonated in a variety of critical locations, such as air traffic control centers. EMP bombs over grid-locked highways might be followed by explosives, gas, or anthrax.

TAN: Technological change and innovation is something that will increasingly dominate society but this very change brings challenges. Technology promises to unleash new means of dealing with the security and terrorism challenges we face, but the danger in building systems—for instance, in data mining, etc.—is that we can be driven too much by technology, neglecting the fact that no one can replace excellent intelligence analysts who have the in-depth training and deep knowledge to be able to make sense of the vast amounts of information and intelligence that is coming through. Ultimately, technology provides the tools for counter-terrorism, but this fixation with technology unfortunately often comes at the expense of developing good human analysis and judgment. These ultimately cannot be replaced by technology.

YOUNG: If certain parts of certain societies continue to believe they are disenfranchised by globalization as represented by technological advances, terrorism will continue to plague the world.

5 – PRIVACY, ONCE A DEFINING RIGHT FOR AMERICANS, IS DYING QUICKLY. (TREND 17)

- Internet communications, a basic part of life for many people, are nearly impossible to protect against interception, and governments around the world are working to ensure their unfettered access to them. Postings to blogs and Web forums are nearly immortal.

    – The contents of most Internet-connected computers are open to virtually unobstructed snooping by anyone with a minimum of skill and the will to examine them. All but the most secure can be invaded by more-capable hackers.

- Corporate databases are collecting and marketing data on individual credit-worthiness, incomes, spending patterns, brand choices, medical conditions, and lifestyles.

    – While privacy regulations bar distribution of much personal information in the European Union, restrictions in the United States are much weaker.

- Widespread surveillance of private individuals is technically feasible and economically viable, as tiny, powerful cameras now cost next to nothing. Increased surveillance has become socially acceptable in an age when many people fear terrorism and crime.

    – In Britain, an estimated 4.2 million surveillance cameras watch over streets, office buildings, schools, and shopping centers, making the U.K. one of the most closely monitored nations in the world. On average, Britons are caught on camera an estimated three hundred times per day.

    – In the United States, the growth of surveillance also is driven by the fear that lawsuits following a future terrorist attack could claim that failure to install monitoring equipment constitutes negligence.

    – Video surveillance systems have been installed in Chicago, New York City, Washington DC, Tampa FL, and other cities around the United States, In most cases, local police departments have been a driving force in this movement. Protests thus far have been small and ineffective.

- The USA Patriot Act of 2001 sets aside the constitutional requirement of a search warrant for government officials who wish to search someone's home in order to thwart possible terrorism. Its provisions have been used to justify searches in pursuit of drug dealers and even, in one attempt thus far blocked by the courts, copyright abusers.

Assessment:

Pessimists could say that privacy already is a thing of the past; society is merely coming to recognize its loss. We believe that enough effective privacy survives outside the most authoritarian countries to justify noting its continued erosion. However, this trend could easily reach its logical conclusion within ten years.

Implications:

In the future, privacy is likely to be defined, not by the ability to keep information truly secret, but by the legal power to restrict its distribution. Even this limited form of privacy will be eroded as both government and private organizations find legal justification for their interest in personal information. Once access is granted to any type of information, it is unlikely ever to be rescinded.

Most surveillance provisions of the USA Patriot Act will survive, even if the law itself is repealed or modified.

In the absence of a major terrorist event, most Americans will continue to consider privacy a "right," and privacy-related lawsuits are likely to proliferate as more people feel violated or inconvenienced by surveillance. However, courts will be unsympathetic to such suits for so long as conservative appointees dominate the bench.

In large and medium-size cities around the world, spaces that remain unwatched by video cameras will continue to shrink.

Growing numbers of companies, and even private citizens, will encrypt their computer data.

The number of criminal cases based on surveillance will grow rapidly in countries with the required technological sophistication and infrastructure.

Private citizens increasingly will use similar technologies to watch over government abuse, as in cases where bystanders have recorded police misconduct with their cell-phone cameras.

Implications for Terrorism:

It will be nearly impossible for terrorists to operate without being observed. However, until artificial intelligence systems "learn" to recognize suspicious activities, manpower will limit use of these observations. Except in obvious target areas, surveillance will be most useful in forensic reconstruction, rather than in active incident prevention.

What remains of privacy protections often conflicts with security needs. A good example is the recent decision to scrap an important data-mining program at the DHS on the grounds that it might implicate the innocent in terrorism or other illegal activities. A more appropriate solution would have been to require that data used by the program be confirmed by at least two independent sources, as is routinely done in the intelligence community.

This is clearly one of the ten most important trends for antiterrorism. It may be one of the top five.

Expert Comments:

Ayers (10): Because of the success of ubiquitous surveillance in the U.K., it would appear that individuals in the U.S. will have to settle for what was previously considered to be the "Big Brother" approach. While this may generally keep people "honest," it might also encourage a collective sense of paranoia—people are, after all, actually being watched. It might additionally make a population which is already litigiously inclined even more determined and/or reckless in pursuit of monetary gain. While some individuals would simply use the system for their own agenda (absolutely anything could be offensive to someone), terrorists could exploit the tendency of others to "give in" when threatened with legal action. Furthermore, if terrorists could tie up specific surveillance procedures in litigation, disruption of terrorist operations would be difficult. It would therefore be beneficial to governing authorities who foresee the dying destiny of privacy in America, to fully consider the unintended consequences and take action to prevent terrorists from exploiting legal loopholes in their efforts to destroy us from within.

Bray (4): Yes, and this loss of privacy has largely occurred without consideration of what will be lost if it does die (in fact, privacy probably already has died). Recent public debates have considered whether the U.S. federal government has the right to conduct electronic surveillance of its citizens, to include monitoring financial transactions and telephone conversations. Most of these debates seem to perceive that ensuring both privacy and protection is not possible—but such a belief is fallacious. Improving the ability of government as an information processing system to better aggregate, filter, act upon, and redirect information must not—and does not—require sacrificing the freedoms of individual citizens.

To prove that privacy and protection are equally obtainable, consider an example where public key encryption allows the masking of collected information from human eyes, but not from processing and linking to other sources of information by trusted information systems themselves. By use of encryption, this masking of collected information provides only "de-identified" information (with personal identifiers removed) to government workers (Straub and Collins, 1990; Rindfleisch, 1997). However, the trusted information systems themselves can access personal identifiers and link different sources of information.

Ideally, these trusted information systems would work non-stop to sort through and identify suspicious patterns of information. Examples of suspicious patterns include an individual living in a large city purchasing a large quantity of castor beans (which can be used to make ricin toxin) with no discernable legitimate purpose, or regular records of large bank deposits from an unclear source of questionable origin. If the patterns are extremely suspicious, the information systems can present the suspicious patterns (de-identified, with personal identifiers removed) to government workers. These workers then decide whether to convene an expedited court hearing to judge if the encrypted personal identifiers associated with the information should be unlocked. Lawyers for a defense—in the absence of the unknown individual(s)—and a prosecution, present opposing sides to the best of their ability. A federal judge decides whether the de-identified pattern of activities provides sufficient cause to lift the freedom of privacy for the collected information. Should the judge rule that the de-identified pattern of information is suspicious enough to merit unlocking the protected identities, an electronic key issued by the court will permit this action. Similar to issuing a warrant, such an approach maintains anonymity of collected information unless a court hearing finds probable cause and temporarily removes this freedom.

Achieving both privacy and protection offers several added benefits: bridging of different government cultures, encouraging collaborations, and increasing the likelihood of positive outcomes. Recall the example of detecting a bioterrorism agent—this situation requires collaboration between the public health and national security communities. Currently, however, collaborations between such communities are few, a result partially from different organizational cultures surrounding information exchange. Exchange of information between public health professionals is open and collegial, whereas the national security community emphasizes compartmentalization and security.

For public health, a central challenge involves linking multiple health records accurately to a common individual across all 50 states without access to a personal identifier. The privacy of individuals is a top priority for public health, specifically the protection of individual health information. The U.S. federal government is limited from collecting personal information as a result of the Health Insurance Portability & Accountability Act of 1996 (HIPAA). Identifying attributes that could be useful in linking different pieces of health information to a common individual—Social Security number, home address, or name—are not available by current law to federal agencies, including the U.S. Centers for Disease Control and Prevention. Health organizations must strip locally stored information of personal identifiers when sent to external partners outside of a state.

For national security, a central challenge involves maintaining the integrity of our national borders despite the sheer volume of traffic that comes in and out daily. Should national security efforts only monitor individual border crossings, they risk security that is either too loose at stopping illegitimate traffic or too restrictive at permitting legitimate traffic. Realistically, our national borders cannot be completely contained and still function. Instead, national security must strive to monitor activity both inside and outside of our borders, to detect threats before they arrive at our borders and catch any that manage to evade detection and enter the country.

Fortunately, the earlier example combining the use of public key encryption and the court system can also help solve these challenges for both public health and national security. By collecting information that is de-identified from human eyes, but not from automated processing by trusted information systems, the privacy of individuals can be maintained for routine government efforts. When a clear danger to either public health or national security presents itself, a court order can be sought to unlock any identities associated with the collected information. Hence, it is possible to meet the needs of both public health and national security without violating the privacy of law-abiding citizens.

CHOBAR: Americans will probably fight to keep their "civil liberties" within privacy, which could delay or significantly slow down the policing and finding of those involved in terrorism or terrorist plots.

COSTIGAN (8): Lack of interest in privacy will accelerate its decline. Younger people, raised in the information technology-driven society, will not learn the values of privacy. Hackers will keep the flame alive in the infotech world, and privacy advocates will do their best. Greater susceptibility to identity theft will make for new terrorist advantages: when people fail to recognize the need for privacy, or expose their network of friends, they will be easier to exploit. In other countries, privacy is not considered ever to be a particular value.

JENKINS: Privacy will continue to be a political battleground as technology improves—more CCTV, smart cameras, face recognition, bulk detection of explosives, etc.

KADTKE: If global terrorist activities continue to increase, the response of nations (particularly in the West) will certainly increase as well. Increasing legal authority for monitoring, search, seizure, and prosecution may accelerate, and political and public support for such reaction will likely grow stronger as well. Information technology will be increasingly relied on for surveillance and tracking of both physical actors as well as cyber-actors. Unfortunately, these trends are already leading to serious degradations of personal privacy, as IT capabilities can already be used to mine for a variety of types of open information on personal activities, and their constraint under current law and regulation is often vague.

KAPINOS: Certainly, with enhanced capability for electronic surveillance across many venues, as well as improving data-mining tools, it is more important than ever that we develop a consensus on the rule sets to govern these capabilities. Laws, policies, and procedures must be established at all levels of government that define how we control, manage, and use the information that we can obtain. We must ensure the proper balance between the legitimate needs of the law enforcement and intelligence communities verses the Constitutional rights of our citizens.

KRIESBERG: Much discussion seems to pit security and freedom against each other as if they were in opposition, when that is not usually the case. Trying to maximize security by restricting freedom is often counterproductive. Enemies are created by overzealous imposition of restrictions. Useful ideas are lost. Resources are wasted in imposing non-essential limitations.

LADUKE (9): Words spoken or transmitted will increasingly be the primary means of detection of hostile interests. But privacy intrusions in efforts to intercept those words are receiving increasing resistance in the U.S. A culture clash between tolerance and privacy intrusions is emerging, for example, the LAPD's "Muslim Mapping Plan." (http://www.latimes.com/news/local/la-me-muslim15nov15,0,6998542.story?coll=la-home-center)

MILLER: This may change, and one can certainly find evidence of push-back by elements on both the far right and the far left of the U.S. political spectrum. It is true that privacy loss tends to ratchet downward without meaningful upticks, but the excesses of the recent past may have created their own antivirus, if only temporarily. The efforts of terrorism should not be hampered unduly by privacy concerns. A claim that terrorism can be obliterated by sufficient abrogation of personal rights is surely unreal. And, it is difficult to argue that the state does not retain sufficient power to effectively pursue and negate the impact of terrorist violence directed at the civilian population—at least in the U.S.

NOLTE: See Don Kerr's remarks on this. (He is principal deputy DNI.) This is, it seems to me, a huge issue. If Kerr is right and we've lost privacy in the traditional sense, what new definition of privacy, if any, will publics insist on?

OSBORNE: Privacy will be redefined in an iterative process as transparency grows within law enforcement and in society. As the public debate around privacy issues grows due to increased use of cameras and other surveillance equipment in urban areas for crime detection/law enforcement, public use of small cameras, recorders, and at home surveillance systems will grow. Police activity will be tracked via GPS on vehicles and perhaps on officers. Videos of officers' interactions will be used for accountability and lawsuit protection. Police will become more accountable to citizenry as crime mapping on the Internet and other types of data are made available for analysis outside of the law enforcement environment, to be used by city planners and private security.

STEELE: Challenges to information security are making levels of intelligence and military secrecy less possible. This will challenge target ascertainment.

TAN: The events of 9/11 have resulted in a massive assault on and erosion of civil liberties throughout the world. Lawyers and civil society activists have since then been engaged in an on-going debate over "security versus freedom"— this debate is important and must be encouraged. Governments and security services must be prepared to participate in it, with a view to negotiating with the rest of civil society where the boundaries and balance might lie. The failure to keep talking and keep negotiating means that we would have lost to the terrorists. Without doing too much, the terrorists have managed to erode some fundamental freedoms such as privacy. The security versus freedom (i.e., freedom from fear, right to privacy, etc.) is an important debate and civil society must agree to where that balance should lie. Without legitimacy, the cause is on the way to being lost.

YOUNGS: Privacy is a right that the public is still reluctant to give up, however, this will change in the event of another attack. If holy warriors wreck havoc in the United States by mass murder and assassination, then citizens will look to the government for protection. Hate crimes will increase against Muslims and more Americans will become armed. Several states have seen an increase in requests for carrying concealed weapons. If chaos prevails, more citizens will take the law into their own hands.

---

6 – THE GLOBAL ECONOMY IS GROWING MORE INTEGRATED. (TREND 8)

- Only half of the world's one hundred largest economies are nation-states. The rest are multinational corporations.

- In the European Union, relaxation of border and capital controls and the adoption of a common currency and uniform product standards continue to make it easier for companies to distribute products and support functions throughout the Continent.

- The Internet continues to bring manufacturers effectively closer to remote suppliers and customers.

- Companies are increasingly farming out high-cost, low-payoff secondary functions to suppliers, service firms, and consultants, many of them located in other countries.

– Parts for the new Boeing 787 "Dreamliner" are being constructed in at least eight countries around the world for assembly in the United States

– Toyota has manufacturing or assembly plants in Japan, Australia, Canada, Indonesia, Poland, South Africa, Turkey, the United Kingdom, the United States, France, Brazil, Pakistan, India, Argentina, Czech Republic, Mexico, Malaysia, Thailand, China, Vietnam, Venezuela, and the Philippines.

• Companies in high-wage countries also are outsourcing management and service jobs to low-wage countries.

– An estimated 3.3 million U.S. jobs are expected to migrate to India and China by 2015. Some 40 million jobs are believed vulnerable to outsourcing.

– There is a nascent countertrend among job-receiving countries to establish branches in the donor lands. For example, in September 2007, India's Wipro announced that it was setting up a programming division in Virginia, both to hire top-quality American programmers and to help tap the lucrative government market.

– Jobs in western Europe are migrating to eastern Europe, the former Soviet Union, and the English- and French-speaking former colonies of Africa. India has begun to ship jobs to even lower-cost countries in Africa.

Assessment:

This trend will continue for at least the next two decades.

Implications:

The growth of e-commerce enables businesses to shop globally for the cheapest raw materials and supplies. In niche markets, the Internet also makes it possible for small companies to compete with giants worldwide with relatively little investment. This has brought new opportunities for quality-control problems and fraudulent cost-cutting by suppliers, as seen in the recent spate of tainted food and other products coming from China.

The Net also has created a generation of "e-preneurs" whose businesses exist largely on the Internet, with production, fulfillment, and other functions all outsourced to specialty firms.

Demand will continue to grow for employee incentives suited to other cultures, aid to executives going overseas, and the many other aspects of doing business in foreign countries

However, rising demand for foreign-language training is likely to be a temporary phenomenon, as more countries adopt English as part of their basic school curricula.

Western companies may have to accept that proprietary information will be shared not just with their immediate partners in Asian joint ventures, but also with other members of the partners' trading conglomerates. In high technology and aerospace, that may expose companies to extra scrutiny due to national-security concerns.

• Establishing overseas branches mitigates this concern by keeping trade secrets within the company, even while gaining the benefits of cheaper foreign labor and other resources.

Economic ties can give richer, more powerful countries considerable influence over their junior partners. Thus far, China has been the most successful at wielding this "soft" power. This has given it the ability to undermine American foreign policy even as it secures its energy and raw-materials needs.

Implications for Terrorism:

International fraud, money laundering, and other economic crimes (particularly carried out via the Internet) are a growing problem, and one that can be expected to spread. At least some of these activities can be expected to finance extremist and terrorist movements.

In addition, entrepreneurial success in global markets could widen the gap between the rich and poor, worsening social strains in countries already vulnerable to extremist movements. It is likely to worsen the problem of international terrorism.

FI rates this one of the top five trends for terrorism.

Expert Comments:

ANONYMOUS (5): This is a very important and largely positive trend because growing global economic integration creates "global consciousness," facilitating inter-governmental and transnational collaboration. Such collaboration among intelligence and security services, industry, and the nongovernmental sector is needed to anticipate and to address boundary crossing terrorist threats. Of course, global integration also provides opportunities for terrorists to cause globally cascading damage by attacking key nodes in global networks. And the rise of global consciousness itself will be challenged by geopolitical divisions caused by the scramble to secure access to oil in an environment of tight supply. (Trend 18: Despite efforts to develop alternative source of energy, oil consumption is still rising rapidly.)

ARMSTRONG: See earlier comments in Trend 1 on local vs. global/U.S.

CHOBAR: It's hard to know who funds what anymore because the global economy is growing more integrated. While local governments struggle to fund policing, national and global terrorist groups easily find funds to communicate on the most sophisticated of levels. This integrated economy makes it more and more difficult to police and more and more likely to enable global terrorism.

FORSTER: All forms of integration dramatically impact the terror paradigm. Economic integration means the potential impact of terrorist attacks is more extreme. For example, the economic impact of a disabled U.S. power grid would quickly surge through the global economy. Integration also eases the flow of individuals, information, and finances and thus improves the capabilities of terrorist organizations. The multi-headed "hydra" that is Al Qaeda today has been facilitated by the ability to train, recruit, plan, finance, and propagandize operations at a distance. The need for a hierarchical command and control structure has been replaced by a networked ideology that inspires, supports, and publicizes action. The space and time paradigm has changed, reducing the importance of geographic proximity. Cyber-attacks, for example, may be launched against any G-8 state from Pakistan. The problems experienced by the Estonian government in the spring 2007 offer insight into the threat of such attacks. The flow of people, goods, finances, and information also increase the cost of protection and prevention and potentially inhibit pursuit and recovery.

However, integration also may be turned into a counter-terror advantage. As a result of increased interdependence, more lives are negatively impacted by terrorist attacks. Under such circumstances, there is hope that impacted innocents will be less inclined to overlook terrorist activities in their locales. The recent Sunni Iraqi shift against Al Qaeda in al-Anbar Province indicates that the support for violence is finite among societal sectors and continued terrorist violence may be a catalyst to anger against the perpetrators and an increase in anti-terror sentiments.

JENKINS: Globalization means increased transnational crime—terrorism, financial fraud, money laundering, cyber-crime, human trafficking, counterfeit goods, smuggling, etc. This complicates issues of jurisdiction, cooperation among police forces, relationships between local law enforcement and federal authorities and the private sector. We will also increasingly see transnational gangs.

KADTKE: The IT revolution and technology-based economies are also driving physical integration of the global economy. As large, and increasingly mid-sized, companies outsource their manufacturing, research, and even management capabilities to many corners of the globe, they become increasingly vulnerable to a wide spectrum of regional and local socio-political woes. The net effect is that local extreme events can have global attention and effect as they propagate throughout the global supply chain.

LaDUKE (1): Because economy generates the power to ensure defense and wage war, it is central to every national interest. But centralizing economy and trade does not automatically centralize nation state interests, so it has the affect of creating a global stage of "actors" with hidden agendas that create diverse alliances and fund terrorism covertly. I see this as the primary root cause behind the growth of global terrorism.

MEILAHN: International fraud, money laundering, etc., via the Internet will be a tool used by terror groups to finance their activities.

MILLER: Actually, it is more interesting to speculate that globalization may have peaked and nations are in a cocooning phase, much like the U.S. just before WWII. One has only to look at the vigorous debate over the "illegal immigrant" issue in the U.S. to see the possible birth of a counter-trend. While this erection of physical and other barriers to entering the country may enhance the level of public fear, I think it may actually offer more opportunities for counter-terrorism—or, at least, counter-transnational-terrorism.

SANDERS (3): See comments under "Complexity and the Future of Terrorism" in Appendix C.

SHTULMAN: The movement of hundreds of billions of dollars to the oil-rich nations and their desire to invest those dollars in everything from high-tech companies with military applications to international shipping companies, airlines, and ports means that it is inevitable that at some point elements with connections to terror will gain control of the means to transport materials and/or men into the United States at will. Corporations that have no connections to terror today can make such acquisitions and later themselves be acquired by others with ties to terror.

SNYDER (6): Economic globalization will continue to depress both wages and job growth in mature industrial economies for at least five more years, fueling domestic political opposition to free-trade and liberalized immigration, and fostering increased xenophobia.

YOUNG: Globalization and distribution of wealth can only help decrease the specter of terror over the long run.

7 – URBANIZATION, ARGUABLY THE WORLD'S OLDEST TREND, CONTINUES RAPIDLY. (TREND 27)

- Forty-eight percent of the world's population currently lives in cities, according to the Population Reference Bureau's 2006 *World Population Data Sheet.* By 2030, that figure will grow to 60 percent, as some 2.1 billion people are added to the world's cities.

  - More than three-fourths of the population in developed countries live in cities. In North America, urbanization is the highest, at 79 percent. But cities are growing fastest in the developing world.

  - The big are getting bigger. In 1950, there were just eight megacities, with populations exceeding 5 million, in the world. By 2015, there will be fifty-nine megacities, forty-eight of them in less developed countries. Of these, twenty-three will have populations over 10 million, all but four in the developing lands.

– Natural increase now accounts for more than half of population increase in the cities; at most, little more than one-third of urban growth results from migration.

• Up to 1 billion city dwellers lack adequate shelter, clean water, toilets, or electricity. The United Nations estimates that these problems cause 10 million needless deaths annually.

• Urbanization has significant environmental consequences.

– Fuels burned in cities account for 75 percent of global carbon emissions from human activity, according to the Worldwatch Institute.

– NASA scientists point out that urbanization also tends to put buildings and blacktop on the most fertile land, eliminating significant quantities of carbon-absorbing plants.

– Urbanization also deprives surrounding areas of water: Instead of sinking into the ground, rain is collected, piped to the city, used, treated as gray water, and then discarded into the ocean. In some regions, such as near Atlanta, water levels in local aquifers are declining rapidly because the water that once replenished them now is lost.

• The United States is the one major exception to the global urbanization trend. This automobile-reliant society built one of the best highway systems in the world and has relatively little mass transit, so more Americans live in the suburbs than in the cities. This could only occur where there are large swaths of land with low population density.

Assessment:

After surviving for some 3,500 years, this trend is unlikely to disappear in the next 50.

Implications:

Cities' contribution to global warming can only increase in the years ahead.

As the world's supply of potable water declines, people are concentrating in those areas where it is hardest to obtain and is used least efficiently. This trend will aggravate water problems for so long as it continues.

Many more people will die due to shortages of shelter, water, and sanitation. Epidemics will become still more common as overcrowding spreads HIV and other communicable diseases more rapidly.

Since urban growth is now due more to natural increase than to migration, programs designed to encourage rural populations to remain in the countryside may be misplaced. Education and family planning seem more likely to rein in the growth of cities.

Implications for Terrorism:

Concentrating the poor and powerless in cities produces conditions ideal for the spread of petty crime, violence, and the kind of religious extremism that lends itself to terror-prone political ideologies. It also provides easy targets for terrorism in some ethnic and sectarian conflicts.

Expert Comments:

ANONYMOUS (6): Third world megacities provide a cauldron in which criminal, radical, and pathologically violent elements can easily blend. Moreover, some are or will become effective "ungoverned territories" as police/domestic intelligence lack the resources to exercise surveillance and control in sprawling slums. This provides an especially fertile environment for the growth of terrorist groups and for unfettered plotting, with easy access to technology, communications, and transportation.

ARMSTRONG: See earlier comments in Trend 1 on local vs. global/U.S.

BRAY (5): Yes, urbanization creates problems both socially and environmentally, but also in terms of urban infrastructure. Specifically, for the government services that try and provide urban stability—and their need to balance protection and privacy of their citizens. For urban governments to achieve both privacy and protection, the ability to authenticate and exchange information securely across multiple departments and agencies is essential to prevent unintentional sharing of government information with incorrect or unidentified third parties (U.S. GAO, 2001, 2003a). If government workers are to collaborate frequently across departments and agencies, they need to locate and validate the identity of each other before they can confidentially share collected information (U.S. GAO, 2006b). This process requires a single security "trust broker" to provide common authentication across all government workers and databases. Such a single authenticating trust broker, when combined with database encryption for all government technology assets (to include files located on laptops), could help to prevent data leak concerns associated with an event similar to a recent laptop theft at the U.S. Department of Veterans Affairs. The stolen government laptop contained the unencrypted personal records of 26.5 million individuals (*New York Times*, 2006d).

Equally, for workers and databases to exchange information successfully, they need to "speak" a similar language. Unfortunately, proprietary databases built by one government agency often cannot share information with other departments and agencies. A common, flexible language for the electronic subcomponents of our system of government: where none currently exists: will address this problem (U.S. GAO, 2002, 2003c, 2004a). Creating a single "big picture" across government requires the ability to query across multiple databases simultaneously. A panel of CIA experts recently echoed the need for better cross-government collaborations: internal fragmentation hurts the intelligence efforts of the national security community (Kerr et al., 2006; U.S. GAO, 2006c). For government as an information processing system, both workers and databases are the important nodes that must frequently interact and exchange information.

CZARNECKI: Humankind still has not come to terms with organizing itself in socially constructive, densely populated cities. Call this trend the catalyst or reactor vessel for the other baseline trends. Driven by resource scarcity and/or perceived wealth (relative) from urban jobs, humans flock to cities, particularly in those places that can least afford to adapt to urbanization. Once again, desperation sets in, coupled with the studied sociological perverse effects of crowded environments with unhealthy social structures. Look to Karachi, Pakistan for the future according to this trend.

JENKINS: Judging by Rio de Janeiro, Sao Paulo, Mexico City, Lagos, Johannesburg, Mumbai, megacities border on ungovernability. Policing has not kept up with growth. The danger is that of creating neo-Medieval societies with people of means residing, working, shopping, and dining behind protected perimeters, dangerous no-man's lands in between, and no-go zones for police. Threatened people are inclined to spend money on private security, not police. This is an important policy issue for financially strapped local governments: public order or private security?

KADTKE: Within a very few decades, nearly half the world's population will reside in urban areas, and the greatest growth will occur in some of the poorest areas. These areas have unique characteristics and exhibit many special problems, including resource requirements, pollution density, and social stresses caused by high population densities. They are also clear breeding grounds for extreme political and terrorist movements, due to the readiness of resources, and they present enormous problems to policing and maintaining of civil order.

MILLER: Now, this is a problem that impacts terrorism, as France and other European countries are discovering. The growing numbers of disaffected will only increase the size of the fertile ground of terrorism recruits.

Osborne: As communities are faced with increasingly limited resources to meet taxpayers' needs, the one-person and small police departments will be incorporated into other entities. Regional police and other modes of policing, including privatization will emerge. Data gathering requirements for intelligence-led policing may require a system wherein commanders and analysts are regionalized while ground troop officers are localized.

Smyre (5): With more large cities in the world, and more people packed in less space, there will be greater loss of hope in times of economic and social problems (lack of food due to extreme oil shocks), potentially leading to multiple reasons for different kinds of terrorism.

Snyder (2): The urbanized share of the world's population will continue to grow rapidly, rising from 50 percent today to 60 percent by 2030. The fastest growing cities lie in Africa, the Middle East, South Asia, and Latin America, where 25 percent to 90 percent of the urban population ALREADY live in mega-slums in which there are no basic utilities and essentially NO effective police presence. This is an invitation for political unrest and violence.

Young: With respect to terror, urbanization can create the seeds for social discontent and possible urban warfare and terror acts. Conversely, if individuals/immigrants are properly assimilated within the host society and jobs are created, urbanization can act as a terror deterrent.

8 – The Internet continues to grow, but at a slower pace. (Trend 34)

- In mid-2007, Internet users numbered about 1.173 billion, up just less than one-fourth in three years.

- Most growth of the Internet population is now taking place outside the United States, which is home to only 19 percent of Internet users.

  - U.S. Internet users now account for about 75 percent of the American population, a figure that has only crept higher for several years.

  - In mid-2007, the most recent available data showed 162 million Internet users in China (12.3 percent of the population), 42 million in India (3.7 percent), and 86.3 million in Japan (67.1 percent.)

  - Internet penetration is lagging badly in Africa, where only 3.6 percent of the population is online. Most Internet users are in the North African countries or in the republic of South Africa. In between, Internet connections are scarce.

- When it comes to percentage of broadband users, the United States ranks only 15th among the developed lands and 24th over all. About 47 percent of American Internet users have broadband service, compared with 90 percent in South Korea.

  - Americans also get poorer service, paying about $35 per month for download speeds of 1.5mbps and only 256kbps upload speeds. Japanese Internet users pay about the same for 50mbps service.

- In mid-2007, there were 2.66 billion IP addresses on the Internet. Of these, nearly 1.4 billion were in the United States, 251 million in the U.K., 154 million in Japan, and 116 million in China.

- E-commerce is still growing, but not as quickly as it once did.

  - In the United States, total retail sales in the first quarter of 2007 came in at about $999.5 billion, Internet retail sales at $31.5 billion, just 3.2 percent of the total and growing by only 0.1 percent of the total for the last three quarters.

- Total Internet sales are expected to reach $116 billion for the year.

- Sales growth, as much as 25 percent per year in 2004, is expected to slow to 9 percent annually by 2010.

• Not long ago, the Internet was predominately English-speaking. In mid-2007, English and "Chinese" (we assume this combines mainland Mandarin, Taiwanese Mandarin, and Cantonese) were tied at 31.7 percent of Internet users.

- More than 5 percent of Netizens spoke Spanish, Japanese, German, or French.

Assessment:

This trend will continue until essentially no one in the world lacks easy access to the Internet, about 30 years by our best estimate.

Implications:

Americans will continue to dominate the Internet so long as they produce a substantial majority of Web pages—but that is not likely to be very long.

Analysts believe that Internet growth will not accelerate again until broadband service becomes less expensive and more widely available. This is a matter of government policy as much as of technology or basic costs.

Demands that the United States relinquish control of the Internet to an international body can only gain broader support and grow more emphatic as Americans make up a smaller part of the Internet population.

B2B sales on the Internet are dramatically reducing business expenses throughout the Internet-connected world, while giving suppliers access to customers they could never have reached by traditional means.

The Internet has made it much easier and cheaper to set up a profitable business. An online marketing site can be set up with just a few minutes' work at a cost of much less than $100. This is fostering a new generation of entrepreneurs.

Internet-based outsourcing to other countries has only just begun. Growth in this field will accelerate again as overseas service firms polish their English, French, and German and find even more business functions they can take on.

Cultural, political, and social isolation has become almost impossible for countries interested in economic development. Even China's attempts to filter the Internet and shield its population from outside influences have been undermined by hackers elsewhere, who provide ways to penetrate the barriers.

Implications for Terrorism:

The Internet will remain a primary tool for the management of terrorist operations, particularly as encryption becomes ever more difficult to break. In addition, Internet-based crime may serve as a funding source for some terrorist organizations. In compensation, the growing availability of large quantities of public records and other information over the Internet should bring new opportunities for investigation and interdiction of terrorist activities.

Expert Comments:

ARMSTRONG: See comments on technology in Trend 28.

AYERS: There is a growing interest among social scientists in the way Internet usage is changing socialization. Rather than being a tool for encouraging harmony and peaceful coexistence through increased communication, it seems that the lack of accountability behind the communication has resulted in aggressive displays of decidedly antisocial behavior. The fringes of society can locate the "like-minded" so easily that they rarely have to deal with "polar opposites" unless they seek out opportunities to do so. Those who are of a mindset to probe for differing points of view may simply be trolling for potential targets (such as blogs or chat rooms) within which to engage in deception, inject argumentation, create disruption, generate conflict, and project power in ways that were inconceivable prior to the advent of the Internet. Considering recent news reports detailing abuse and other types of violence documented by the perpetrators themselves in film and text with the specific intention of placing the evidence in "e-space," it would appear that "e-inspired" vilification and assault is on the rise. As aggressively anti-social behavior becomes "the norm" on the Internet, it is also becoming more evident in the physical world. As individuals adopt the role of agitator (whether in "e-space" or physical space) more will follow, if only out of a need for self-defense. This willful polarization of society only serves to enhance terrorist objectives. A population with large and increasing numbers of "sociopaths online" is a target-rich environment for recruitment by terrorists. If Western teens can be coerced into beating up other teens or innocent strangers for a few seconds of "fame," what else might they be capable of?

BRAY (7): Depends on what you mean by the Internet. If by "World Wide Web" yes, it is slowing down and in fact the World Wide Web is ready to die and be replaced with a newer generation concept yet unknown. The Internet itself (as infrastructure) will always exist, but in several areas (VoIP, video) the Internet has experienced dramatic, accelerating growth as more Internet users employ such technologies. So it's difficult to say generically that the Internet is growing/ slowing, but you need to consider specific technologies and why specific technologies might be slowing to make way for something newer.

CHOBAR (2): There is no way local or national policing can monitor all the Internet activity, or if policing does occur it is difficult to do well. Thus, the Internet has given terrorists a "silent," speedy, and effective method for high-speed communication and dissemination of information. This information can provide instant information from the location of troops to the actual providing of classes on building newer, more sophisticated weapons of destruction.

COSTIGAN (6): Many governments will attempt to slow the growth of the Internet or, more precisely, decrease their population's ability to inform themselves in a direct effort to control information flow. In the face of renewed terrorist attacks, even democrat governments may seek ways to reduce information flow. For example, instead of letting the world know which group perpetrated an attack, in an effort to not boost the stature of one terrorist group a government might say it was any number of terrorist groups, but the effect will be the same: reduced information. Additionally, for terrorists, temporary defacement will remain the most likely outcome of "web attacks," but they will continue to exploit weaknesses in Internet-connected systems, potentially using the Internet to mount lightweight attacks against certain systems (supervisory control and data acquisition [SCADA] networks, etc.) if the effort is manageable, cheap and, ideally, an insider is available. Were they to succeed, the damage could be considerable, but it will likely be hit or miss and the overriding question is whether they believe their time would be better spent elsewhere. Importantly, the Internet's value as the cheapest and best communications and propaganda delivery method will override any attempt to fundamentally "crash the system."

KADTKE: With the increasing spread of cyberspace, we are currently witnessing a host of new social networking capabilities and online virtual communities. We have recently seen the first cyberspace enabled-political debate, and governmental as well as private sector organizations are holding meetings and doing business in Second Life and similar virtual worlds. Sociologists observe that many users of these communities relate more closely to the virtual environment than their real lives. Are we trending toward a time when much of the world's population relates more closely to virtual online communities of interest, rather than their traditional physical social organizations or even their nation? What will be the effects as these virtual communities seek to exert political power locally and globally?

MILLER: Conducting counter-terrorism in cyberspace is clearly one of the critical battlefronts. This will increase in activity and importance.

NOLTE: The Internet will remain a source of friction in civil liberties discussions in the U.S. (and elsewhere), as we attempt to rebalance the security/privacy understanding in a very different environment. This clearly impacts the domestic security effort and may have effects internationally as well.

SMYRE (7): This is a two-edged sword related to terrorism. If the increase in the use of the Internet can bring more in poverty to be able to take care of themselves, the cause of terrorism should be reduced. On the other hand, the more on the Internet spreading knowledge of how to make bombs and how to network with other terrorists, the great the level of terrorism that could result.

SNYDER (4): At current growth rates, rising volumes of video-graphic materials transmitted via the Web are now expected to saturate the Internet's carrying capacity by 2010 to 2012, making the entire network increasingly vulnerable to hacker attack and "cybertage."

The IT press reflects a widespread professional consensus that the hacker community has long had the capacity to compromise the Internet, and there is open debate over why no serious attack on the Net has been launched since 2002. One speculative conclusion to this debate has been that the Internet is so vital to the terrorist community's capacity to organize, recruit, and operate that there is a tacit agreement NOT to shut it down.

YOUNG: Most people recognize that without the Internet, the terrorist would be without one of his most valuable tools. The Internet is used for recruiting, fund raising, communication, financial transfers, training, and proselytizing. It has become so valuable that most if not all terror groups have their own websites recognizing that they must keep in the public forefront in order to remain relevant. While the Internet may grow at a slower pace in the future, terrorists will continue to rely on its existence for their existence.

---

9 – ADVANCED COMMUNICATIONS TECHNOLOGIES ARE CHANGING THE WAY WE WORK AND LIVE. (TREND 35)

- The Internet is as much a communications medium as it is an information resource.

- Telecommuting is growing rapidly, thanks largely to e-mail and other high-tech forms of communication. About 80 percent of companies worldwide now have employees who work at home, up from 54 percent in 2003. The number of telecommuters in the United States reached an estimated 20 million in 2006.

    - AT&T says that 90 percent of its employees do some work away from the office, while 41 percent work at home one or two days per week. This saves the company a reported $180 million a year.

    - However, Millennials already have abandoned e-mail for most purposes other than communicating with "clueless" parents and grandparents. Most have adopted instant messaging and social-network Websites to communicate with their peers.

- "Podcasting"—recording college lectures, news stories, business reports, and the like for playback on the Apple iPod—allows users to listen at their convenience.

- Better communications is a major goal of many government agencies, particularly in law enforcement and disaster services, which need to coordinate the activities of many different agencies under emergency conditions.

- So-called "Web 2.0" services are building communities nearly as complex and involving as those existing wholly in the real world.

  - Second Life is a 3-D virtual world entirely built and owned by its residents. Launched in 2003, by May 2007 it had 6.8 million residents, 1.75 million of whom had logged on in the previous two months. Here in the real world, designers earn substantial incomes creating fashions and other paraphernalia for Second Life characters. One resident was banned when his character raped another "avatar" in virtual reality.

  - MySpace and Facebook have a total of more than 180 million members who form communities of friends, most of whom have never met except on the Internet.

  - A number of people have taken to wearing a small Web camera, either recording their entire lives or broadcasting them over the Internet.

Assessment:

Again, this trend has only just begun.

Implications:

E-mail promised to speed business. Instead, it absorbs more time than busy executives can afford to lose. Expect the nascent reaction against e-mail to grow as many people eliminate mailing lists, demand precise e-communications rather than open-ended conversation, and schedule only brief periods for dealing with mail.

Instant messaging is likely to be even more destructive of time for the under-thirty set.

However, e-mail is a major contributor to globalization and outsourcing, because it eliminates many of the obstacles of doing business across long distances and many time zones.

Unfortunately, e-mail and other modern communications techniques also have made possible a variety of crimes, from online fraud to some forms of identity theft.

They also make it virtually impossible to retract ill-considered statements or embarrassing online activities. Once something exists on the Internet, it is all but immortal and nearly impossible to hide.

Implications for Terrorism:

See Trend 34 (item 8 of this list.)

Expert Comments:

ARMSTRONG: See comments on technology in Trend 28.

AYERS (8): "The enemy of the enemy is my friend." There will be ever-increasing communication and cooperation between various criminal elements (drug cartels, ID theft rings, and black-marketers), dissidents, anarchists, terrorists, and rogue elements operating from within the governments of nation-states. With global communications, war planning on a global scale—by coalitions of terrorist and criminal groups as well as coalitions of states—is not only possible, but probable. Instantaneous communications make simultaneous operations an easy task (as seen with the attacks of 9/11). Conversely, the massive amounts and differing modes of communications, combined with antiquated hierarchical structures within Western governments, will make the West more vulnerable, unless or until a method of instantaneous and ubiquitous information gathering and threat warning can be achieved. In the meantime, psychological "blowback," in the form of technology abandonment by the many, could become an issue. Communications might become more difficult because of the overwhelming nature of such, thus limiting the adoption of new technology (or the use of high-tech communications in general). Threat information might therefore ultimately be unattainable or stalled in the process of distribution.

BRAY (8): See Trend 5.

COSTIGAN (7): Of course, but there may be a backlash. Trust is easiest to establish in direct meetings. Banks and financial services companies will attempt io develop better technical systems for trust, but costs will be passed on to the consumer. With continued clever schemes by criminals, establishing a trusted (electronic) connection with your bank will become more difficult still, perhaps even too cumbersome for many. Will that lead to a desire to bank and shop locally? Despite terrorists using communications technologies much in the same ways as other groups, they will continue primary recruiting in trusted spaces—face to face, group to group, with online outreach being a method of last resort. Terrorists and other criminal elements will exploit communications technologies for spreading fear, psychological warfare, making and moving money, planning and research, performing operational assessments, recruiting and encouraging sympathy, and maybe—a low probability—for destruction.

KRIESBERG: Advanced communication technologies will foster diffusion of ideas and awareness of circumstances of others. Diaspora communities will flourish. There are more risks of intense conflicts as cultural differences have more chances to produce clashes.

But it can also generate more appreciation of diversity.

Attention to the implications of these developments is vitally important.

LADUKE (8): Ubiquitous publication of news will increase publicity and will continue to increase the "instantaneous" stakes of changes in global public sentiment. U.S. weakness in managing with public sentiment is helping fuel sponsorship and recruitment for terrorism, which is being used as a tool to dissuade U.S. interests.

The military is waging war with what Barnett calls a "leviathan force," and he contends that the military needs a network of "system administrators" (http://www.ted.com/index.php/talks/view/id/33) to manage humanitarian aid and public sentiment.

Communications in the military tactical sense is not designed to support the kind of culturally sensitive communications that need to occur to change public sentiment in cultures that are very foreign to our own. Essentially, the discipline of public relations needs to increase dramatically within the military and the defense department and globally thread the needle between silence and propaganda.

SANDERS (8): See comments under "Complexity and the Future of Terrorism" in Appendix C.

STEELE: Harnessing the "Medici Effect" [Johansson, Frans, *Medici Effect: What Elephants and Epidemics Can Teach Us About Innovation* Cambridge: Harvard Business School Press, 2006] Proactively searching for the interaction effects and using multivariate thinking in the interaction of Proteus "planes of influence" might increase potential target awareness. The world as a complex cross-impact matrix, not just wildcard thinking.

TAN: This trend also facilitates the spread of radical Islamist and indeed any type of millenarian/apocalyptic ideology in this post-modernist age. It creates a virtual world where these ideologies take root and grow, affecting the real world through its ability to self-radicalize individuals, link up cells, develop terrorist ideas and plans, and help organize actual attacks. The most insidious is the ability to enable a worldwide network of jihadists to emerge and develop. How do you better contain this trend?

Young: There is hardly any terrorist who is not familiar with the common cell phone or satellite phone. As encryption becomes more in the public domain, terrorist communications will become more difficult to intercept.

10: The United States is ceding its scientific and technical leadership to other countries. (Trend 30)

- "The scientific and technical building blocks of our economic leadership are eroding at a time when many other nations are gathering strength," the National Academy of Sciences warns. "Although many people assume that the United States will always be a world leader in science and technology [S&T], this may not continue to be the case inasmuch as great minds and ideas exist throughout the world. We fear the abruptness with which a lead in science and technology can be lost—and the difficulty of recovering a lead once lost, if indeed it can be regained at all."

- Although research and development (R&D) spending is growing in raw-dollar terms, when measured as a percentage of the total federal budget or as a fraction of the U.S. GDP, research funding has been shrinking for some 15 years. In 2005, the United States spent about 2.68 percent of its GDP on R&D, down from 2.76 percent in 2001.

  - Washington has often reduced the post-inflation buying power of its R&D funding request. In the FY 2007 budget, for the first time, it cut R&D funds in absolute dollars as well. The 2007 funding request for R&D totaled about $137 billion, down about 1 percent from FY 2006.

  - Some areas were harder hit. The National Science Foundation lost 3.2 percent of its previous budget; the National Institute of Science and Technology lost 6 percent. Some programs funded by the Federal Energy Efficiency and Renewable Energy Office lost 18 percent.

- Military research now absorbs much of the money that once supported basic science.

  - Since 2000, U.S. federal spending on defense research has risen an average of 7.4 percent per year, compared with only 4.5 percent for civilian research.

  - In 2006, 59 percent of U.S. federal research funding went to defense projects.

  - Of that, an estimated 40 percent went to "earmarks," congressional pet projects often of doubtful value.

  - DARPA has been legendary for its support of "blue sky" research that led to dramatic technical advances, including the creation of the Internet. Today it focuses increasingly on immediate military needs and low-risk development efforts.

- Washington's neglect of basic science is being felt in many ways.

  - Only half of American patents are granted to Americans, a number that has been declining for decades.

– Only 29 percent of the research papers published in the prestigious *Physical Review* in 2003 were by American authors, down from 61 percent in 1983.

• More than half of American scientists and engineers are nearing retirement. At the rate American students are entering these fields, the retirees cannot be replaced except by recruiting foreign scientists.

  – Between 25 percent and 30 percent of high school graduates who enter college plan to major in science or engineering. Fewer than half of them receive a degree in those fields.

  – The number of U.S. bachelor's degrees awarded in engineering in 2005 was nearly 15 percent below the peak 20 years earlier. The United States needs 114,000 engineering graduates each year, according to the Department of Labor. According to most reports, it graduates about 65,000.

  – According to the National Academy of Engineering, the United States produces only about 7 percent of the world's engineers.

  – Only 6 percent of American undergraduates are engineering majors. In Europe, the number is 12 percent; in China, it is 40 percent.

  – Of the doctoral degrees in science awarded by American universities, about 30 percent go to foreign students. In engineering, it is 60 percent.

• By inhibiting stem-cell research, cloning, and other specialties the United States has made itself less attractive to cutting-edge biomedical scientists.

  – The United Kingdom is capitalizing on this to become the world's leader in stem-cell research. In the process, it is reversing the brain drain that once brought top British scientists to the United States, More than seventy leading American biomedical researchers have moved to the UK, along with many less-noted colleagues.

  – Latin America also has been receiving scientific emigrés from the U.S.

• Since post-9/11 immigration restrictions were enacted, the number of foreign students taking the Graduate Record Exam has declined sharply.

  – Applications were off by 50 percent from China, 37 percent from India, 15 percent from South Korea, and 43 percent from Taiwan as of 2004. Though recovering slowly, their numbers remain depressed.

  – Instead of building relationships in the United States—professional loyalties that could contribute to American S&T—these missing students will form their attachments to U.S. competitors.

  – This is significant. About 25 percent of America's science and engineering workforce are immigrants, including nearly half of those with doctoral degrees. During the 15 years ending in 2007, one-third of the American scientists receiving Nobel Prizes were foreign-born.

• According to Purdue president Martin Jischke, by 2010 more than 90 percent of all scientists and engineers in the world will live in Asia.

Assessment:

This trend emerged from a wide variety of ill-conceived political decisions made over the last 30 years. It will take a generation to reverse.

Implications:

If this trend is not reversed, it will begin to undermine the U.S. economy and shift both economic and political power to other lands. According to some estimates, about half of the improvement in the American standard of living is directly attributable to research and development carried out by scientists and engineers.

The Bureau of Labor Statistics predicts that the number of job openings in science and engineering will grow by 47 percent in the five years ending 2010—three times as fast as non-technical fields. The United States will not produce nearly enough home-grown technical specialists to fill them.

Demand to import foreign scientists and engineers on H-1B visas also will continue to grow.

Publicity about the H1-B program, and about the offshoring of R&D to company divisions and consulting labs in Asia, in turn, will discourage American students from entering technical fields. This has already been blamed for shrinking student rolls in computer science.

In 2005, China for the first time exported more IT and communications goods ($180 million) than the United States ($145 million.) Its lead has grown each year since then.

Implications for Terrorism:

The growing sophistication of scientists and engineers in the developing world threatens to put chemical, biological, and nuclear weapons in the hands of international terrorist organizations. The success of A.Q. Khan in creating Pakistan's nuclear program and spreading his knowledge to the Middle East is likely to be just the first of what could be many such examples. This will make intelligence and security duties much more difficult to carry out successfully.

Expert Comments:

ANONYMOUS (9): This exacerbates the effects of rapid technological advance because it diminishes the capabilities of the leading counter-terrorism power to monitor the emergence of new technologies that could be put to terrorist use or diversions of existing technologies. To keep tabs on technological threats, new global or multilateral scientific and technological monitoring mechanisms will be needed, although concerns about safeguarding intellectual property will complicate such efforts.

ARMSTRONG: The U.S. is not ceding its leadership. In fact, S&T is one of the few areas where the U.S. retains global respect, even in the Muslim countries with extremely poor (and violent) views of America. While many look at S&T as almost a liability, that we're dependent on it and that we're not developing enough talent, the rest of the world is mimicking our skills and building on it because of the value they see in it. I have hosted two discussion panels on using S&T as diplomacy for DHS science and technology conferences. The key take-away has been the value of enhancing S&T relationships for long-term benefit. Working with foreign scientists, as well as their communities, either here or abroad, not only taps into and develops additional research and development capacity, it also promotes changes in commercial, academic, infrastructure, and legal systems that form the foundation of democratic institutions, a potential win-win for people and societies and S&T. A promising reality is polling showing American S&T continues to be admired by countries that are increasingly opposed to American politics. The real risk is not empowerment of other countries (see earlier comments on technology and globalization), but on outsourcing, which is a different strategic threat than terrorism, although it increases our liability as disruption on our periphery or in countries beyond our control will have implications for the United States.

CHOBAR (5): I worked for a huge global corporation before returning to education. I watched as this company brought in new employees to various U.S. divisions, from every nation on the planet, to train them in the latest communication, transportation, power generation, water processing, aviation, electrical distribution, security, and water desalination. Policing of people's backgrounds was seldom done. These people went back to their home countries with huge 6" spiral bound notebooks, as well as hundreds of CDs and DVDs of product information. We hand [over] this phenomenal scientific and technical information under the umbrella of being "corporate employees." However, in the hands of terrorists or terrorism supporters, this same scientific and technical leadership is used against us and other nations of the world.

COSTIGAN (5): Fine educations are now available elsewhere, perhaps closer to home, and the response to pre-9/11 immigration policy lead to fewer foreign students in U.S. universities, making them a harder sell. Vigorous attempts by government, and perhaps just the passing of time, have lead to a recent rebounding of foreign enrollment after the 9/11 slowdown. Needless to say, universities are a primary engine for the U.S. S&T and the economy. Thus, it is critical that foreign students, with their leads in sci/tech, seek their education in the U.S. Perhaps just as important as the economic factors, when fewer students come to the United States, the U.S. also loses the opportunity to influence future worldwide corporate and governmental leadership. While high technology may assist in capturing terrorists or reducing the need for interests in terrorism-prone areas, friendly governments and organizations are key to continued strength.

NOZAWA: In the long run, we can recapture the S&T leadership since we still own the knowledge. We have a head start in winning the knowledge war. Charles Sanders Peirce did all the homework and tradeoff analyses and gave us the answers on a golden platter. For the moment, we see neither the knowledge nor the golden platter.

SANDERS (7): See comments under "Complexity and the Future of Terrorism" in Appendix C.

SNYDER (3): Growing shortages in our domestic supply of STEM (Scientists, Technicians, Engineers, and Mathematicians) recruits will make the U.S. increasingly dependent on imported high-skill labor, 25 percent to 30 percent of whom have come from Muslim countries in recent years.

Note that U.S. employers and business lobbies are urgently seeking to double or triple the H-1B visa cap from its current limit of 65,000 per year. Imported personnel could be placed in the U.S. as "sleepers"—for which we are already screening applicants—or could subsequently be suborned into collaborating with terrorists by threats to family members back home. Conversely, Islamists may inveigh against Muslims who work for Americans as traitors, in an attempt to deprive the U.S. of critically needed skills.

ADDITIONAL FINDINGS OF NOTE

While the trends above were of widespread interest, they were far from being the only subjects about which the participants offered valuable observations. All of their comments can be found in the *55 Trends* section that follows and in Appendix C. However, some deserve to be singled out for special attention. We considered the following items to be of particular value:

Reacting to Trend 4, which cites the growth of the world's elderly population, one of our anonymous respondents pointed out a concern that the rest of us had overlooked:

The problem is more one of age structure than of aging per se: not only are there more elderly but, in the developed world in particular, fewer young people. This means that Western militaries will have fewer troops to deploy abroad and a lower tolerance for casualties. They will thus be less inclined to help police ungoverned areas in the lesser-developed world where terrorist groups could find sanctuary.

This participant, a highly placed official with the American government whose responsibilities include antiterrorism activities, cited this trend as the fourth most important for terrorism.

Several members of our expert panel cited the role of local police in the battle against terrorism. This also was a major finding of last summer's SHARP 2007 conference. For example, Dr. William Nolte of the University of Maryland wrote:

This is one instance in which local authorities can help to avert potential terrorism. Good policing can facilitate the process whereby an "alien" population, in this case Muslim, integrates effectively into society, rather than being further alienated from it.

RAND's Brian Jenkins noted:

High levels of immigration will exacerbate ethnic tensions and provoke powerful reactions against both legal and illegal immigration. The major issue for police will be the role of local police in enforcing national policies against illegal immigration. Pressure from local citizens and Washington will push police to play a greater role in reducing illegal immigrant populations with possible adverse effects on community relations and law enforcement.

And:

Globalization means increased transnational crime—terrorism, financial fraud, money laundering, cyber-crime, human trafficking, counterfeit goods, smuggling, etc. This complicates issues of jurisdiction, cooperation among police forces, relationships between local law enforcement and federal authorities and the private sector. We will also increasingly see transnational gangs.

Although no single trend received more than one or two comments about this issue, the role of local policing clearly was a common concern for our panelists.

While this report has been in preparation, a few new issues have presented themselves for consideration. They were too late for inclusion in our expert survey, yet seem too significant to be ignored. We mention them here because we believe that anyone concerned with terrorism should be aware of these potential problems.

One of these is the dirty bomb, a hazard that FI has long considered more likely to materialize than most other proposed high-impact attacks. Although dirty bombs have received considerable attention, they still present unmet challenges. Conventional explosives designed to distribute radioactive materials such as radiological medical wastes over a wide area are not generally counted among weapons of mass destruction. Yet, they could prove more destructive than a limited chemical or biological attack. They also could prove equally difficult to prevent.

Early in 2008, a major exercise in New York City, using a helicopter-borne radiation detector, attempted to locate a cache of cesium-137 being carried in an SUV somewhere in the city. It failed. The attempt, described by Spencer S. Hsu in the February 4, 2008, *Washington Post*, was called off after half an hour owing to technical problems. More encouragingly, a ground unit managed to detect the simulated bomb on 42nd Street, just west of Times Square.

The test was part of the $90 million "Securing the Cities" program, which aims to develop the means to detect and head off radiological attacks on major cities. According to some critics, that goal may be technologically unfeasible. The problem is that an improvised dirty bomb is likely to be shielded with lead or some other material to reduce its radiation signature, making it far more difficult to find. Developing more sensitive detectors capable of finding a shielded bomb is an urgent necessity if cities like New York and Washington are to be relatively safe from radiological attack.

Richard A. Falkenrath, NYPD's deputy commissioner for counterterrorism and formerly a homeland security aide with the Bush White House, says there are at least two more: better communications and data transfer systems for managing the work of monitoring for radiation sources, and better procedures so that the police can check out any alarms without disrupting traffic—which is already possible within Manhattan, but not on the highways on and off the island.

New York City is not without defenses against dirty bombs. More than 1,400 local police officers have been trained to participate in radiation detection efforts. Several thousand radiation detectors have been distributed to police officers and others whose work takes them around the city. In Manhattan, there are half a dozen $500,000 trucks with advanced detectors. And twice a day, the police set up checkpoints on Manhattan streets to train officers in radiation detection procedures and to deter would-be bombers. All this is considerably more protection than any American city enjoyed a few years ago.

Nonetheless, at Forecasting International, we rate improved radiation detectors, communications facilities, and management systems as among the most urgent requirements for improved security against terrorism in the United States.

The second issue is the vulnerability to attack of one of the country's most important, and softest, targets: the passenger rail system. Unlike air travel, which can be watched over quite successfully at boarding gates and other well-defined choke points, trains and subways would be almost impossible to protect, even if they did not have many times the passenger load carried by airlines. Any attempt to do so would instantly bring rail travel to a halt.

The Madrid attacks of March 11, 2004, showed all too clearly what a few pounds of explosives can accomplish when used against rail transport. Yet, three years later the United States has 4.5 million passengers riding New York's trains and subways, Washington has about 550,000 more, and there still is no effective way to defend any of them against a simple bomb.

Other possible attacks on rail systems could be even harder to prevent or interrupt. A suicide bomber could easily detonate his explosives in, say, one of the 42nd street subway stations at rush hour. And the attempt by Aum Shinrikyo to release Sarin nerve gas in the Tokyo subways on March 20, 1995, could easily be repeated, to greater effect, in New York or Washington, D.C.

This situation could change in the near future. In February 2008, the Department of Homeland Security is hosting a major gathering of security experts specifically to examine the question of how to prevent terrorist bombings without interrupting the nation's passenger train service. However, it is difficult to see what can be done about the enormous vulnerability of the rails.

The third item is a development in terrorist relations. It has not happened yet, so far as we know, but the evidence of a new axis of cooperation could arrive at any time. Not long ago, Admiral James Stavridis, head of the U.S. Southern Command, was speaking at a conference in Latin America. "I fear greatly that the connectivity between narcoterrorism and Islamic radical terrorism could be disastrous in this region," he told the assembled officials.

As evidence that such an alliance could be possible, he cited several key associations. Venezuelan president Hugo Chavez met at least seven times with his Iranian counterpart, Mahmud Ahmadinejad. After his fourth visit to Iran, Chavez and Ahmadinejad pledged to cooperate in defense of their national interests and ideals. Other meetings Admiral Stavridis considered worth mentioning included visits between Ahmadinejad and Bolivian president Evo Morales and between Morales and Chavez and Morales and President Rafael Correa of Ecuador.

"Today in Latin America there is a competitive environment for us politically," Stavridis said. "The United States needs to be a good competitor in this marketplace. We need to show why our ideas are better, are sensible [and] will produce good results,"

At FI, we believe that the possibility of a working relationship between Islamic terrorists and their counterparts in the Latin America is significant. Both have important issues with the United States and have shown the willingness to use horrific violence in pursuing their interests. The latter are devoted to money, the former have it in adequate supply. The two groups are natural allies. When they discover their common interests, they could easily turn America's porous southern border from a theoretical danger into a very practical one. This situation would be worse still if narcoterrorists gained a state sponsor in their campaign to defend their commercial interests against the efforts of American law enforcement.

In his talk, Admiral Stavridis suggested a number of ideas to push in striving to recruit or recover friends in Latin America. These included capitalism, free trade agreements, human rights, democracy, and liberty. These all are worthy ideas, with varying degrees of marketability in that region. However, it will take considerably more than a philosophical PR campaign to keep the influence of Al Qaeda and its allies from America's southern doorstep.

Winning over South America's leaders and citizens will require a sustained policy of investment, development aid with no obvious strings attached, human-rights assistance, and visible and effective efforts to improve the well-being of the region's poor. It would help also to ratchet down the widely unpopular Iraq war as soon as possible and to quell any saber-rattling impulse that might be felt in Washington toward any part of the world, not just Latin America.

However, none of this will have any effect on the narcoterrorists, whether or not they ally themselves with Muslim extremism. We see little evidence that anyone knows how to deal effectively with them—not, at least, within the limits of action generally observed between sovereign nations.

55 Trends for the Future of Terrorism

Note that where the text of a comment is preceded by a number, the participant has rank ordered the ten most important trends. The number is that contributor's ranking for the trend.

Note also that in order to be complete, the comments in the section, "Ten Most Important Trends for the Future of Terrorism," above are repeated in the list below.

GENERAL LONG-TERM ECONOMIC AND SOCIETAL TRENDS

1. THE ECONOMY OF THE DEVELOPED WORLD IS ON PATH TO GROW FOR AT LEAST THE NEXT FIVE YEARS.

- The U.S. economy has been expanding continuously, though often weakly, since the fourth quarter of 2001. GDP grew by 3.2 percent in 2006, slowing to 2.6 percent in the fourth quarter of the year and just 0.7 percent in the first quarter of 2007. The consensus forecast calls for a rebound to 2.8 percent growth from the second quarter through year's end, but this depends heavily on the course of private consumption.

- Job creation and unemployment numbers are puzzling. Unemployment rates hovered around 4.5 percent in the first half of 2007, which counts as nearly full employment. About 145,000 new jobs were created each month for the first six months of 2007, according to the official data, compared with 186,000 reported in 2006.

    - Washington says it takes 140,000 new jobs each month to absorb the new workers coming into the labor market. However, a year or two ago, when the population was smaller, 150,000 new workers were said to enter the market each month. New jobs are either drawing down unemployment or leaving some new workers jobless, depending on which number you believe.

    - But that is true only if the job creation numbers are reliable. They aren't. There also is a major conflict between job surveys. For example, in April 2007, the Bureau of Labor Statistics (BLS) reported that its survey of establishments, which tallies payrolls at selected companies, found 88,000 new jobs for the month, including 25,000 in government. In contrast, the BLS household survey, which actually asks people whether they are working, reported a loss of 468,000 jobs for the month! Most economists believe the survey of establishments gives a more accurate picture of employment than the household survey, and in general we agree. Yet there are a number of "fudge factors" built into the establishment survey that may or may not be valid. At the very least, the United States needs to get a better handle on its employment situation.

- Inflation remains under control according to official reports. Both the consumer price index (CPI) and core inflation, neglecting energy and food prices, came in at 2.6 percent in 2006. In 2007, CPI has been sharply higher—up 7 percent, annualized, for the three months ending in May—thanks to spikes in the cost of energy and food. Core inflation rose by only 1.6 percent annualized for the three months ending in May. Government officials argue that core inflation is a more accurate reflection of long-term price trends because the cost of food and energy is so erratic. However, current increases in food and energy are due to long-term problems—the continuing imbalance between supply and demand of refined petroleum products and the growing diversion of corn to ethanol production. We believe CPI is now a much better measure of the economy than core inflation. If so, there may be trouble ahead for consumers.

- For the moment, those consumers do not seem to be seriously worried. In the first quarter of 2007, consumers spent 4.2 percent more than in the previous three months. Spending was off a bit in April, May, and June, but nowhere near as much as the rising CPI and monthly declines of about 0.1 percent in real household income might have suggested. Thus far, it seems consumers will continue to keep the economy growing.

- How does all this add up? At Forecasting International, we believe the growth rate will average about 2.3 percent annually through 2008—a bit more in 2007, slightly less the following year. Until the employment picture becomes much clearer, we will not be truly confident of that number. However, we see no prospect of a significant downturn in the near future.

- The world's second economic dynamo, China, continues to whir. Its GDP officially grew by 10.7 percent—adjusted for inflation—in 2006, with 10.4 percent forecast for 2007 and 2008. Thanks to China's hot export markets, the country's current-account surplus is huge, equivalent to 10.7 percent of GDP in 2007, with 9.8 percent expected in 2008.

  – In fact, China may be even wealthier than it seems. A study of its gray market in 2005, including "all illegal incomes, questionable incomes, and incomes of dubious origins," suggested the true GDP may be 24 percent larger than the official numbers. This powerhouse will keep the global economy humming even if the United States cannot.

- In Germany, Europe's biggest economy is performing well. The country's GDP grew by 3 percent in 2006, its fastest growth since 2000. Inflation is at just 1.9 percent, and real incomes are rising, if only a little. There even are signs that German consumers are beginning to spend for the first time in years. The Conference Board's leading index for Germany was up 1.6 percent for the six months ending in April, with a sharp spike at the end of that period. Economists now predict that the GDP will grow by 2.9 percent in 2007 and 2.2 percent in 2008. The German economy still has structural problems that could worsen any future downturn. Yet for the moment it seems good times should continue at least into 2010.

- The French GDP rose 2.1 percent in 2006, with growth of 2.2 percent expected in 2007 and 2008. That is the good news. Unfortunately, there is bad news as well. Unemployment is stuck above 8 percent. The Conference Board's leading indicator for France has been leveling off and actually declined slightly in May 2007. The government absorbs 50.7 percent of the GDP in taxes but spends more, giving a budget deficit of 2.4 percent. Plans to cut taxes more than spending could put the deficit over the 3 percent allowed by the European Union. In all, there is room to wonder how long France can sustain its growth beyond 2008.

- The British economy grew by 2.8 percent in 2006 and continued growing at that rate, on average, through the first half of 2007.

  – This is even better news than it sounds, as the second quarter of 2007 marks the 60th consecutive quarter of growth in Britain. Measured by GDP and inflation, the British economy has been more stable than at any other time in memory; the longest previous run of continuous growth was just nineteen quarters. Unemployment was only 5.5 percent in early 2007. Consumer spending has been strong, but was softening in early to mid-2007. Yet at mid-year, the Conference Board's leading index for the United Kingdom was growing at an annual rate of 4.5 percent. Short of a global recession, the UK's GDP seems destined to continue growing by 2.5 percent annually, or better, for the next few years.

- All this adds up to fairly good prospects for the European economy as a whole. Its aggregate GDP grew by 2.8 percent in 2006, its fastest rate in six years, with 2.7 percent growth forecast for 2007 and 2.3 percent for 2008. Modest weakness in France and Italy will be more than offset by the strength of Germany and the U.K. Europe will remain a sound trading partner for the United States and China for at least the next five years.

- Japan's GDP rose by 2.2 percent in 2006. In the fourth quarter of the year, growth hit 4.8 percent, its best showing in three years. This growth rate has slowed in 2007 but remains positive. Between November 2006 and May 2007, the Conference Board's index of leading indicators for Japan sank at a rate of 1.8 percent per year. Continued growth depends on spending by notoriously wary Japanese consumers. Nonetheless, the Organization for Economic Cooperation and Development predicts that Japan's GDP will grow by 2.4 percent in 2007 and 2.1 percent in 2008. The Japanese economy seems likely to remain healthy for at least a few years beyond 2008.

  - In the long run, Japan faces significant problems. Its population is aging, its working-age population is shrinking, and its birth rate is the lowest in the industrialized world and still declining. By 2030, the number of workers in Japan will shrink from its current 66 million to about 56 million. Over all, the country's population is expected to decline by 50 percent by 2075 and by two-thirds through 2100. At the same time, government debt equals 176 percent of GDP. This will make it extremely difficult for Tokyo to provide necessary services for tomorrow's elderly. Yet these are problems for the future. They will not affect Japan's economy during the period now under study.

- Both prices and wages should remain under control.

  - Worldwide, improved manufacturing technology will continue to boost productivity and reduce the unit cost of goods.

  - At the same time, workers who remain on the job longer will offset slow growth in the labor force and the globalization of business will keep pressure on salaries in the developed countries.

AUTHORS' COMMENT:

The data above remain as originally supplied to our expert panel. There have been a number of gloomy developments in the world economy since then. In the United States, we have had the weakest Christmas retail season in years, a collapse in the real-estate market, declining job growth, the reappearance of significant inflation, and of course the crunch in subprime mortgages, which has spread to Britain and threatens prime mortgages as well. GDP growth in 2007 came in at 2.2 percent, sliding to an anemic 0.6 percent in the fourth quarter. In Germany, inflation is up to 3.3 percent, well above the level allowed by the European central bank, and fears are rising that the strength of the Euro will throttle exports. Inflation is threatening China, Australia, Eastern Europe, Russia, and the Middle East as well. In all, it seems that the economies of the United States and the world are not as healthy as they were just a few months ago.

Nonetheless, at Forecasting International we believe that the U.S. economy will continue to grow in 2008, though perhaps not as quickly as once anticipated. The global economy will remain reasonably strong as well. Our expectations for the United States would change abruptly if today's credit problems were to infect the prime mortgage market, but for the moment that continues to seem unlikely.

Assessment:

These trends have been revised many times since they were first codified in the late 1980s. Some trends have fallen out of the list as they matured or as circumstances came along to change them. Others have been added as they were recognized. This trend has remained a constant, and with each revision its effective period has been extended. To invalidate this trend would take a catastrophe on the order of the loss of Middle Eastern oil from the Western economies. No such dramatic reversal of global fortune can be foreseen.

Implications:

New growth among all these trading partners should create a "benevolent cycle," in which the health of each partner helps to ensure the continued health of the rest at least through 2012. Global growth is expected to come in at 5 percent in 2007, 4.8 percent in 2008, and 4.4 percent, on average, in the five years ending in 2013.

China has developed into an effective counterbalance for the U.S. economy. When America hits hard times, China can keep the world from following into recession. We first saw this in the post 9/11 crunch in the United States. This should make the global economy much more stable for so long as China remains a vibrant trading nation.

Any interruptions in economic growth should be relatively short-lived.

By 2012 or so, India will expand faster than any other market in the world, with China falling into a close second place.

In the long run, the newly capitalist lands of the former Soviet Union should be among the fastest growing new markets, particularly if the oil industries of Kazakhstan and its neighbors, Kyrgyzstan and Uzbekistan, can be developed promptly.

Labor markets will remain tight, particularly in skilled fields. This calls for new creativity in recruiting, benefits, and perks, especially profit sharing. This hypercompetitive business environment demands new emphasis on rewarding speed, creativity, and innovation within the workforce.

Implications for Terrorism:

This is a top-ten trend.

The growing gap in wealth between the rich and poor nations will further destabilize the world order, continuing to inspire potential terrorists in the developing countries to strike at the wealthy in their home countries and, in some cases, at the richer lands. The growing gap in wealth between the rich and poor within many western lands will feed discontent among the less well-off, possibly helping to inspire both random violence and native terrorists in the West. This development will increase the security-related workload of intelligence and law enforcement agencies around the world. It also will help to drive continued growth in the private security industry.

The growing gap in wealth and income between the rich and the poor also will help to inspire conversion to Islam in the West, particularly among the poor and powerless. As we have seen in England, Germany, and Australia, this can be a source of violent extremism among both immigrant and native populations.

Expert Comments:

Anonymous (1): This is a trend with important, if mixed implications for terrorism. On the one hand, it will provide opportunities for young people (including migrants) who, un- or under-employed, might otherwise drift off into violence prone cults. Moreover, it will provide governments with revenues to pursue robust counter-terrorist policies, including the acquisition of needed surveillance and information processing technologies. On the other hand, such growth will exacerbate international inequalities providing motivation for terrorist actions (although inequality per se, has not been, to date, a major driver of terrorism). More significantly, growth will drive more migration, technological advance, and global warming, all of which may contribute to the problem.

ARMSTRONG: The gap itself is not the problem; the local situation is the problem. The world does not necessarily care how others are doing, but how they are doing. Local poverty and disillusionment fuel extremism and hope for a better future. Failure to address issues of security, humanitarian relief, governance, economic stabilization, and development in countries and neighborhoods creates fertile breeding grounds for extremists, terrorists, and insurgents to attack the national interests of the United States. This can be seen in inner-city development in the U.S. as well as in Iraq and elsewhere. Comparisons of the U.S. and our Western allies to "Gap" countries mean little. The response to the strategic American public diplomacy campaigns showing how great Muslims have it in the U.S. was a giant yawn, followed by "What's that got to do with me here in [pick your country: Egypt, Jordan, Palestine, Iraq, etc.]?"

KADTKE: In many regions of the world, the left-behind economies, political instability, and extremist activity will result in failed states, which will serve as breeding grounds and staging areas for further terrorist activities and recruitment. As the number of these areas increases, the UN and Western powers will not have the resources to commit globally.

KRIESBERG: One other effect of growing inequality within the United States may be worth noting. That is the impact of increased concentration of great wealth upon political decision making and policy implementation. At least some of the inadequate U.S. responses in dealing with terrorism are attributable to undue attention to the views of major political contributors, in procurement and in outsourcing.

LADUKE (3): The U.S. housing market fallout, the trade deficit, and the decline of the U.S. dollar alongside the economic advance and alliances of other developing nations is eroding the balance of power. If the U.S. economy falters and this flows into national defense, we should expect terrorist confrontations from many directions to end what is perceived (by terrorist groups and hostile nations) to be a long-standing negative imperialistic influence on our world.

MEILAHN: I disagree that the gap between rich and poor will inspire would-be terrorists in developing states to strike at wealthy in their home states and at wealthier states. Most evidence that I have seen indicates that there are other reasons, other motivations. It is not generally the poor and/or disenfranchised that become terrorists. It is the people who are already fairly fundamental in their beliefs, who are "pushed over the edge" by U.S. consumptionism, what they perceive as poor values, "easy" women, etc.—and they feel that the U.S. influence is bad for Islam. I am doing some work on this but believe there are many other factors involved, including a desire to make up for failings or sins (when you become a martyr, all is forgiven and you go to heaven), desire to become a part of something bigger than one's self (think psychology of cults), etc.

MILLER: At the moment, this looks like a pretty shaky prediction. The concern might be that, in the face of an economic downturn, the federal government might be forced to cut back on its counter-terrorism efforts. Such curtailment would, of course, become the single most negative impact on the prevention of future attacks on civilian populations by terrorists. At this time, I would give the possibility of a federal bailout (relatively) on GWOT less than a 50-50 chance, but the rise of environmental, social, and economic pressures on the next administration may prove decisive.

OSBORNE: The demand for materials from China and India will continue to affect crime problems around the world. For example, theft of copper has increased globally due to the changing markets—theft of this and similar resources (such as water) will grow and affect crime rates and types all over the world.

SANDERS (1): See comments under "Complexity and the Future of Terrorism" in Appendix C.

SMYRE (1): As the gap widens between the economy of the developed world and the two billion plus who live on $2 per day, there will be an increased ability to recruit young terrorists who have little to no economic hope…especially as the real-time media rubs this gap into the faces of those unable to find employment.

SNYDER (8): Rising costs for food, and for oil and other basic industrial commodities due to rapid growth in global demand—plus increased energy taxes and surcharges designed to promote fuel conservation and reduce greenhouse gases—will increase long-term inflation rates in most industrial nations, especially the U.S.

Stagflationary economics and the continued dismantling of the industrial era "social contract" will sustain the widening gap between "haves" and "have-nots" in most free market economies.

So long as info-mation and globalization fail to produce a general rise in prosperity among mature industrial economies, there will be increasing political disaffection in those countries, giving rise to neo-Luddism and anarchism aimed both at multi-national corporations and central governments. Unlike international terrorists, domestic anarchists can be expected to commit increasingly sophisticated acts of cybertage in order to reduce public confidence in—and business reliance on—the Internet, thereby diminishing the technology's power as a force for transformational economic, social, and political change.

Barring a reversal of current long-term socioeconomic trends in the U.S., a populist-anarchist backlash is likely to be a greater source of overt terrorist acts in America within ten years than will international terrorism.

YOUNG: Economic expansion can only help development in the Middle East. The result may lead to an increase in the middle class, currently almost non-existent in countries readily identified with terrorism. It is likely that once the populace begins to accumulate individual wealth that support for terror will abate.

2. THE WORLD'S POPULATION IS ON COURSE TO REACH 9.2 BILLION BY 2050.

- Average annual growth worldwide peaked at 2.19 percent in 1963 and has fallen steadily since. The U.S. Census Bureau's International Data Base projects that annual growth will fall below 1 percent in 2016 and below 0.5 percent by 2047.

- The greatest fertility is found in those countries least able to support their existing populations: the largest population increases projected between 2000 and 2050 include the Palestinian Territory (217 percent), Niger (205 percent), Yemen (168 percent), Angola (162 percent), the Democratic Republic of Congo (161 percent), and Uganda (133 percent).

    - The Muslim world is especially fertile, with fertility rates of 7.5 in Afghanistan, 6.0 in Yemen, and 4.9 in Iraq.

    - Of the 2.7 billion extra people in the world in 2050, about 40 percent will live in sub-Saharan Africa and 30 percent in the Muslim world.

- Even these estimates may be much too low. According to the Center for Strategic and International Studies (CSIS), most official projections underestimate both fertility and future gains in longevity. They also assume that life expectancy will grow more slowly in the future, which seems unlikely.

- In contrast to the developing world, many industrialized countries will see fertility rates below the replacement level and hence significant declines in populations, excluding the effects of immigration. This means the population of the developed nations will fall from 14 percent of the total world population in 2000 to only 10 percent in 2050.

- By 2015, the workforce in Japan and much of Europe will be shrinking by 1 percent per year. By the 2030s, it will contract by 1.5 percent annually.

Assessment:

Demographic trends such as this are among the most easily recognized and difficult to derail. Barring a global plague or nuclear war—wildcard possibilities that cannot be predicted with any validity—there is little chance that the population forecast for 2050 will err on the high side.

Implications:

Rapid population growth in the United States compared with its industrialized competitors will reinforce American domination of the global economy, as the European Union falls to third place behind the United States and China.

To meet human nutritional needs over the next forty years, global agriculture will have to supply as much food as has been produced during all of human history.

Unless fertility in the developed lands climbs dramatically, either would-be retirees will have to remain on the job, or the industrialized nations will have to encourage even more immigration from the developing world. The third alternative is a sharp economic contraction and lower living standards.

A fourth alternative is the widespread automation of service jobs as well as manufacturing, to accomplish the work needed to support accustomed living standards. However, this requires development of a means other than wages to distribute wealth and to provide both a living income and a fulfilling occupation for workers and would-be workers displaced by machines and software.

Barring enactment of strict immigration controls, rapid migration will continue from the Southern Hemisphere to the North, and especially from former colonies to Europe. A growing percentage of job applicants in the United States and Europe will be recent immigrants from developing countries.

Implications for Terrorism:

This is a top-ten trend.

Growing American prosperity relative to other countries with rapidly growing populations and overburdened economies will continue to make the United States a target for terrorism.

As one aspect of poverty, shortages of food could help to inspire extremism unless the industrialized nations make a determined, visible effort to provide for the world's poor.

In the long run, American restrictions on immigration from Latin America could inspire extremism among both documented and undocumented aliens, conceivably resulting in a modest amount of terrorist activity. However, this will have little support among Hispanics, whether legal residents or not. There is little prospect that a Latin extremist movement could ally itself with Muslim extremists.

Expert Comments:

CHOBAR (8): With significant global population growth, there will be additional problems of hunger, poverty, poor health, and illness—especially in light of the numerous hurricanes, flooding and other global warming issues facing our planet. These will lead to serious policing issues, as people struggle to survive. If terrorists appeal to children, people and teenagers who are hungry and living in poverty, by filling their basic needs, especially children of the growing population will go over to terrorism and the glory it brings them fighting against those who have affluence and wealth.

CZARNECKI: This is one of three baseline trends that forecast a near-perfect social storm for increased societal violence, much of it expressed as terrorism. Although UN reports indicate a slowing of world population growth, this will not be a uniform slowing. Some places, especially those that can least afford and adapt to population growth, will exhibit massive growth without the resources/information to sustain that growth. The competition for the scarce resources that are available will be great and extreme. Those who find their position(s) hopeless or near-hopeless can be expected to lash out at those whom they perceive have taken their survival from them. Wherever this kind of growth-resources mismatch occurs, expect violence of the most terrible kind.

JENKINS: High levels of immigration will exacerbate ethnic tensions and provoke powerful reactions against both legal and illegal immigration. The major issue for police will be the role of local police in enforcing national policies against illegal immigration. Pressure from local citizens and Washington will push police to play a greater role in reducing illegal immigrant populations with possible adverse effects on community relations and law enforcement.

LaDUKE (7): Increased population density and megacities, largely emerging in developing nations, will be juxtaposed against advances in technology that could be applied to terrorism and destructive force. Attacks will potentially be more devastating.

MILLER: Alas, this one is more likely to be exceeded than undershot. I would put this rapidly increasing pool of potential terrorism adherents as one of the most critical in terms of its importance as a driver of future terrorism. I don't see any way to seriously affect global population growth, but it is the primary reason that the GWOT is a "long war" much like the "war" on crime.

SANDERS (2): See comments under "Complexity and the Future of Terrorism" in Appendix C.

SMYRE (2): It is expected that 80 percent of the growth in population from now to 2050 will be in poverty. This will increase the potential for more terrorism in more places unless the developed world begins to see the importance of helping the impoverished of the world improve their quality of life. This will become as important as will any foreign policy initiative and will challenge the conservative philosophies of much of the U.S. population.

SNYDER (1): With 1 billion people born between 1975 and 1995, the Third-World Baby Boom will increase the labor supply of most developing countries faster than the local economies create jobs. This will curtail economic opportunity for an entire generation of young people in Africa, the Middle East, South Asia, and Latin America, and give rise to a growing population of unemployed.

STEELE: Disproportionate segments of the world's population growth in the developing world will produce a widening gap between developed and developing worlds. This produces environments of anomie and alienation as a breeding ground for terrorist ideology.

YOUNG: Much of the increase in the world's population will reside within the world's poorer countries. Lack of status and resources has been a favorite motivation for terror recruiters, and it is a situation that melds easily with question one.

3. LIFE EXPECTANCY IN THE DEVELOPED WORLD IS STEADILY GROWING LONGER.

- Each generation lives longer and remains healthier than the last. Since the beginning of the twentieth century, every generation in the United States has lived three years longer than the previous one. An 80-year-old in 1950 could expect 6.5 more years of life; today's 80-year-olds are likely to survive 8.5 more years.

- Life expectancy in Australia, Japan, and Switzerland is now over 75 years for males and over 80 for females.

- A major reason for this improvement is the development of new pharmaceuticals and medical technologies that are making it possible to prevent or cure diseases that would have been fatal to earlier generations. In many developed countries, credit also goes to government health programs, which have made these treatments available to many or all residents. In the developing lands, the primary reason is the availability of generic drugs, which cut the cost of care and make health affordable even for the poor.

• Medical advances that slow the fundamental process of aging now seem to be within reach. (This is a controversial issue within the medical community, but the evidence appears quite strong.) Such treatments could well help today's middle-aged Baby Boomers to live far longer than even CSIS anticipates. In the developed world, younger generations are likely to live routinely beyond the century mark.

Assessment:

See the assessment for Trend 2.

_____

Implications:

Global demand for products and services aimed at the elderly will grow quickly in the immediate future, but this trend may pass as geriatric medicine improves the health of the elderly.

Developed countries may face social instability as a result of competition for resources between retirement-age Boomers and their working-age children and grandchildren. At the present rate of growth, public spending on retirement benefits in the United States and other developed countries could be one-fourth of GDP by 2050, even as the number of workers available to support each retiree declines sharply.

Barring dramatic advances in geriatric medicine, the cost of health care is destined to skyrocket throughout the developed lands. This could create the long-expected crisis in health-care financing and delivery.

However, dramatic advances in geriatric medicine are all but inevitable. Paying the high cost of new drugs, technologies, and therapies will reduce the overall cost of caring for patients who otherwise would have suffered from disorders delayed, eased, or cured by such advances. In the end, these reductions will offset many of the expected increases, leaving the average health-care bill in the developed lands much lower than the doomsayers predict.

Any practical extension of the human life span will prolong health as well and will reduce the incidence of late-life disorders such as cancer, heart disease, arthritis, and possibly Alzheimer's disease. This would dramatically reduce demand for products and services in the senior market, at least in the developed world. FI believes this development is nearer than even many researchers expect.

Healthier aging in the developed world may offer new hope to the world's poorer, sicker lands. Faced with declining growth in their pharmaceutical industries, western nations—and particularly the United States—are likely to subsidize research and treatment for diseases that burden the poor countries of Africa and Asia. This will give those lands their first real prospects for economic growth and improved quality of life.

Implications for Terrorism:

Longer life expectancies mean extended careers and longer retirements. This trend will raise pension costs for intelligence and security departments throughout the industrialized world. It also will encourage senior personnel to remain on the job longer, making it difficult to promote their younger colleagues and give them the broad experience needed for senior-level positions in turn. In compensation, this trend will ensure that intelligence and security services can maintain their institutional memory, an asset that is often lost today. In the long run, this should improve the efficiency of antiterrorist and counterterrorist efforts.

Expert Comments:

BRUH: I do believe that law enforcement agencies can solve the "aging" problem, if it is a problem, by having mandatory age retirements based upon years of service and or age. This can be justified by the positions being dangerous and requiring certain physical attributes. It is important that officers can best serve in such dangerous occupations when they are within a certain age group; i.e., not older then 60. Of course, departments can have justifiable exceptions to a mandatory age limitation.

LANOTTE: With the increased age expectancy and the increasing population, having experienced law enforcement officers willing to stay on the job will be a positive result. One possible solution to the problem of bringing younger officers up through the ranks would be to place older, experienced officers on the retired list, but keep them at their highest rank and keep them working. The military has used this method to keep expertise on the rolls longer, and keep personnel active when they may otherwise not desire to do so.

4. THE ELDERLY POPULATION IS GROWING DRAMATICALLY THROUGHOUT THE WORLD.

- Worldwide, the elderly (age 65 and older) numbered 440 million and represented 6 percent of the global population in 2002. Their numbers will nearly double by 2020 (to over 9 percent of total population) and more than triple by 2050 (to nearly 17 percent), according to the U.S. Census Bureau's International Data Base.

- In the developed world, people age 60 and over made up one-fifth of the population in 2000 and will grow to one-third in the next half century.

- Between 2000 and 2050, the 60+ age group in the less developed countries will grow from only one in twelve to one in five.

- The first Baby Boomers turn 65 in 2011. Thereafter, 10,000 Americans will turn 65 every day. Only half will maintain their standard of living in retirement. One in four will be dependent on government programs.

  – Only one American in 25 was over age 65 in 1900. Between 2030 and 2050, one in five will be over age 65.

- Throughout the developed world, population growth is fastest among the elderly. In the United States, there are 4.2 million people age 85 and up. By 2050, there will be 19.3 million.

– In Germany, the retirement-age population will near 19 percent of the total in 2010 and will reach 31 percent in 2050.

– By 2050, one in three Italians will be over 65, nearly double the proportion today.

– Japan's over-65 population will be 22 percent of the total in 2010 and nearly 37 percent in 2050.

• In Europe, the United States, and Japan, the aged also form the wealthiest segment of society.

• In the United States, at least, suburban populations are aging faster than those in the cities.

Assessment:

Again, this is a demographic trend, difficult to derail and unlikely to change while the massive Baby Boom generation remains on the scene.

Implications:

Not counting immigration, the ratio of working-age people to retirees needing their support will drop dramatically in the United States, Germany, Italy, Russia, Japan, and other countries. This represents a burden on national economies that will be difficult to sustain under current medical and social security systems.

In the next two to three decades, shortages of health workers will loom large in "aging vulnerable" countries. The United States in particular will need at least twice as many physicians specializing in geriatrics as its current 9,000, as well as half a million more nurses by 2020.

Suburban communities are likely to face a growing demand for social services such as senior day-care, public transportation, and other programs for the elderly. This will place a growing strain on local government budgets.

In the developing countries, where the elderly have traditionally relied on their children for support, this system will begin to break down as middle-aged "children" find themselves still supporting their parents while anticipating their own retirement.

Implications for Terrorism:

> **[CSIS Aging Vulnerability Index (2003)**
>
> Rankings from Least to Most Vulnerable
>
> **Low Vulnerability**
>
> 1. Australia
> 2. United Kingdom
> 3. United States
>
> **Medium Vulnerability**
>
> 4. Canada
> 5. Sweden
> 6. Japan
> 7. Netherlands
> 8. Belgium
>
> **High Vulnerability**
>
> 10. France
> 11. Italy
> 12. Spain

In many of the capitalist economies, the elderly are the wealthiest segment of society. As the senior population expands, this implies a growing concentration of wealth and a corresponding deprivation of the young. In the long run, this could inspire instability that, while not amounting to terrorism in itself, could complicate antiterrorist efforts. It also could raise the demand for social services, competing with security functions for government funding.

Of lesser significance, an older population is likely to be more concerned with security and to be more destabilized by terrorist events. This could raise political pressures on intelligence and security services to produce results by any means necessary.

However, the greatest age-related effects will be in those countries where this trend is weakest. In many of the developing countries, population growth is due mostly to out-of-control birth rates. This means that a growing number of volatile young men with few prospects for a satisfying life will be available for recruitment to extremist causes. Some will become terrorists, and their numbers are likely to be much larger the terrorist population today.

Expert Comments:

ANONYMOUS (4): The problem is more one of age structure than of aging per se: not only are there more elderly but, in the developed world in particular, fewer young people. This means that Western militaries will have fewer troops to deploy abroad and a lower tolerance for casualties. They will thus be less inclined to help police ungoverned areas in the lesser-developed world where terrorist groups could find sanctuary.

I think this issue and the points that you make are woefully underrated by too many others (who are likely largely unaware of the types of stats which you have assembled).

ROBERTS: Two risks can be pegged:

1. The elderly are a more vulnerable and less resilient population: more easily attacked and less able to recover—a good target for higher casualties if struck in 'ghettoes' (seniors' communities.)

2. Your point about possible resentment on the part of the younger, burden-carrying generation(s) could have several negative implications and lead to hostile currents.

YOUNGS: As the baby boom generation begins to retire, healthcare and affordable housing will become key issues. Genetic predisposition to certain diseases or conditions will be readily tested for, and issues concerning insurability or the willingness of insurance companies to cover these individuals will become a debatable issue. Diseases, such as Alzheimer's, will critically impact long-term care facilities and burden the Medicaid system. The issue of length of time on the job will be impacted as we see a larger aging population. Even now, the age when you can receive full social security benefits has been extended. With recruitment being an issue and the age of retirement being extended, the cost of health insurance for municipalities and private companies will go up as older workers remain on the job.

5. TECHNOLOGY IS CREATING A KNOWLEDGE-DEPENDENT GLOBAL SOCIETY.

- More and more businesses, and entire industries, are based on the production and exchange of information and ideas rather than exclusively on manufactured goods or other tangible products.

- At the same time, manufacturers and sellers of physical products are able to capture and analyze much more information about buyers' needs and preferences, making the selling process more efficient and effective.

- The Internet makes it possible for small businesses throughout the world to compete for market share on an even footing with industry leaders.

- It also makes it possible for international organizations such as businesses, nonprofits, and political movements to coordinate their operations more effectively.

- The number of Internet users in the United States more than doubled between 2000 and 2007, to nearly 231 million, or 69 percent of the population. Yet the percent of the population online has remained almost unchanged since 2004. About 70 percent now use broadband connections, but adoption of broadband has slowed markedly since 2005.

- In the United States, the "digital divide" seems to be disappearing. Internet access is increasing faster in black and Hispanic households as they catch up with white households. As of 2001, 32 percent of Hispanic and 30.8 percent of African American households were online. By early 2004, 61 percent of black children and 67 percent of Hispanic youngsters had Internet access at home, compared with 80 percent of white children.

- Digital appliances—whether computers or telephones—are becoming more integrated, portable, and powerful.

Assessment:

This trend will not reach even its half-way mark until the rural populations of China and India gain modern educations and easy access to the Web.

Implications:

This trend is raising the level of education required for a productive role in today's workforce. For many workers, the opportunity for training thus is becoming one of the most desirable benefits any job can offer.

Even entry-level workers and those in formerly unskilled positions require a growing level of education. For a good career in almost any field, computer competence is mandatory.

Knowledge workers are generally better paid than less-skilled workers, and their proliferation may raise overall prosperity.

However, data and communications technologies also are exposing workers in the developed world to competition from low-wage countries. It is not yet clear at what pay level these competing forces will balance.

This trend also is enlarging the income gap between well-educated workers and those with a high school degree or less. That gap will continue to grow.

In ten years, most digital devices will combine multimedia communication functions and real-time voice translation, so that conversations originating in one of seven or eight common languages can be heard in any of the others. These technologies will enable even more people to become knowledge workers or, at least, knowledge-enhanced workers.

Telecommuting will make many companies more efficient, cutting their expenses in the process.

New technologies create new industries, jobs, and career paths, which can bring new income to developing countries. An example is the transfer of functions such as technical support, and more recently R&D, to Asian divisions and service firms.

For some developing countries, computer skills are making it faster and easier to create wealth than a manufacturing economy ever could. India, for example, is rapidly growing a middle class, largely on the strength of its computer and telecom industries. Other lands will follow its example.

Implications for Terrorism:

For terrorism, this is clearly an important trend. As technology transforms society, it provides new opportunities to sow chaos. From interbank networks to air traffic control systems to the computerized controls at an oil refinery, the critical systems of the industrialized world are increasingly open to tampering and interference, often from afar via the Internet. A high-tech society is a vulnerable society, almost by definition. We believe that such vulnerabilities are more significant in dealing with governments, rather than when facing terrorists, because terrorists by nature prefer the drama of low-tech carnage, but the threat of high-tech terrorism cannot be overlooked.

Technology also provides new opportunities to combat terrorism. From advanced communications systems to affordable video surveillance cameras to data mining, technology allows intelligence and law enforcement agencies to carry out much of their work faster and more effectively. Owing to the limited personnel available for real-time observation, many of these technologies—particularly video surveillance—will be used mostly for forensic reconstruction of terrorist events until artificial intelligence becomes powerful enough to recognize incidents in progress.

Expert Comments:

Bray (2): Yes, we live in interesting times. Never before has humanity created and had access to so much knowledge. *TIME* Magazine's recent recognition of every individual (i.e., "you") as the 2006 Person of the Year represents the accelerating trend where anyone can find, analyze, produce, and remix various media on the Internet. For academia, the growth of new knowledge is exponential. In the year 1900, there were 9,000 scientific articles published. In 1950, there were 90,000, and by 2000 there were 900,000 scientific articles published in that year.

It is becoming difficult to "keep up" with all this new knowledge. Entrusted with the responsibility of protecting their civilian populous and maintaining stability, national governments face tremendous challenges in addressing the increasing amount of knowledge. Workers from multiple government agencies must search through, prioritize, and potentially act upon knowledge of both national opportunities and threats. Unfortunately, the founders of our federal government may have included some organizational obstacles and redundancies intentionally. Preventing an individual from consolidating too much political power represented a significant concern, as published in *The Federalist Papers*. Both the fragmentation and slow pace of our system of government intentionally limit a political official from becoming synonymous to a monarch. Yet in an age of increasing amounts of knowledge, government fragmentation hurts more than it helps.

Chobar (9): Several years ago on National Public Radio (NPR) a noted computer expert declared, "Give me five computer experts and 5-million dollars, and I can bring the entire U.S. computer system down!" Policing and safety of our technology is extremely important because such terrorism could bring down our entire U.S., and global economy, if terrorists were able to devise massive "computer viruses" which infected every businesses computer system in such a knowledge-dependent global society.

Czarnecki: Technology provides information on a vast scale for a cheap price. The problem is that technology itself is very expensive and that one must know how to use technology to take advantage of it. (Think of the classic programming problem of VCRs—and now HDTVs!) Where technological capability exists and where there is relative social equality, there will be a tendency towards decreased violence as information provides an equalizer for competitors for resources. However, the worst situation will be where technological capability exists in a socially inequitable condition; then those who "have not" will also have the ability to know what they do not have, and the have-nots will not like that one bit. Whether that in itself leads to increased violence depends on other trends, like social stability of the state/tribe/group.

Jenkins: Criminals will always exploit new technology faster than authorities can develop countermeasures. When technology develops rapidly, law enforcement falls further behind. The frontiers of technology, especially the Internet, will remain lawless. Specialized units with specialized training will be required, but it is not merely a matter of training. Younger generations raised with the technology think differently than even well-trained older generations. It will be a matter of recruiting even more than of training.

Kadtke: For the short term, the single most important driver of terrorist activity globally is the information revolution. Terrorist groups, along with trans-national criminals and upstart political movements, are being greatly facilitated by the rapidly spreading and extremely low-cost communication capabilities such as the Internet and cell phones. These allow vastly increased capabilities for organization building, command-control, fundraising, and strategic communication. IT technologies are leveling the geopolitical playing field.

Economic growth and sustainability increasingly depends on high-tech manufacturing and scientific and research capabilities. While there is a general trend toward increasing global wealth, and there are many new winners in the high-tech economy, there are many nations which have virtually no resources to compete. This will increasingly create pockets of have-nots with deepening poverty and despair.

Kapinos: With regard to terrorism, technology is the proverbial double-edged sword. Technology provides our enemies advanced tools and weapons to use against us, but also provides us with outstanding tools and weapons of our own. Obviously, the current and future war may be fought as much through cyber-space as on the battlefield; the winner being they who can harness the technology and transfer the available knowledge faster and more effectively.

On our side, we are challenged more by our self-created bureaucratic and political obstacles to effective information-sharing and knowledge management than by the level of our technology. The sharing of information between government agencies at the Federal, state, and local levels is hampered tremendously by outdated rule sets that have been used to manage this process. Federal policies and procedures around intelligence information were established at the height of the Cold War to serve the specific needs of that period. What is needed are more flexible rule sets to reflect the 21st-century model for broader network-based information management. Our enemies are already mastering this model in their operations: We need to quickly play catch-up in order to stay ahead.

Meilahn: Growth of the Internet—and more importantly access to it by people worldwide—is a tremendous asset for Al Qaeda and other terror organizations. It allows them to spread their rhetoric and radical view of Islam, as well as to share information regarding tactics, techniques, and procedures for executing acts of terror.

Nolte: Much of the attention devoted to technology has focused on how it will change law enforcement operations. I would think that how technology will change the way criminals, such as terrorists, operate will be at least as important.

Osborne: As issues of homeland security continue to place attention on the need for data sharing and analysis at all levels of policing and law enforcement, new tools will emerge that are more user friendly and affordable, leading to a truly knowledge-based, intelligence-led police network more suited to combating terrorism. Progress will be slow, requiring retraining a workforce, enlightened managers, increased civilianization of analysts/experts, and more research on crime/terrorism threat pattern detection as well as crime/terrorism threat prevention.

Shtulman: The more technologically dependent our society becomes, the more vulnerable it becomes to technological attack, and the more potentially devastating such attacks will be. Hackers don't need to move traceable materials to prepare for an attack or go to training camps in Afghanistan to learn their trade. They can remain invisible until they strike. Everything from terror financing through identity and credit theft to attacks on the national infrastructure can be expected on-line in the future.

Young: Technology has been an enabler for terror as the Iraq War has shown. Terrorists adopt new, more lethal technologies as countermeasures are created. This has been the case in all wars and should be no different in future low-intensity conflicts.

6. Mass migration is redistributing the world's population.

- There are nearly 100 million international migrant workers in the world, according to the United Nations. About 30 million live in Europe, 20 million in Africa, and 18 million in North America.

  - These figures include only the workers themselves, not their dependents.

- About 4 million people immigrated permanently to the countries of the Organization for Economic Cooperation and Development in 2005, 10.4 percent more than the year before.

- Immigration to Western Europe from Eastern Europe, North Africa, the Middle East, and the Indian subcontinent continues despite controls enacted in the wake of terrorist attacks.

  - More than 400,000 legal immigrants from Central Europe now live and work in Western Europe. Between 3 million and 4 million more migrants are expected to join them in the next twenty-five years.

- In China, about 160 million people have moved from rural areas to cities in recent years.

- Immigration is quickly changing the ethnic composition of the U.S. population. In 2000, Latinos made up 12.6 percent of the U.S. population; by 2050, they will account for 24.5 percent. Asians in the United States, currently 3.8 percent of the population, will comprise 8 percent by 2050, according to the latest U.S. Census Bureau figures.

  - Higher fertility rates among the immigrant Latino population will accelerate this trend. As of 2002, women in the United States produced about two children during their lives, just enough to maintain the population. Among Hispanics, the average was more than 2.7 births per woman. Among Mexican immigrants, it was nearly 2.9.

  - At the same time, there is a small countertrend of Generation Xers and, especially, Millennials moving to other countries to pursue business opportunities or for cultural interest.

Assessment:

As native workforces shrink in most industrialized lands, economic opportunities will draw people from the developing world to the developed in growing numbers. Thus, this trend will continue for at least the next generation.

Implications:

Impoverished migrants will place a growing strain on social-security systems in the industrialized countries of Europe and North America. Similar problems will continue to afflict the urban infrastructures of China and India.

Remittances from migrants to their native lands are helping to relieve poverty in many developing countries. Globally, these payments exceeded US$230 billion in 2005, according to the World Bank.

Significant backlashes against foreign migrants, such as the skinhead movement in Europe, will be seen more frequently in the years ahead. They will appear even in the most peaceful lands. For example, in Scandinavia, resentment against foreign workers is strong, in part because they can return to their native lands after three years of employment and collect a pension equal to the minimum wage for the rest of their lives.

- Since the terrorist attacks of September 11, 2001, and the rail bombings in London and Madrid, the large number of Muslim immigrants in Britain, France, and other European lands has inspired suspicion, and some persecution.

- Unfortunately, suspicion is to some extent justified. A tiny minority of Muslim immigrants have proved to be linked to terrorist groups, and some have plotted or carried out terrorist attacks. So have native-born Muslims and converts to Islam.

Implications for Terrorism:

Some of the most fervent "culturist" movements will continue to spring from religious fundamentalism that would-be dictators and strongmen can exploit to promote their own interests. Others will appear, or gain strength, as a response to the growth of foreign populations in once-homogeneous societies.

Terrorism will be a continuing problem long into the future, particularly in European nations with large, poorly integrated Muslim immigrant populations. Security concerns therefore will take up more time and resources in the future, both for the intelligence community and for the big-city police departments that provide neighborhood-level surveillance.

Expert Comments:

Anonymous (2): This is the most obvious and important driver of terrorism in the next decade or so. Immigrant Diasporas contain small pools of alienated individuals who—because they do not "fit in" or because their traditional sensibilities are offended by modernist values—are prone to violent radicalization. This will continue to be a particular problem in Europe given the limited prospects for social integration of migrants, and the sharp clash between the "post-modern" values of the host culture and the very traditional values of the Islamic migrant worker force.

Ayers (3): Regardless of pervasive anti-Western sentiment, Western nations remain popular places for immigration from third world nations. A massive influx of displaced refugees, political asylum cases, legal immigration, and illegal immigration combined with falling birthrates throughout the Western world, will no doubt exacerbate the tendency of immigrants to establish and stay within the boundaries of familiar cultures—the essence of multiculturalism. Even a slight expansion of liberalism within American politics would increase the standing of ideas consistent with cultural relativism. Given a scenario where there is a general public endorsement of cultural relativism coupled with a lack of incentives for assimilation, it would seem likely that immigrant communities within the U.S. will follow the same path as many of those within the Netherlands (or much of Western Europe, for that matter)—with each community's cultural norms and laws (interpretations of *shari'a* specific to certain cultures, for example) being the acceptable, or the only acceptable, regulatory system for the members within these social groupings.

As former Dutch parliamentarian Ayaan Hirsi Ali noted, women are often adversely affected by the lack of cultural assimilation. Indeed, "honor killings" are not unknown within the U.S. and may unfortunately become more common over the next twenty years. And as Hirsi Ali (among others) has shown, the low status and poor treatment of women has a direct correlation to the development and growth of extremist ideologies and activities within these communities.

If multiculturalism and cultural relativism were to become more prevalent within the U.S., it would not take much for practices such as female infanticide, primogeniture, and polygamy to change the male-to-female relationships within immigrant communities. The resultant glut of young males looking for an identity and a purpose would be 20 years or more in the future, but could be devastating in regard to the conflict scenarios that could play out on the streets of U.S. and other Western cities. (See *Bare Branches* by Hudson and den Boer [2004] for a complete description of how statistical gaps based on gender create conditions ripe for conflict.)

Bruh: There is every indication that immigration and emigration, depending upon the nation, will continue to grow; i.e., 2007 is showing the largest number of immigrants yet to come to the U.S. All this also can change if the U.S. or other western countries are hit hard by terrorism. Borders may close in a way not yet seen.

Chobar: Travel and movement among the world's population is so easy these days, policing and detection of terrorist movement are extremely difficult to follow.

Jenkins: See Trend 2.

Kadtke: Demographic changes and mass population movements after the end of the Cold War were the largest in nearly a century, and economic changes will continue to drive such trends. An unfortunate by-product of these activities is the lack of security induced by the inability to control borders in many regions, and the inability to identify terrorist suspects and their movements. In spite of major changes in Federal law (e.g., the Patriot Act) the U.S. still faces enormous challenges for security, and many say this has come at the cost of personal privacy.

Kriesberg: Yes, mass migration is changing the composition of many countries. Combined with the new communication technologies, the importance of diaspora communities will grow. They will be more permanent and maintain engagement in more than one country. Dual citizenships are increasing.

Members of such communities can be bridge builders, contributing to better inter-cultural understandings. They can affect government policies relevant to terror by their political engagement.

However, if they are isolated and face discrimination, the risks of alienation are great, and even if only a tiny percentage are drawn into small militant cells considerable damage may be done, as has been the case in Spain, the U.K., Bali, etc.

LaDuke (10): Immigrants are largely leaving areas known to house terrorist threats and coming to the U.S. and NATO countries. (http://www.nytimes.com/ref/world/20070622_CAPEVERDE_GRAPHIC.html) Migration can obviously import/export terrorism or extremism. It also increases the need to homogenize diverse cultures and simultaneously quell threats. (See my comments on diversity [in Trend 7])

Lanotte: The common view of the immigrant in the Western World today is that the immigrant will settle in a new country but retain all of their old customs and mores, as opposed to adopting and adapting to their new home. This is an erroneous view of immigration. If the immigrants are unwilling to assimilate, they should not be allowed to stay.

Miller: This is a concern for counter-terrorism, as it tends to break down the insulation between states and allows agents for terrorist groups to infiltrate currently stable populations. It is not clear how much further into the future nations will allow such mass movements into their sovereign territory. Arguably, however, the genie is out of the bottle and the fertile breeding grounds are already in place. Future traffic may be only a trickle, but still be devastating, as key individuals arrive to take advantage of the fact that the existing alien collections remain un-acculturated or even unassimilated. Pockets of aliens remain relatively compact, cohesive, and volatile.

Shtulman: Our open southern borders make a mockery of everything else we do. What is the point of no-fly lists when we know that tens of thousands of illegals walk across our borders every year? If the drug trade is a source of funding for Mexican smugglers and Middle Eastern terror organizations, then we must assume that the two groups are in contact with one another and that Mexican smugglers are bringing in Middle Eastern terrorists as well as drugs to the U.S. If they can bring in people and drugs, why not weapons, explosives, and everything else necessary to launch a wave of simple attacks whenever they choose to do so?

Smyre: The developed world will face tremendous challenges as the push of immigration explodes in times of economic downturn and water shortages. This will not only increase the potential for border wars and water wars, but also will create friction internally among different cultural and age groups…even leading to the possibility of a new concept of "generational terrorism," since the developed world is older and the developing world is younger.

STEELE: Global cultural interactions will produce unexpected outcomes and potential challenges to global stability—the intersection of at least three planes of cultural cross impact: "Multicultural Tsunami" (Dator), "Cultures in Collision" (Cornish, E. *Exploring the Future*, World Future Society, 2004),"Deculturation" (ibid.)

YOUNG: Migration and immigration are two of the population problems Western Europe especially will have to deal with in the coming years. With respect to terror, it often is second-generation immigrants who become disenchanted with their new country of residence and are not quite assimilated. It is these individuals who have given rise to homegrown terror in the United Kingdom. France and Spain recently have seen acts of terror from their immigrant populations, and radical Islam already has a foothold in the remainder of Western Europe. The migration trend will only exacerbate the current problems and will be a source of turmoil unless and until measures are taken to rectify the societal and economic differences.

7. DESPITE SOME XENOPHOBIC REACTIONS TO IMMIGRANTS, THERE IS GROWING ACCEPTANCE OF DIVERSITY.

- Migration is mixing disparate peoples and forcing them to find ways to coexist peacefully and productively. Because of this, the interaction of diverse cultures will continue to grow, both internationally and intranationally, throughout much of the world.

- The Internet and other technologies promote long-distance communication and build links between distant, and disparate, people.

- Mass media, including television, radio, films, interactive games, and music tend to homogenize global culture as they promote a common language, mores, and cultural reference points.

  – In the United States, for instance, television encourages the spread of standard accents and language patterns.

- The globalization of business is having a similar impact. Throughout the United States and Europe, regional differences, attitudes, incomes, and lifestyles are blurring as business carries people from one area to another.

- Intermarriage also continues to mix cultures geographically, ethnically, socially, and economically.

- Minorities are beginning to exert more influence over national agendas.

  – The growing number of African-Americans, Hispanics, and Asians in the United States is mirrored by the expanding population of refugees and former "guest workers" throughout Europe.

- Britons increasingly support staying in the European Union, according to a September 2007 survey by the polling firm Ipsos MORI. In March 2001, 39 percent of those surveyed said they would vote to keep the U.K. in the European Union, and 42 percent favored getting out. By 2007, 51 percent supported staying in while 39 percent wanted out.

- However, in many countries there are powerful reactions against these changes.

– The growth of the German neo-Nazi movement after unification in 1992 is one obvious example, though public distaste for these views has tended to keep extremist activities in check.

– American hostility toward undocumented aliens also may be viewed as a reaction against the growing political and cultural influence of a minority.

– Japan has chosen to develop robotic technologies for industry and the home, rather than opening its traditionally closed society to substantial immigration and foreign influence.

Assessment:

This trend applies most clearly to the West, where it will continue for as long as we can foresee. In other regions, including Japan and large parts of the Muslim world, it remains weak, if it exists at all.

Implications:

Groups with highly varied customs, languages, and histories of necessity will develop ways to coexist peacefully.

Nonetheless, local conflicts will continue to erupt in societies where xenophobia is common.

Companies will hire ever more minority workers and will be expected to adapt to their values and needs. Much of the burden of accommodating foreign-born residents will continue to fall on employers, who must make room for their languages and cultures in the workplace.

Public schools and libraries must find more effective ways to educate this future workforce.

Implications for Terrorism:

Where acceptance breaks down, terrorism can begin. This is the source of skinhead movements from Russia through much of Western Europe. If these fascist movements do not themselves rise to the level of terrorism, they can inspire it in their victims.

There is at least a possibility that a similar movement could arise in the United States in response to continued Hispanic immigration.

In practice, acceptance of diversity can help to enable the refusal of newcomers to assimilate into the majority culture. This can weaken national cohesion and make it more difficult to combat internal threats.

Expert Comments:

AYERS: Acceptance of diversity by citizens of host nations is one thing. Acceptance by the immigrants themselves may be a completely different story. New immigrants are more likely to remain within enclaves of individuals from countries with cultures and linguistic dialects similar to their own, than they are to venture into environments where they may feel socially uncomfortable. Western European nations have been happy to oblige, allowing sections within urban areas (and in some cases, entire cities) to become culturally segregated from the host nation population. This inclination has been difficult to reverse, as multiculturalism has long been considered "politically correct"—those who question its value have been labeled "racist" (and yes, "xenophobic"). The scenario is, however, easily exploited by terrorist organizations as well as "movements" devoted to propagating extremist ideologies via non-violent means. Hizb ut-Tahrir and associated splinter groups, for instance, focus on a "grand plan" that involves revolution via demographic change—attempts to establish communities of extremists in sufficient numbers to "infiltrate" local government via legal means (direct hire or election). Their plan involves specific stages necessary to achieve a non-violent governmental takeover for the ultimate aim of the "establish[ment of] a state ruled by sharia." (See Zeyno Baran's article "Fighting the War of Ideas" in *Foreign Affairs*, Vol 84[6], 2005.) Thus, while there most probably will be a greater acceptance of diversity, "national cohesion" could well be undermined by "demographic sabotage" in the long-term.

JENKINS: See Trend 2.

KAPINOS: In recent months, there has been a significant focus on the problems that states and localities are facing as a result of failed immigration policies. Communities that are feeling unduly impacted by large numbers of immigrants (legal or not) are reacting by enacting harsh policies and implementing their own de-facto immigration laws. While much of this is driven by political opportunism, latent xenophobia, and demagoguery, there are some valid underlying concerns present.

The Federal government must act to address the holes in the current immigration system, and develop viable policies that address all concerns. Otherwise, we run the risk of continuing to contend with uncontrolled movement of people into the United States and potential foreign terrorist infiltration. In addition, we will end up encouraging more corrosive actions at state and local levels, which could eventually undermine support among overseas allies.

KRIESBERG: Yes, the norms respecting diversity are becoming more widespread. And the inclusion of diverse people fosters economic development. Good police work is needed to monitor hate groups of all stripes, include the local xenophobic ones. Carefully targeted arrests are effective, while broad roundups are counterproductive.

LADUKE (6): Diversity programs encourage the acceptance of the differences of others. Some nations, for example, Spain, do not have a strong concept of, or perceived need for, diversity programs. The concept is stronger in developing nations with high immigration because it helps solve issues of internal strife and, as such, is particularly strong in U.S. enterprises and institutions.

Generally speaking, wide acceptance that increases group tolerance, supplies badly needed skilled labor, and fuels a knowledge economy can equally create opportunities for terrorist operations, cell network expansion, or the giving away of technology critical to national interests. This tension already exists in the U.S. and unchecked will develop further into a power struggle between corporate/institutional interests and national defense interests. A proactive collaboration between industry, education, and defense interests is badly needed in the U.S.

MILLER: This seems more like Pollyanna thinking. I would not recommend counting on the base population to somehow become more tolerant, and would discourage the belief that some society will somehow police itself.

SHTULMAN: See Trend 6.

TAN: Muslim migrant communities in Western Europe have found it hard, for various reasons, to integrate with their host countries. The result is that second and third generation Muslims have become alienated by the general lack of social acceptance and have to suffer discrimination on a daily basis. There is now evidence that the same trend is occurring in Australia. In the U.S.A., the anti-Muslim backlash from 9/11 does not yet seem to have the same alienating effect, primarily because of the liberal freedoms, particularly of religion, that are enjoyed and respected in the U.S.A. Yet, moderate Muslim intellectuals have warned that it is now, before the kind of problems experienced with European Muslim communities, that law enforcement and government in general [must] build ties of deep trust and cooperation with their local Muslim communities and work hard towards integrating Muslims into mainstream society. This is to prevent the kind of social and other forms of discrimination that would alienate Muslims and provide fodder for radical Islamist recruitment or result in self-radicalization. Growing acceptance of diversity is not enough. There needs to be active political will to embrace local Muslims in the community and make American Muslims feel very much part of society. Indeed, only Muslims themselves can police their own communities most effectively, especially in rooting out the extremists in their midst.

YOUNG: Establishment of immigrant enclaves within host countries does not help the assimilation process. Discrimination will likely prevail until there is a general acceptance of the immigrants' presence. As long as there is discrimination and economic disparity between the immigrant and host population, there are grounds for terror attacks on host country institutions.

YOUNGS: Illegal aliens are in many cases overwhelming local law enforcement resources. Congress seems reluctant to deal effectively with the immigration issue. Many municipalities are adopting their own local ordinances regarding this subject. As the United States moves into a recession, jobs will become more valuable and many immigrants will leave states that do not offer support. Hospitals and schools are changing policies drastically due to this pressure. Currently the United States Senate is considering a bill which would force local and state law enforcement to enforce immigration laws. This is another in a series of unfunded mandates.

8. THE GLOBAL ECONOMY IS GROWING MORE INTEGRATED.

- Only half of the world's one hundred largest economies are nation-states. The rest are multinational corporations.

- In the European Union, relaxation of border and capital controls and the adoption of a common currency and uniform product standards continue to make it easier for companies to distribute products and support functions throughout the continent.

- The Internet continues to bring manufacturers effectively closer to remote suppliers and customers.

- Companies are increasingly farming out high-cost, low-payoff secondary functions to suppliers, service firms, and consultants, many of them located in other countries.

  - Parts for the new Boeing 787 "Dreamliner" are being constructed in at least eight countries around the world for assembly in the United States

  - Toyota has manufacturing or assembly plants in Japan, Australia, Canada, Indonesia, Poland, South Africa, Turkey, the United Kingdom, the United States, France, Brazil, Pakistan, India, Argentina, the Czech Republic, Mexico, Malaysia, Thailand, China, Vietnam, Venezuela, and the Philippines.

- Companies in high-wage countries also are outsourcing management and service jobs to low-wage countries.

  - An estimated 3.3 million U.S. jobs are expected to migrate to India and China by 2015. Some 40 million jobs are believed vulnerable to outsourcing.

  - There is a nascent countertrend among job-receiving countries to establish branches in the donor lands. For example, in September 2007, India's Wipro announced that it was setting up a programming division in Virginia, both to hire top-quality American programmers and to help tap the lucrative government market.

  - Jobs in western Europe are migrating to eastern Europe, the former Soviet Union, and the English- and French-speaking former colonies of Africa. India has begun to ship jobs to even lower-cost countries in Africa.

Assessment:

This trend will continue for at least the next two decades.

Implications:

The growth of e-commerce enables businesses to shop globally for the cheapest raw materials and supplies. In niche markets, the Internet also makes it possible for small companies to compete with giants worldwide with relatively little investment. This has brought new opportunities for quality-control problems and fraudulent cost-cutting by suppliers, as seen in the recent spate of tainted food and other products coming from China.

The Net also has created a generation of "e-preneurs" whose businesses exist largely on the Internet, with production, fulfillment, and other functions all outsourced to specialty firms.

Demand will continue to grow for employee incentives suited to other cultures, aid to executives going overseas, and the many other aspects of doing business in foreign countries

However, rising demand for foreign-language training is likely to be a temporary phenomenon, as more countries adopt English as part of their basic school curricula.

Western companies may have to accept that proprietary information will be shared not just with their immediate partners in Asian joint ventures, but also with other members of the partners' trading conglomerates. In high technology and aerospace, that may expose companies to extra scrutiny due to national-security concerns.

  – Establishing overseas branches mitigates this concern by keeping trade secrets within the company, even while gaining the benefits of cheaper foreign labor and other resources.

Economic ties can give richer, more powerful countries considerable influence over their junior partners. Thus far, China has been the most successful at wielding this "soft" power. This has given it the ability to undermine American foreign policy even as it secures its energy and raw-materials needs.

Implications for Terrorism:

This is a top-ten trend.

International fraud, money laundering, and other economic crimes (particularly carried out via the Internet) are a growing problem, and one that can be expected to spread. At least some of these activities can be expected to finance extremist and terrorist movements.

In addition, entrepreneurial success in global markets could widen the gap between the rich and poor, worsening social strains in countries already vulnerable to extremist movements. It is likely to worsen the problem of international terrorism.

Expert Comments:

ANONYMOUS (5): This is a very important and largely positive trend because growing global economic integration creates "global consciousness," facilitating inter-governmental and transnational collaboration. Such collaboration among intelligence and security services, industry, and the non-governmental sector is needed to anticipate and to address boundary crossing terrorist threats. Of course, global integration also provides opportunities for terrorists to cause globally cascading damage by attacking key nodes in global networks. And the rise of global consciousness itself will be challenged by geopolitical divisions caused by the scramble to secure access to oil in an environment of tight supply. (Trend 18: Despite efforts to develop alternative source of energy, oil consumption is still rising rapidly.)

ARMSTRONG: See earlier comments in Trend 1 on local vs. global/U.S.

CHOBAR: It's hard to know who funds what anymore because the global economy is growing more integrated. While local governments struggle to fund policing, national and global terrorist groups easily find funds to communicate on the most sophisticated of levels. This integrated economy makes it more and more difficult to police and more and more likely to enable global terrorism.

FORSTER: All forms of integration dramatically impact the terror paradigm. Economic integration means the potential impact of terrorist attacks is more extreme. For example, the economic impact of a disabled U.S. power grid would quickly surge through the global economy. Integration also eases the flow of individuals, information, and finances and thus improves the capabilities of terrorist organizations. The multi-headed "hydra" that is Al Qaeda today has been facilitated by the ability to train, recruit, plan, finance, and propagandize operations at a distance. The need for a hierarchical command and control structure has been replaced by a networked ideology that inspires, supports, and publicizes action. The space and time paradigm has changed, reducing the importance of geographic proximity. Cyber-attacks, for example, may be launched against any G-8 state from Pakistan. The problems experienced by the Estonian government in the spring 2007 offer insight into the threat of such attacks. The flow of people, goods, finances, and information also increase the cost of protection and prevention and potentially inhibit pursuit and recovery.

However, integration also may be turned into a counter-terror advantage. As a result of increased interdependence, more lives are negatively impacted by terrorist attacks. Under such circumstances, there is hope that impacted innocents will be less inclined to overlook terrorist activities in their locales. The recent Sunni Iraqi shift against Al Qaeda in al-Anbar Province indicates that the support for violence is finite among societal sectors and continued terrorist violence may be a catalyst to anger against the perpetrators and an increase in anti-terror sentiments.

JENKINS: Globalization means increased transnational crime—terrorism, financial fraud, money laundering, cyber-crime, human trafficking, counterfeit goods, smuggling, etc. This complicates issues of jurisdiction, cooperation among police forces, relationships between local law enforcement and federal authorities and the private sector. We will also increasingly see transnational gangs.

KADTKE: The IT revolution and technology-based economies are also driving physical integration of the global economy. As large, and increasingly mid-sized, companies outsource their manufacturing, research, and even management capabilities to many corners of the globe, they become increasingly vulnerable to a wide spectrum of regional and local socio-political woes. The net effect is that local extreme events can have global attention and effect as they propagate throughout the global supply chain.

LaDUKE (1): Because economy generates the power to ensure defense and wage war, it is central to every national interest. But centralizing economy and trade does not automatically centralize nation-state interests, so it has the affect of creating a global stage of "actors" with hidden agendas that create diverse alliances and fund terrorism covertly. I see this as the primary root cause behind the growth of global terrorism.

MEILAHN: International fraud, money laundering, etc., via the internet will be a tool used by terror groups to finance their activities.

MILLER: Actually, it is more interesting to speculate that globalization may have peaked and nations are in a cocooning phase, much like the U.S. just before World War II. One has only to look at the vigorous debate over the "illegal immigrant" issue in the U.S. to see the possible birth of a counter-trend. While this erection of physical and other barriers to entering the country may enhance the level of public fear, I think it may actually offer more opportunities for counter-terrorism—or, at least, counter-transnational-terrorism.

SANDERS (3): See comments under "Complexity and the Future of Terrorism" in Appendix C.

SHTULMAN: The movement of hundreds of billions of dollars to the oil-rich nations and their desire to invest those dollars in everything from high-tech companies with military applications to international shipping companies, airlines, and ports means that it is inevitable that at some point elements with connections to terror will gain control of the means to transport materials and/or men into the United States at will. Corporations that have no connections to terror today can make such acquisitions and later themselves be acquired by others with ties to terror.

SNYDER (6): Economic globalization will continue to depress both wages and job growth in mature industrial economies for at least 5 more years, fueling domestic political opposition to free-trade and liberalized immigration, and fostering increased xenophobia.

YOUNG: Globalization and distribution of wealth can only help decrease the specter of terror over the long run.

---

9. MILITANT ISLAM CONTINUES TO SPREAD AND GAIN POWER.

- It has been clear for years that the Muslim lands face severe problems with religious extremists dedicated to advancing their political, social, and doctrinal views by any means necessary.

- Most of the Muslim lands are overcrowded and short of resources. Many are poor, save for the oil-rich states of the Middle East. Virtually all have large populations of young men, often unemployed, who are frequently attracted to violent extremist movements.

- During its proxy war with the Soviet Union in Afghanistan, the United States massively fortified the Muslim extremist infrastructure by supplying it with money, arms, and, above all, training.

- It is making a similar mistake today. The overthrow of Saddam Hussein and the American occupation of Iraq has inspired a new generation of *jihadis*, who have been trained and battle-hardened in the growing insurgency.

- In a now-declassified National Security Estimate, the American intelligence community concluded that Al Qaeda was more powerful in 2007 than it had been before the so-called "war on terror" began—more dangerous even than it had been when it planned the attacks of September 11, 2001.

- American support for Israel has also made the United States a target for the hatred of Muslim extremists.

Assessment:

This trend may wax and wane, but it seems unlikely to disappear this side of a Muslim reformation comparable to those that transformed Christianity and Judaism.

Implications:

Virtually all of the Muslim lands face an uncertain, and possibly bleak, future of political instability and growing violence. The exceptions are the oil states, where money can still buy relative peace, at least for now.

These problems often have spilled over into the rest of the world. They will do so again.

In a 1994 terrorism study for the Department of Defense and other government clients, Forecasting International predicted that by 2020 a strong majority of the world's twenty-five or so most important Muslim lands could be in the hands of extremist religious governments. At the time, only Iran was ruled by such a regime. That forecast still appears sound.

Iraq is likely to become the next fundamentalist Muslim regime. Once American forces leave, Iran will support the establishment of a Shiite regime much like its own in Baghdad.

There is a one-in-ten chance that this will set off a general war in the Middle East, as Sunni-dominated states intercede to protect Iraqi Sunnis against Shi'a domination. However, Iraq and Saudi Arabia already are negotiating to keep this situation under control.

Any attempt to reduce the commitment of Western forces to the task of stabilizing Afghanistan will result in the restoration of the Taliban to power.

Implications for Terrorism:

This is a top-ten trend.

The West, and particularly the United States, must expect more—and more violent—acts of terrorism for at least the next 20 years.

Europe faces a significant homegrown Muslim extremist movement, and the United States may do so in the near future. Thanks largely to waves of immigration since the 1980s, Islam is the fastest-growing religion in both regions. Extremist clerics in Europe are recruiting young Muslims to the cause of *jihad* against their adopted homes. So far, their colleagues in the United States have been much less successful. That may not always be true.

Western interests also will be vulnerable in many countries outside the Muslim core. International ties formed among Islamic militants during the anti-Soviet war in Afghanistan produced an extremist infrastructure that can support terrorist activities almost anywhere in the world. The war in Iraq is doing so even more efficiently.

This development must be taken even more seriously because, for the first time, a Muslim country—Pakistan—has nuclear weapons. Muslim extremists view this technology as an "Islamic bomb" that could be used to promote their cause. From here on out, nuclear terrorism is a realistic threat.

This risk will grow as Sudan, Iraq, and probably other countries establish fundamentalist regimes sympathetic to the cause of *jihad* against the West.

Saudi Arabia easily could be taken over by a fundamentalist regime. The Saudi rulers may well try to avoid this by providing even more support to extremists and directing their attention to the West.

The overthrow of the Taliban in Afghanistan and, especially, of Saddam Hussein in Iraq, have made future fundamentalist revolutions more likely, rather than less so, because it has strengthened the global *jihadi* movement.

This is clearly the single most important trend for terrorism.

Expert Comments:

ANONYMOUS (3): Obviously important for inspiring disaffected individuals and small groups but perhaps of diminishing significance as a driver of an organized "global guerilla" campaign. Militant Islam has failed to capture a foothold in the Maghreb or the Arab world, and may now be facing a "Thermidor-style" popular rejection due to its excesses against co-religionists in several Middle Eastern countries.

ARMSTRONG: While militant Islam does continue to spread, we must consider the Taliban's increasing reliance on foreigners as well as the rejection of Al Qaeda in parts of Iraq, both because their extremist message fails to resonate with the locals. Information drives this train, and frustration with the present condition drives recruitment. Failure to understand the Koran, the Hadith, or Islam in general permits acts otherwise abhorrent.

General Douglas Stone, chief of detainee operations in Iraq, has noted the distinction between ideologues and tag-alongs:

> *We are able to determine the guys that don't really give a shit about the Koran in the first place—they're using it as a discipline—those guys are beginning to fall into the category of irreconcilables, and that's helpful to me. I want to know who they are. They're like rotten eggs, you know, hiding in the Easter basket, so that's very helpful. Then it's also equally helpful to have guys who come out and say, "I didn't know that. Now that I know that, I'm going to change my life." And we poly[graph] them. You'd be...interesting to know, because we are trying to figure out if they are messing with us. But we are convinced that they have made a significant change. Now, you're not talking about, you know, radicals going to choir boys, but you're talking about radicals who won't use violence without a very clear understanding that they are damned if they do.*

While we debate the merits of *Qutb* and its value to extremist ideology, we too often forget to ask how many extremists actually read *Qutb* in the same analytic framework as we do and aren't just spoon fed select passages from the Koran to support their violence. Also, it's worth bearing in mind that Christianity, Judaism, and Hinduism do not have the promotion and outreach campaigns for the needy and less fortunate that Islam does. We must look at what gives militant Islam its power, something we do not fully understand. The answers more likely lie in my response to Trend 1 than in the inherent attractiveness of extremism and hate.

AYERS (1): Every success claimed (whether or not the assessment of success is an honest one) by Islamic terrorists supports their efforts to expand the scope of their activities and, in their own minds, validates the extremist agenda—to establish the global domination of Islam. In addition to the looming specter of nuclear weapons in the hands of Islamists, we now see limited support for anti-U.S., anti-Israeli terrorist operations among elements of non-Islamic rogue regimes. If, as it now appears may be the case, leaders of former or potential superpowers are added to the mix—providing assistance in the form of planning and weapons (however covertly) to increasingly dangerous state sponsors of terrorism—it might be possible for a nuclear supported and/or nuclear armed Islamist state (such as Iran) to arrange large and small-scale attacks (terrorist as well as state-to-state) around the world, simultaneously. In fact, with sufficient assistance and pre-action infiltration, it might be possible to remove the major Western powers from global connectivity long enough to create desired effects (such as the destruction of Israel followed by major and minor terrorist attacks throughout all Western countries.) Arguments over the value of multiculturalism and cultural relativism aside, calls for "demographic jihad" and attempts to indoctrinate susceptible members of immigrant populations with extremist rhetoric by organizations like Hizb ut-Tahrir (see Zeyno Baran's 2005 article "Fighting the War of Ideas" in *Foreign Affairs*, vol. 84 [6]) may increase the likelihood of pre-attack infiltration throughout Europe and the United States.

BRUH: Islamic fundmentalism is a serious law enforcement problem as well as one that affects national security. It will likely continue resulting in greater serious crime with not just economics behind the activities.

CHOBAR (3): Most local law enforcement personnel are ill informed regarding "militant Islam." Thus, places like Pakistan, England, the United States, and Canada are "harbors" for any number of Muslims who may be communicating by Internet, satellite dish, etc. There may also be significant caches of wealth being accumulated in these countries which are unknown to policing agencies but well know to terrorists.

Forster: I have addressed this extensively in the point on undemocratic governance. [See Appendix C.] Here I would only add that extremism is an increasing challenge as it permeates new regions and extremist movements with varying objectives coalesce. New regions of militant Islam-incited conflict include sub-Saharan Africa, particularly the Horn and Nigeria. However, the most serious threat is the increasing militancy in Western Europe's Muslim population, which lives "below the radar" until they take action. While the coalescence between the GSPC [*Groupe Salafiste pour la Prédication et le Combat*—the Salafist Group for Call and Combat—a Sunni militia that aims to overthrow the Algerian government and establish an Islamic state] and Al Qaeda is most probably the result of declining capabilities of the GSPC, these alliances often include increased radicalization of and violence by the weaker partner (e.g. GSPC). The case of the Taliban's integration of foreign fighters also has changed tactics by increasing the use of suicide bombers in Afghanistan. More strategically, the integration of foreign fighters threatens to regionalize the conflict because of regime instability in the broader area.

Two counter-terrorism issues that deserve attention involve the ultimate appeal of Islamic extremism as a "way of life" for a general population and the emergence of reform in Islam. First, the 2006 National Intelligence Estimate correctly concluded that "sharia-based extremism is neither popular nor likely to ultimately address the frustrations evident in Islamic society today." As a result, programs aimed at political modernization and economic development may defuse much of the militancy. Tied to a development strategy is the encouragement of moderate Islam among those who are tired of having their religion perverted and seek to lead an "Islamic Reformation."

Jenkins: Terrorism will continue to be a threat for the foreseeable future. The Internet has become an increasingly important venue for recruitment, exhortation, instruction, and propaganda. Terrorists are ahead of the authorities here. There will be continuing pressure on local law enforcement agencies to enhance their own intelligence capabilities. The rest of the world will be dealing with the terrorist tactics and know-how developed in Iraq for the next fifteen years. Terrorists' determination to carry out large-scale, indiscriminate violence is pushing authorities from a traditional investigations approach to preventive intervention. We do not have a well-developed corpus of law in this area.

Kadtke: While a spectrum of terrorist organizations exist globally, their total net power is overshadowed by the terror activities of militant Islamic groups, and the latter continues to expand. Moreover, these activities have caused a political awakening among Islamic groups and nations that continues to grow, and they are beginning to engage aggressively with modern public diplomacy tools such as Al Jazeera. Whether or not a clash of civilizations will occur in the future, clandestine sponsorship of militant Islamic groups will remain a major driver of these activities.

Kriesberg: Militant Islam may be spreading to some degree. But as it overreaches and fails, it generates counter forces and resistance from other Muslims. That should be recognized. Allowing space for the highly doctrinaire to participate in governance can be part of their transformation.

Another consideration is the division within Islam between the Sunni and the Shia. The intensity of that schism could at some point become a source of support for norms of tolerance, as happened within Christianity after years of intense struggle between Catholics and Protestants.

LaDuke (4): An obviously huge threat to the U.S. because militant Islam is seated in the midst of the interests of multiple superpower agendas, has a massive population for recruitment, and has potential to publicly or covertly gain access to advanced technology.

Lanotte: Since the mid 19th century, there has been a distinct separation between internal law enforcement and external "instrument of foreign policy." Understanding that changing this arrangement can create a "slippery slope," it may be time to re-think the use of military assets, especially intelligence assets, to combat jihadi-like threats.

Leffler: Research in the Middle East, published in the peer-reviewed *Journal of Conflict Resolution*, demonstrated that a sufficiently large group of Invincible Defense Technology experts in Israel affected the war in nearby Lebanon. The Lebanon War intensity dropped 45 percent, war deaths dropped 76 percent, and quality of life improved by 0.75

standard deviation units. In Israel, crime dropped by 12 percent and quality of life improved by 1.3 standard deviation units. Areas with a low quality of life can be a breeding ground for terrorism. Based on this research, it is clear that Invincible Defense Technology is capable of greatly reducing the protracted sectarian violence in the Middle East.

Meilahn: This is a Muslim problem that can only be fought by Muslims. The more moderate Muslims must take on this fight, and the U.S. can help them. Currently only about 2 percent are radicals; but that is still a large number. According to a Gallup analysis of polls representing 90 percent of the world's Muslim population, another 7 percent are "politically radicalized." That is, they believe the 9/11 attacks were completely justified and have an unfavorable view of the United States. And in 2006, the Pew Research Center found that 17.7 percent of Muslim respondents believed that violence against civilian targets in order to defend Islam can be justified "often" or "sometimes." At least some of the radicalized 2 percent can be re-educated about Islam and "de-radicalized," prevented from executing acts of terror. This group is the one the USG should concern itself with from a preventive standpoint.

Another point is that most of the Muslims who condoned attacks on 9/11 believe that it was justifiable because of U.S. "colonizing" and the way we are too controlling of other countries. The USG could do much with regard to its foreign policy to change its image from "occupier" to cooperative member of the world community. That would do much to decrease motivations for jihad, and keep terrorists away from our borders or our interests worldwide.

Oil states will also suffer problems (a disagreement with your list of trends) because the Shi'ia-Sunni divide will be aggravated as both militant Sunni groups (such as Al Qaeda) and militant Shi'ia groups (Hizb'Allah) influence others of like kind by their example and successes. For example, the Shi'ia in Saudi Arabia may rise up and demand their rights and representation in a mostly Sunni land. Although Iran is an "extremist" government, they are actually fairly democratic the way they operate. Frankly, this is one government that is less concerning to me (because they have fairly good control of their state, and they are moderating politically as a somewhat post-revolutionary government—Ahmadi-Nejad's comments not withstanding—he is not the leader here, Ayatollah Khamenei is) than are other governments that are more precarious; state failure leaves the conditions ripe for extremism to grow (as along the Pakistani-Afghan border in the FATA [Federally Administered Tribal Areas of Pakistan]).Iraq is currently the center of a proxy war for influence between Saudi and Iran—the winner will be identified by what type of long term government resides there, Shi'ia or Sunni.

Miller: Obviously, this looms large in our thinking about terrorism. I am not sure how significantly Islam's growth or even the increase in fundamentalist Muslim trained youth (in Saudi Arabia, e.g.) actually translates directly into a U.S. problem, unless we choose to make it so. There is certainly not a linear cause and effect between Muslim growth and terrorist threat to the U.S. However, there may well be a "tipping point" when the cork pops and local mid-East regimes become actively engaged in violence, and the U.S. becomes involved as an agent for the regime. The recent Iraq experience may suggest that, barring the presence of outside forces, Muslim internecine violence can be controlled, if not eliminated.

Nolte: This is one instance in which local authorities can help to avert potential terrorism. Good policing can facilitate the process whereby an "alien" population, in this case Muslim, integrates effectively into society, rather than being further alienated from it.

Probst: The most troubling manifestation of militant Islam is the cult of Global jihad that has found expression under the tutelage of Usama bin Laden and the Al Qaeda organization. Due to continued success of intelligence and security services working, "al Qaeda Central" has largely been decimated. Despite reverses, its malignant ideology has metastasized, infecting the body politic of Muslim communities worldwide. The ideology has developed a global following and a global reach. Bin Laden himself has achieved the iconic status that had previously been reserved for secular revolutionaries such as Lenin and Che Guevara. Even in the secular West and even among non-Muslims, we see efforts to "canonize" bin Laden as a freedom fighter who has defended the interests of the Muslim masses. The aim is to have the ideology of jihad transcend Islam and speak to the angry, oppressed, and wretched of the earth regardless of class, nationality, or religion.

Rabasa: I would argue that this trend is not very cut and that, in fact, there are indications that militant Islam may have reached a high-water mark globally and may be retreating in some areas. Al-Qaeda-influenced terrorist campaigns have lost ground in Iraq, Saudi Arabia, and Indonesia. In Europe there is greater awareness on the part of political elites of the threat of radicalization of its homegrown Muslim population and steps are being taken in some countries to counter this trend.

SANDERS (4): See comments under "Complexity and the Future of Terrorism" in Appendix C.

TAN: The startling failures of U.S. grand strategy after 9/11, particularly its disastrous strategy in Iraq, have been counter-productive to the global war on terrorism. From relative stability albeit under Saddam's dictatorial hand, Iraq has slid into chaos and has become the training ground for the global jihad much as Afghanistan had become the training ground from which Al Qaeda emerged. However, the jihadists in Iraq are honing their skills in combating the world's technologically most advanced armed forces and are learning to perfect techniques in IEDs, sabotage, sniping, kidnappings, assassinations, urban warfare, etc. Once dispersed throughout the world, these jihadists will re-constitute a post-Al Qaeda network that will be much more competent, effective, and deadly. Unfortunately, their first targets will be likely Muslim governments and allies of the U.S.A. throughout the Middle East. Can these regimes meet the emerging challenge of the post-Iraq militants? Will the radicalization being spawned in Iraq today seep through its borders to destabilize the entire Middle East? The question today is not how to win Iraq. The questions are: What can the U.S.A. and the West do to meet and contain the growing threat from radical Islam? How can we contain Iranian Shi'ite fundamentalism from threatening the stability of the entire Middle East?

YOUNG: As long as the conditions for Islamic extremism exist worldwide terror activities will not subside over the short term. These conditions include but are not limited to political and economic conditions in the extremists' home countries such as corrupt leadership; lack of general, non-religious, education opportunities; support for anti-Western religious teachings and high unemployment amongst Muslim youth. Should these conditions be addressed by a new type of Muslim leader then extremists will always have a recruiting base.

TRENDS IN VALUES, CONCERNS, AND LIFESTYLES

10. SOCIETAL VALUES ARE CHANGING RAPIDLY.

- Industrialization raises educational levels, changes attitudes toward authority, reduces fertility, alters gender roles, and encourages broader political participation.

  - This process is just beginning throughout the developing world. Witness the growing literacy, declining fertility, and broad voter turnout seen in India over the last decade.

- Developed societies increasingly take their cue from Generation X and the Millennial generation (aka Gen Y or Generation Dot-com), rather than the Baby Boomers who dominated the industrialized world's thinking for most of four decades.

- Millennials value, and display, both self-reliance and cooperation. They need self-reliance because they believe individuals can no longer count on government social-security income, pensions, or other benefits. They value, and are good at, cooperation because group action often is the best way to optimize the use of scarce resources, such as retirement savings.

- Post-September 11 fear of terrorist attacks has led Americans to accept almost without comment security measures that their traditional love of privacy once would have made intolerable.

  - This continues a long-established tendency in the United States to prefer a greater sense of safety at the cost of increased government surveillance and intervention in their lives.

Assessment:

This trend will continue for at least the next two decades in the industrialized lands and two generations in the developing world.

Implications:

The growing influence of the post-Baby-Boom generations will tend to homogenize basic attitudes throughout the world, because Generation Xers and especially the Millennials around the globe have more in common with each other than with their parents.

The highly polarized political environment that has plagued the United States since the 1980s will slowly moderate as results-oriented Generation Xers and Millennials begin to dominate the national dialogue.

As national security concerns have begun to lose their immediacy, family issues are regaining their significance in American society: long-term health care, day care, early childhood education, antidrug campaigns, and the environment. Concerns about health care, education, and the environment already are shaping the 2008 presidential campaign.

Demand for greater accountability and transparency in business will be crucial for countries that wish to attract international investors.

Implications for Terrorism:

This is a top-ten trend.

Reaction against changing values is one of the prime motives for cultural extremism, not only in the Muslim world and in parts of India, but in the United States and Europe, where it appears in the form of hate crimes against immigrants.

The spread of westernized Generation X and Dot-com values in the developing world will provoke an even greater reaction from fundamentalists, who will see it as cultural imperialism by America and Europe and as a threat to the piety of their children, and therefore to their afterlife in paradise. This is likely to make the anti-West movement among Muslims even more violent and widespread.

At the same time, a reaction against immigrants could trigger hate crimes against the foreign-born on a scale not recently seen in the United States, conceivably inspiring a small native terrorist movement in response.

Expert Comments:

BRAY (3): They are and different "niche" values are emerging. To try and say all Generation X'ers are the same would be untrue. Same with Generation Y. Whereas the Baby Boomers did seem to have a similar (if not cohesive) identity, partly due to the television media and its one-way interactivity, the Internet is allowing for several different sub-groups of social values to exist and thrive across great distances even if the number of members subscribing to those views are few.

CHOBAR (10): With global terrorism and societal values changing rapidly, many in U.S. society don't really know what to believe. Drug trafficking and other high-dollar crime may well be lending financial support to the financing of technology for terrorists. Right here in the "bread basket of the world," gangs and significant crime is moving in. Policing it is becoming more and more difficult.

JENKINS: Societal values are constantly in flux. As society redefines what is legal and what is tolerable, enforcement will be continuously affected.

KRIESBERG: Societal values are changing; significantly so are global values. The diffusion of values relating to the protection of individual and collective human rights is significant for countering terrorism. Personal security is an important human right.

Norms supporting popular governance also are diffusing.

LaDUKE (5): Behind the global shift in values is a society that feels increasingly impacted by larger global issues and superpower interests with far less trust in the capabilities of social institutions and nation states to solve those issues. Failed states are rampant (http://www.foreignpolicy.com/story/cms.php?story_id=3865), and citizens feel a loss of control over their own individual and societal destinies. Depending on which direction group values shift, this energy can translate into efforts like the advance of social causes or discontent and extremism. The simultaneous rapid rise of causes like environmentalism and terrorism are really two sides of the same coin. Integral dialogue creates an inclusive climate and gives citizens in any culture a sense of control over integral issues that are larger than individual nation states.

LANOTTE: Culturally, the Western World was developed on the Judeo-Christian ethos. Among those ethical mores is a common respect for all citizens, including women. The lack of respect for certain classes, including sex and religion, is not a problem for Western Civilization. However, it is a problem for those religions unable to share this ethical boundary. It is unacceptable to allow hate crimes, but there is a case to be made that crimes that are common and normal in the Muslim world should be prosecutable in the Western World. This should be our focus, not whether the rest of the world accepts our value system.

MEILAHN: I agree that changing societal values are a prime motive for extremism. See my note for Trend 1 above.

MILLER: It is not clear that this will impact terrorism in either a net-positive or net-negative way.

YOUNG: One of the main complaints Muslim extremists have is that their traditional society and its values are being Westernized. Extremists use this tactic to recruit new extremists and will continue to use terror to prevent events such as the Middle East Peace Process from occurring.

11. YOUNG PEOPLE PLACE INCREASING IMPORTANCE ON ECONOMIC SUCCESS, WHICH THEY HAVE COME TO EXPECT.

- Throughout the 1990s—effectively, their entire adult lives—Generation Xers and the Millennials knew only good economic times, and the economic downturn at the turn of the century seemed to them a confusing aberration rather than a predictable part of the business cycle.

    – Most expect to see hardship on a national level, but they both want and expect prosperity for themselves.

- Generation Xers and the Millennials are the most entrepreneurial generations in history.

- In the United States especially, most young people have high aspirations, but many lack the means to achieve them.

    – High-school dropout rates average between 18 and 30 percent, depending on who does the counting.

    – Inner-city rates are much higher by anyone's measure, with up to half of all students leaving high school before graduation in the worst districts.

    – Only about one high-school graduate in four goes on to receive a college degree. Many of the rest wish to go, and are qualified to do so, but cannot afford the high cost of further schooling.

    – On average, someone with a bachelor's degree in the United States earned nearly $54,689 in 2004, compared with less than $29,448 for someone with only a high school diploma.

    – High-school dropouts earned just $19,915, while those with a professional degree raked in $119,009.

Assessment:

This trend appeared with the Baby Boom generation and has strengthened with the later cohorts. It will be interesting to see what develops among the children of the Millennials, something we find it difficult to predict with any confidence.

Implications:

Disappointed ambitions will be a major source of political unrest in the United States and many other countries in the next two decades. Most of the other countries seriously affected by this trend will be in the developing world or will be host to large numbers of disadvantaged immigrants.

Entrepreneurialism will be a global trend, as members of Generation X and the Millennials throughout the world tend to share values. Generation X and Millennial entrepreneurs are largely responsible for the current economic growth in India and China, where they are becoming a major force in the Communist party. In India, the younger generations dress and think more like their American counterparts than their parents. In China, the democratic fervor that spawned Tiananmen Square has been replaced by capitalist entrepreneurialism.

If younger-generation workers find their ambitions thwarted, they will create growing pressure for economic and social reform. If change does not come fast enough in the developing world, disappointed expectations will raise the number of young people who emigrate to the developed lands.

In the United States, pressure will grow to provide more, and less burdensome, economic assistance to qualified high school graduates who cannot afford to go on to college.

Pressure also will grow to make sure that all American students have access to an education capable of preparing them for college or a rewarding career.

Implications for Terrorism:

Disappointment also will drive underemployed young men in the developing world into fringe political and religious movements. This will add to future terrorism and instability, with profound effects on the cultures and economies of both their homelands and the target countries.

This basic materialism may be the single greatest complaint of Muslim fundamentalists against the West.

Expert Comments:

Bray (10): See Trend 10.

Chobar (7): We need to really encourage our Generation X and Millennials to understand the complexities of policing and terrorism. Many of them, especially in the Midwest portion of the United States, live very "sheltered" lives and do not understand worldviews. They are totally unfamiliar with global politics, global relations, and definitely global terrorism. They could help significantly, if we assist them to focus less on economic success, which they have come to expect. I work with teacher candidates every day and know there are many Generation X and Millennials who want to sacrifice economic success for the good of teaching children, for the good of society, and the good of families.

Miller: Oddly, this may be more of a driver of terrorism than one might think. Given that many of the suicide bombers and terrorists in general, are not common thugs (Zarqawi) but are educated engineers, doctors, and other professionals (Al-Zawahiri), I would put the disparity between young educated persons' expectations and actualities high on the list of motivators for future terrorist violence.

Sanders (5): See comments under "Complexity and the Future of Terrorism" in Appendix C.

Tan: The march of the global interlinked economy and the values it espouses are breaking down traditional value systems everywhere. Globalization emphasizes materialism and individualism, in contrast to spiritual values, the community, and the environment. It spawns a culture of expectations; whereas people in the past were relatively content even in relative poverty, young people today want to have all the material goods and the good life that they see in images propagated by the global media. This revolution in expectations cannot be met. Instead, what has happened are masses of frustrated youth in teeming third-world cities unable to meet these expectations. In Muslim lands, in the context of a population explosion, corrupt and nepotistic regimes, poor governance, and wide socio-economic disparities, radical Islam ideology offers a plausible explanation, a radical solution, a plan of action, and a system of rewards for signing up. Globalization will spawn millenarian and apocalyptic religious cults, many possibly not Islamic in character (remember the *Aum Shinrikyo*) that will have quite radical and violent solutions to this problem.

YOUNG: As stated previously, in some Muslim countries, young people believe they have no future when they are unemployed and see the globalized world begin to pass them by. When people believe they have no economic future, it affects their daily lives and they easily turn to terrorism.

12. TOURISM, VACATIONING, AND TRAVEL (ESPECIALLY INTERNATIONAL) CONTINUE TO GROW WITH EACH PASSING YEAR.

- International tourism grew by more than 6 percent in the first half of 2007, thanks in part to global prosperity. By 2020, international tourist arrivals are expected to reach 1.6 billion annually, up from 842 million in 2006.

  - The number of Americans traveling to foreign countries (excluding Canada and Mexico) crashed following the September 11 attacks. More recently, their numbers have been growing by about 5.5 percent annually, even faster than before 2001.

  - In contrast, the United States received only 21.7 million visitors from countries other than Canada and Mexico, down 17 percent from the peak in 2001, even though the dollar's weakness on foreign exchange markets should have made the United States a more attractive destination. The decline stems from tighter American entry restrictions enacted in the name of security and from international hostility inspired by the Iraq war.

- However, U.S. domestic tourism is growing about 2.3 percent each year.

- By 2020, according to the World Trade Organization, 100 million Chinese will fan out across the globe, replacing Americans, Japanese, and Germans as the world's most numerous travelers.

  - Chinese spending for international travel will reach $100 billion by 2008.

  - Some 50 million Indian tourists will join them.

- China soon will become the world's most popular destination as well, as preparations for the 2008 Summer Olympic Games focus international attention on Beijing.

  - By 2020, China can expect 130 million international arrivals.

- Online travel services are displacing traditional travel agencies in all but cruises and other luxury markets.

  - In the United States, the online travel industry grossed $79 billion in 2006. It is expected to take in more than $94 billion in 2007 and $146 billion by 2010.

• Multiple, shorter vacations spread throughout the year continue to replace the traditional two-week vacation.

Assessment:

Travel seems to be in the DNA of the middle and upper economic classes. This trend will continue so long as national economies continue to generate new prosperity for the formerly poor.

Implications:

Travel will grow by at least 5 percent per year for the foreseeable future.

Tourism offers growing opportunities for out-of-the-way destinations that have not yet cashed in on the boom. This will make it an important industry for still more developing countries.

American domestic tourism will continue to grow by an average of 2.3 percent per year through at least 2011.

The tourism industry will create 3.3 million new jobs worldwide. Jobs dependent on tourism will comprise nearly 14 percent of the global workforce.

Direct employment will not grow quite as quickly, but it will be up 1.7 percent annually, to nearly 87.5 million jobs, while indirect employment will account for some 260 million jobs around the world.

This will bring major opportunities for the travel industries of Southeast Asia and Africa, where Chinese and Indian tourists can take quick, inexpensive vacations.

Retirees who travel off-season will further ease the cyclical peaks and valleys typical of the industry.

Cruise ships will continue to lure retirees. Some liners are offering full-time residency—creating new options for assisted living arrangements.

Implications for Terrorism:

The continuing growth of tourism will increase the contact between Westerners and residents of the developing world, to the frustration and dismay of culturally motivated extremists in the recipient lands.

Western tourists are more vulnerable to kidnapping and killing when abroad than they are at home.

Expert Comments:

BRUH: As we have seen, terrorism can quickly change the habits of people such as if civilian planes and cruise ships are attacked, travel and tourism will fall off in major ways and if "enough" serious attacks take place, travel and tourism could be virtually shut down at least of the kind that crosses international borders for many years at a time.

CHOBAR: Tourism, vacationing and travel may decline if terrorism were to begin targeting such large devices as cruise ships, major tourist attractions (The Eiffel Tower, etc.) and/or large travel beginning points such as JFK airport, Heathrow Airport, Union Station in New York City, etc.

Forster: This trend obviously increases terrorist targets, has a greater economic impact from attacks, and provides a high publicity opportunity. A massive explosion at Disney World might well rival the 9/11 attack from a terrorist publicity perspective and potentially even casualties. Furthermore, we know that transportation infrastructure has become a popular target because it has the probably of a relatively high casualty rate while shaking society's confidence and instilling fear that can have a long-term residual economic impact.

Miller: While air hijacking has been stanched at the moment, tourism and even air travel are surely going to remain attractive targets for future terrorist innovators.

Shtulman: Attacks on tourists are not new, especially for Israelis. The hijacking to Entebbe and attempt to shoot down an Israeli airliner in Kenya following an attack on a hotel known to be patronized by Israelis are only the most famous incidents. The bombing of the nightclub in Bali took mostly Australian lives and Germany saw an attack on a club that was a favorite of American servicemen. If tensions between America and Iran rise, American tourists in Europe will potentially be easy targets for Iranian proxy groups like Hezbollah.

Young: As tourism increases, more populations become vulnerable to terrorist attack. Terrorists have tended to strike at certain countries, such as Egypt, which rely on the tourism industry for their economic livelihood. This trend will surely continue as more areas of the world become more accessible.

---

13. The physical-culture and personal-health movements are improving health in much of the world, but they are far from universal.

- Emphasis on preventive medicine continues to grow.

  – Of late, a few insurance carriers—but more each year—have expanded coverage or reduced premiums for policyholders with healthy lifestyles.

- Where change has been slow, legislation has sometimes mandated it.

  – Since 2005, more than half of states have required insurers to pay for mammograms.

- Health is continuing to improve in the United States, but less quickly.

  – During the 1990s, health in the United States improved by 1.5 percent annually, based on such measures as smoking prevalence, health-insurance coverage, infant mortality rates, and premature deaths.

  – During the 2000s, health improvement has slowed to just 0.2 percent a year, largely due to personal choices.

- Health consciousness is spreading to Europe. For example, a recent poll found that two-thirds of Britons now spend more to maintain a healthy lifestyle than they did a decade ago, and three out of four say they enjoy leading a healthy lifestyle.

  – Unfortunately, much of the developing world still worries more about eating enough than about eating well.

- Smoking is in general decline in the United States. Only 21 percent of Americans smoked cigarettes as of 2005, down from 30 percent in 1983. About 42.5 percent of current smokers reported that they had tried to stop smoking within the last year. However, the percentage of smokers has stabilized since 2000.

- The antismoking movement also has made its way to Europe. Ireland banned smoking from its pubs late in April 2004. In 2006, France banned smoking in public facilities. Britain followed suit in 2007.

- The global obesity crisis is a significant countertrend to the physical-culture movement. Poor diet, physical inactivity, and associated obesity contribute to 47 percent of diseases and 60 percent of deaths worldwide.

  – Developing countries that "westernize" their diets by consuming more foods high in fat, sugar, and salt are at risk of epidemic obesity, including among children and adolescents.

- The current epidemic of obesity in the United States is especially troubling. Among children, overweight has tripled since 1980, to about 18 percent for those age six or older.

  – However, there is some evidence that obesity has begun to stabilize among American adults. The rate of obesity among women appears to have reached a plateau in the last six years.

Assessment:

This trend always seems a case of two steps forward, at least one step back. We expect it to continue for at least the next generation.

Implications:

As the nutrition and wellness movements spread, they will further improve the health of the elderly.

Better health in later life will make us still more conscious of our appearance and physical condition.

Thus, health clubs will continue to boom, and some will specialize in the needs of older fitness buffs. Diet, fitness, stress control, and wellness programs will prosper.

States will continue to mandate insurance coverage of mammography. By 2012, they will begin to require coverage of sigmoidoscopy.

By 2015, Congress will add coverage of many preventive-care activities to Medicare.

The cost of health care for American Baby Boomers and their children could be much lower in later life than is now believed. However, Asia faces an epidemic of cancer, heart disease, emphysema, and other chronic and fatal illnesses related to health habits.

Like tobacco companies, producers of snack foods, liquor, and other unhealthy products will increasingly target markets in developing countries where this trend has yet to be felt.

Continuing health improvements in the industrialized world will be accompanied by a dramatic rise in heart disease, diabetes, cancer, and other such "lifestyle" disorders in the developing lands.

Chronic diseases related to obesity burden national economies and could thwart economic progress in developing countries.

Implications for Terrorism:

We see no obvious implications for terrorism.

Expert Comments:

ROBERTS: The increasing preoccupation with personal health is a benefit for the state of public health and the purse of the individuals. A side-effect with respect to this growth in consciousness, though, is a potentially enhanced psychological vulnerability to the threat of chemical, biological, radiological, and nuclear weapons, which can have long-term deleterious effects on health; e.g., radiological contamination.

14. CONSUMERISM IS STILL GROWING.

- A networked society is a consumerist society.

    - Shoppers increasingly have access to information about pricing, services, delivery time, and customer reviews on the Internet.

    - Marketers, of course, can also check the competition's offerings. This may gradually halt the decline of prices and shift competition increasingly to improvements in service and salesmanship.

- A possible reaction to this trend began in June 2007, when the U.S. Supreme Court threw out a longstanding rule and decreed that manufacturers have the right to set minimum retail prices for their products.

- Children in the United States become shoppers as young as age six and become aware of brands at age two or three, due largely to child-focused advertising.

- The Millennial generation is becoming increasingly prone to compulsive spending.

    - In the United States, 10 percent of Millennials can be classified as clinically compulsive spenders, compared with 5 percent of Generation Xers and perhaps 3 percent of Baby Boomers.

Assessment:

This trend seems likely to remain healthy for the at least the next 15 years.

Implications:

Consumer advocacy agencies and organizations will continue to proliferate, promoting improved content labels, warning notices, nutrition data, and the like on packaging, TV, the Internet, and even restaurant menus.

Europe, Japan, China, and other markets are undergoing the same revolution that has replaced America's neighborhood stores with cost-cutting warehouse operations, discounters such as Wal-Mart, and "category killers" like Staples and Home Depot.

However, the cultural and political power of farmers and small shop owners has slowed this trend in some areas, particularly in Japan.

Thanks to recent contamination of food imported from China, the U.S. Food and Drug Administration will be required to improve screening of incoming food products. However, it will not receive adequate funding to do the job effectively.

As prices fall to commodity levels and online stores can list virtually every product and brand in their industry without significant overhead, service is the only field left in which marketers on and off the Internet can compete effectively.

Branded items with good reputations are even more important for developing repeat business.

Consumer debt may be an even greater problem for Millennials than it has been for their elders.

Implications for Terrorism:

The growth of consumerism in Muslim lands will provide one more incentive for a fundamentalist reaction and a further inspiration for terrorism. This may also inspire a return to strict Islam among Muslims in Western lands, and perhaps help turn some younger Muslims toward extremist movements. In this, consumerism represents a security issue for law enforcement.

Expert Comments:

MEILAHN: Consumerism is a symptom of the commercialism and materialism that Al Qaeda finds anathema about the West. This will be a prime motive for extremism. Generally concur with findings.

NOLTE: It is not a given that consumerism in Muslim societies will work to the advantage of the fundamentalists. We are in the second generation of post-Revolutionary Iran, and I would think one of the things the mullahs should worry about is that Iranians 15 to 25 are more interested in iPods than the Koran.

ROBERTS: Concur with your position and that of Meilahn. At the same time, commercialism and materialism do not provide a solid psycho-cultural base in beliefs and values for the type of resiliency in spirit that may be needed if we face a nastier variety of extremist; e.g., mass-casualty or catastrophic terrorism (say through chemical, biological, radiological, and nuclear weapons or high explosives) carried into Western cities with the ferocity that has appeared in Islamic societies (Iran, Afghanistan, and other Asian venues) or 911-NYC, London, and Madrid on a repeated basis.

15. THE WOMEN'S EQUALITY MOVEMENT IS LOSING ITS SIGNIFICANCE, THANKS LARGELY TO PAST SUCCESSES.

- According to some, though not all, studies, women have nearly achieved pay parity with men in the United States when factors such as educational level, responsibilities, and seniority are taken into account.

  - From 1979 to 2005, median wages for women in the United States with college degrees rose by 58 percent.

  - Their male counterparts saw pay hikes of only 24 percent over the period.

– In 2004, one-third of American women earned more than their husbands, up from 24 percent in 1987.

• Some 70 million women, 59 percent of those age 16 and older, participated in the U.S. labor force in 2006.

  – Among those ages 25 to 54, more than three-fourths either held a job or were looking for one.

  – Three-fourths of employed women worked full-time.

• Younger generations of women are better educated.

  – Fully 58 percent of American college students were women as of 2006.

  – Among whites, only 56 percent are female, but 60 percent of African-American college students are women.

  – Among students over age 25, nearly two-thirds are women.

  – And women earn nearly 60 percent of the bachelor's and master's degrees awarded in the United States.

• Nearly 10.4 million American businesses were owned by women in 2006, up 42 percent from 1997.

  – Women-owned firms currently employ 13 million people and generate $1.9 trillion in sales, according to the Center for Women's Business Research.

  – However, most are small retail and service operations that offer few opportunities to build major corporations.

• Corporations are adding more women to their boards of directors.

  – In Britain's top 20 firms, 90 percent now have at least one female director on their boards, reports the U.K. Department of Trade and Industry.

  – In the United States, 14.6 percent of the directors at *Fortune* 500 companies were women as of 2006.

• Generation Xers and Millennials are virtually gender-blind in the workplace, compared with older generations. This is true even in societies such as India and Japan, which have long been male-dominated, though not yet in conservative Muslim lands.

• An infrastructure is evolving that allows women to make more decisions and to exercise political power, especially where both spouses work.

  – One indication of growing dependence on the wife: life insurance companies are selling more policies to women than to men.

• More women are entering the professions, politics, and the judiciary. As we have seen in Iraq, they also are finding roles in combat.

Assessment:

This trend is valid only in the developed lands. In the developing world, the movement toward women's equality is barely beginning. In the United States, the trend could be seen as complete, with women's equality now taken for granted and only mopping-up operations required to complete the process. However, we believe that the women's equality movement will continue to retain some importance, less with each passing year, until the gender-blind Generation X and Millennials accede to leadership in business and politics.

Implications:

In most of the developed world, whatever careers remain relatively closed to women will open wide in the years ahead. Japan will remain some years behind the curve, owing to the strength of its traditionally male-dominated culture.

Women's increasing entrepreneurialism will allow the formation of entrenched "old girl" networks comparable to the men's relationships that once dominated business.

The fraction of women entering the American labor force has leveled off in recent years. The percentage of female workers is likely to remain approximately stable until some force appears to begin a new trend.

Demand for child care, universal health coverage, and other family-oriented services will continue to grow, particularly in the United States, where national services have yet to develop. Over the next twenty years, American companies may increasingly follow the example of their counterparts in Europe, whose taxes pay for national daycare programs and other social services the United States lacks.

There is little sign of progress for women in much of the developing world. India is an exception, because growing literacy has given women the chance to earn income outside the home and, with it, value other than as wives and mothers.

Implications for Terrorism:

Any strong feminist movement in the Muslim lands will inspire terrorism, particularly against the movement's members in their home countries. To the extent that feminist movements are viewed as being inspired or supported by the West, they will provide another grievance for extremists to hold against the United States and its allies. In this, the international women's movement becomes yet another potential source of terrorism.

Expert Comments:

AYERS: When I first looked at this, the topic appeared to be too overwhelming to address in this format. I could render a book on the specific issues listed, but I've tried to narrow the focus a bit. Unfortunately, it is still a rather lengthy response (in three parts).

In the West: While Western women have had a great deal of success in regard to general notions of equality, a gender gap currently remains in the leadership positions of government, companies, corporations, and political organizations. This is not necessarily due, however, to discrimination based on gender, per se. It certainly cannot be addressed with the usual (and usually very vocal) proclamations of a need for diversity, or with the regulations so often prescribed to "fix" the problem. Contrary to popular (current) opinion, gaps associated with gender, race, and ethnicity are increasingly caused by a lack of diversity in attitude—and the attitude at issue is no longer one that is simply prejudiced against visible or overt facets of an individual's makeup. The main obstacle to diversity is the elitist attitude of superiority based on pride of placement, narcissism, assumptions of merit based on position, aggregate disinterest in and dismissal of alternative views, and the tendency of individuals "in charge" to promote based on similarity of thought patterns and confirmation of beliefs, if not political expediency and/or agendas of self-serving aggrandizement.

In government, women and minorities who have already made it to the senior ranks, are likely to have succumbed to the same "superior" attitude (consciously or sub-consciously), either as a method of "fitting in" or by virtue of expecting to gain exactly what others have received—that is, all that comes with a "superior" status. Indeed, many who have "made it" have done so by manipulating the system with the intent to maintain a level of systemic discomfort—a level that can be coincidentally sustained by continually harping on the need for "diversity" which, in turn, offers proponents the latitude of rarely (if ever) being questioned about their own professional competence.

Past and current methods of obtaining and retaining "diversity" among the powerful, when combined with the "elitist" mentality within which the powerful are ensconced, have contributed to an even bigger gap that is specifically rooted in competence (or perhaps more appropriately, incompetence)—a gap between the competence of those in leadership positions (no matter what the gender, race, or ethnicity) and those who are supposedly being led. When incompetence is promoted by mandate in order to achieve diversity, incompetence becomes the default "norm" and the "elitist" mentality rises to take the place of true leadership based on professionalism, in-depth knowledge, and expertise. Even more unfortunately, the system is not only self-sustaining—it is virtually impossible to reform.

Needless to say, none of this bodes well for the Global War on Terrorism. A bureaucracy that is bogged down in political correctness as well as with the maintenance of a supremely self-absorbed leadership cadre formed through the use of politically expedient and/or mandated methods of fostering the careers of "a chosen few" will not be able to successfully foresee or address external threat.

In Islamic countries or communities: It has been recently noted by several female reformists from Islamic countries (or countries with large Islamic populations) that spokespersons from the major women's movements in the West have apparently disavowed any interest in or knowledge of the culturally-accepted mistreatment and abuse that many women are subjected to under the rule of radical Islam and/or radical interpretations of *shari'a*. The blanket Western acceptance of socially "progressive" concepts such as cultural relativism and multiculturalism has masked distasteful subjects like honor killing, female infanticide, female genital mutilation, stoning, gang rape, immolation, beheading, imprisonment (to include solitary confinement) within the home, and other types of torture, keeping the liberal sensibilities of those who would normally be outraged (especially if these things were happening to them) from even accepting the possibility that these abuses occur. In fact, one of the few Western feminists (and quite possibly the only leading feminist) who has recently attempted to discuss the status of women in the Middle East with anything other than favorable verbiage, placed blame squarely on the Western feminist movement for not having "sounded the alarm" and for not insisting on a global "single standard of human rights." (see Phyllis Chesler's 2006 article "How Afghan Captivity Shaped my Feminism" in the *Middle East Quarterly*, Vol 13[1], p. 10).

Yet, the silence of Western feminists has in the past been encouraged by the outrage of a few from the ranks of an educated Arab and/or Muslim female elite who—apparently by virtue of birthright—claim to be best able to speak for Middle Eastern, Arab, or simply Muslim women. (For an example, see Suha Sabbaugh's compilation of works entitled *Arab Women: Between Defiance and Restraint*, 1996. It should be noted that Sabbaugh specifically complained about what she perceived as a Western feminist intent to establish Western superiority or "domination" over Muslim women [when and if Western females did speak about issues related to women in Arab or Muslim societies] as opposed to any beneficent attempt to "form bonds of sisterhood across cultures." [p. xiii] Her strong and lengthy diatribe against Western women's attempts to raise awareness about abuses such as honor killing could be indicative of the reasoning behind the fear of Western women's organizations to speak out on behalf of the abused in other cultures.) These self-appointed spokespersons for Muslim women have, in the past, denied a great deal of what is known about the abuse of females in their societies—possibly for the sake of retaining "cultural honor"—thus relegating any negative discussion of the general status of women within communities that adhere to a strict form of *shari'a*, to that of "myth." Indeed, if abuse is acknowledged, it is often only with the caveat that mistreatment of women is a cultural, vice a religious issue. But regardless of the issue's origin, the abuse will persist until addressed.

We have, therefore, a conundrum. Do Western women's rights advocates speak out about the status of women under *shari'a* and risk the wrath of Muslim women (or women who are otherwise connected to the region and/or culture) who claim that right for themselves, even when their rhetoric differs substantially from what is known to be true? Or do Western feminists shy away from the fray, professing only a positive understanding of the issue in order to be politically correct? Thus far, it seems the latter scenario has won out. Currently, because of what appears to be a basic acceptance of radical Islam, a complete and unyielding acceptance of multiculturalism and cultural relativism, and an almost willful degree of ignorance by the very organizations formed to protect women's rights (supposedly on a global basis), the West's women's liberation movement holds little meaning for the women who are most often subjected to torturous abuse based on various rigid interpretations of *shari'a*.

But what does this mean for the GWOT? Barbara Victor, in her book *Army of Roses: Inside the World of Palestinian Women Suicide Bombers* (2003), pointed out the propensity of women who are perceived as having been "dishonored" (or as having somehow dishonored the family) to become martyrs–suicide bombers for the jihad. "Dishonored" women are trapped between cultures that may be predisposed to kill them and their own intense desire for the equality that has been consistently denied them.

Volunteering for suicide operations could be seen as the "only way out." Rather than being sentenced to die and killed at the hand of a family member or a stranger, these women regain honor for themselves and their families by controlling their own deaths while in the process of killing others for the purpose of jihad. They thereby ensure their continued existence as martyrs for Islam in the minds of those left behind—as opposed to leaving a legacy of shame, if thought of at all after death. They are assured of a path to paradise, vice being condemned to hell for having committed dishonor—and they are given "intercession rights" for 70 other relatives. If not threatened with "honor killing," they might avoid hastily arranged marriages that could easily result in lives of continued abuse or neglect. Additionally, what they believe they will find in death is something close to equality—more, at least, than they could ever hope for in the earthly realm.

The initial onslaught of dishonored female volunteers for the intifada and *jihad* may possibly have been followed by women who sought martyrdom simply because they were "true believers"—it is difficult to tell, as suicide bombings are always portrayed as an act of complicit heroism on the part of the "martyr," and any form of dishonor would have been erased in the ultimate act of martyrdom. Regardless of the reasons, however, there will be more women used in suicide operations in the future. Terrorist organizations may actively seek to dishonor young girls in order to subsequently recruit them (in fact, there have been rumors that this has already occurred). Women will feel increasingly "trapped" between cultures that are polar opposites and see martyrdom (in the form of suicide bombings) as the only "positive" path open to them. And, if a global rise in extremism of all sorts is any indication, women will become increasingly susceptible to indoctrination into the global jihadist mentality.

The outlook for an increasingly "diverse" (but multicultural) western population: Radical Islamists are highly unlikely to agree to women's rights; and Muslim women—especially, but not limited to those in poor, rural areas—will be likely to suffer even more severely in the future because of "blowback."

Here again, as cultural enclaves within the United States continue to grow—especially those held together by rigid socio-religious mores and extreme fear—incidents similar to those that are currently plaguing Western Europe will increase in number. The U.S. will see violent riots, murders, and an increasingly polarized society. These issues will include a severe treatment of women and curtailment of women's rights in certain areas of the country. There have already been honor killings as well as cases of outright female slavery within the United States. Terrorism perpetrated by women due to "dishonor" may only be a matter of time.

KRIESBERG: From a global perspective, the women's movement continues to spread and deepen. Most relevant for countering terrorism, women are increasingly engaged in governance. Quantitative research indicates that countries with higher rates of women's civic engagement are less prone to be in wars. Greater engagement by women may tend to result in less militarized ways of countering terrorist attacks and thereby be less likely to be counterproductive.

MILLER: Of course, this trend has had nothing to do with the Muslim nations, which are now breeding grounds for terrorists. It is absolutely fascinating, however, to see one Muslim terrorist group after another adopt suicide bombing by female recruits. As the feminist movement in the U.S. showed tradition being trumped by economic rationalism, so this adoption of female bombers demonstrates the superiority of practicality over religion.

SMYRE (4): With the slowing of the women's equality movement, there will be a lessening of pressure on Islamic cultures to give their women more freedom of expression, thereby causing greater internal tension in those countries. This could either lead to less terrorism due to internal Islamic conflict or more terrorism as a result of increased male cultural control.

YOUNG: While not having a direct bearing on the future of terrorism, it is well know that women' equality is extremely variable in Middle Eastern societies, varying from the very strict Wahhabist culture of Saudi Arabia to the relatively liberal culture of Lebanon, Indonesia, and Jordan.

16. FAMILY STRUCTURES ARE BECOMING MORE DIVERSE.

- In periods of economic difficulty, children and grandchildren move back in with parents and grandparents to save on living expenses. Many bring their own children with them. In the United States, one-third of Generation Xers have returned home at some point in their early lives. Among Millennials, the figure is even higher.

  – The 2001 Census found that so-called "multigenerational households" are the fastest growing group in the United States.

  – Among the poor, grandparents also provide live-in day care for the children of single mothers trying to gain an education or build a career.

- The average age of marriage is rising, and growing numbers of people either do not marry or remain single after divorce. The number of people living together outside marriage thus continues to rise.

- Nonetheless, the fastest growing "family" structure consists of a single adult living alone.

- Yet the nuclear family also is rebounding in the United States, as Baby-Boom and Generation X parents focus on their children and grandparents retain more independence and mobility.

- Same-sex households also are gaining new acceptance.

  – At least five American states now permit same-sex marriage or have enacted domestic-partnership laws that provide similar protections: Massachusetts, California, New Jersey, Connecticut, and New Hampshire.

  – In this, they join such countries as Denmark, Germany, the Czech Republic, the United Kingdom, and most recently Switzerland.

  – Many American companies now grant spousal benefits to the same-sex partners of employees, even where states do not.

- Many grandparents are raising their grandchildren because drugs and AIDS have left the middle generation either unable or unavailable to care for their children.

— This trend is strongest in Africa, where AIDS has orphaned some 12 million children, half between the ages of 10 and 14. In Botswana, Lesotho, Swaziland, and Zimbabwe more than one in five children will be orphaned by 2010. According to UNICEF. At that time, there will be 25 million AIDS orphans in sub-Saharan Africa. In the seven African countries most affected by AIDS, life expectancy at birth has now dropped below 40 years.

Assessment:

This trend will remain in effect for at least a generation in the United States, longer in the rest of the world.

Implications:

Where many European countries have largely adjusted to this trend, the United States has not.

Tax and welfare policies need adjustment to cope with families in which heads of households are retired or unable to work.

Policies also need modification for those who receive Social Security and work to support an extended family.

In the United States, the debates over homosexuality and the "decline of the family" will remain polarizing for the foreseeable future.

The next debate is likely to focus on granting parental rights to more than two parents, as when a sperm or egg donor wants a role in the life of a child whose official parents are the recipients.

Implications for Terrorism:

Government agencies of all sorts will have to adjust benefits and other policies to fit the needs of non-traditional families, much as private organizations must. This includes intelligence, security, and police departments.

Direct influences on terrorism, if any, seem negligible.

Expert Comments:

CZARNECKI: I generalized this trend to mean that traditional social structures are changing more rapidly. More diversity threatens stability; it means significant, strategic, and irreversible change. Such change, while acceptable to many in societies, is absolutely abhorrent, even condemnatory, to some very fundamentalist traditionalists. There is ample evidence in recent, as well as ancient, times that such traditionalists, even though a small minority within societies, can cause great trouble and tragedy. Coupled with the increased access of technology, captured in Trend 5 and Trend 28, such potential for trouble increases nonlinearly.

YOUNG: Especially in Muslim society, this is almost certainly not the case. With respect to terror, for example, the *shahid*, or martyr, is revered in Palestinian society. There are many examples where Middle Eastern families support their terrorist sons or daughters because of the deeply held religious and political beliefs.

17. Privacy, once a defining right for Americans, is dying quickly.

- Internet communications, a basic part of life for many people, are nearly impossible to protect against interception, and governments around the world are working to ensure their unfettered access to them. Postings to blogs and Web forums are nearly immortal.

  - The contents of most Internet-connected computers are open to virtually unobstructed snooping by anyone with a minimum of skill and the will to examine them. All but the most secure can be invaded by more-capable hackers.

- Corporate databases are collecting and marketing data on individual credit-worthiness, incomes, spending patterns, brand choices, medical conditions, and lifestyles.

  - While privacy regulations bar distribution of much personal information in the European Union, restrictions in the United States are much weaker.

- Widespread surveillance of private individuals is technically feasible and economically viable, as tiny, powerful cameras now cost next to nothing. Increased surveillance has become socially acceptable in an age when many people fear terrorism and crime.

  - In Britain, an estimated 4.2 million surveillance cameras watch over streets, office buildings, schools, and shopping centers, making the U.K. one of the most closely monitored nations in the world. On average, Britons are caught on camera an estimated three hundred times per day.

  - In the United States, the growth of surveillance also is driven by the fear that lawsuits following a future terrorist attack could claim that failure to install monitoring equipment constitutes negligence.

  - Video surveillance systems have been installed in Chicago, New York City, Washington DC, Tampa FL, and other cities around the United States, In most cases, local police departments have been a driving force in this movement. Protests thus far have been small and ineffective.

- The USA Patriot Act of 2001 sets aside the constitutional requirement of a search warrant for government officials who wish to search someone's home in order to thwart possible terrorism. Its provisions have been used to justify searches in pursuit of drug dealers and even, in one attempt thus far blocked by the courts, copyright abusers.

Assessment:

Pessimists could say that privacy already is a thing of the past; society is merely coming to recognize its loss. We believe that enough effective privacy survives outside the most authoritarian countries to justify noting its continued erosion. However, this trend could easily reach its logical conclusion within ten years.

Implications:

In the future, privacy is likely to be defined, not by the ability to keep information truly secret, but by the legal power to restrict its distribution. Even this limited form of privacy will be eroded as both government and private organizations find legal justification for their interest in personal information. Once access is granted to any type of information, it is unlikely ever to be rescinded.

Most surveillance provisions of the USA Patriot Act will survive, even if the law itself is repealed or modified.

In the absence of a major terrorist event, most Americans will continue to consider privacy a "right," and privacy-related lawsuits are likely to proliferate as more people feel violated or inconvenienced by surveillance. However, courts will be unsympathetic to such suits for so long as conservative appointees dominate the bench.

In large and medium-size cities around the world, spaces that remain unwatched by video cameras will continue to shrink.

Growing numbers of companies, and even private citizens, will encrypt their computer data.

The number of criminal cases based on surveillance will grow rapidly in countries with the required technological sophistication and infrastructure.

Private citizens increasingly will use similar technologies to watch over government abuse, as in cases where bystanders have recorded police misconduct with their cell-phone cameras.

Implications for Terrorism:

This is a top-ten trend.

It will be nearly impossible for terrorists to operate without being observed. However, until artificial intelligence systems "learn" to recognize suspicious activities manpower will limit use of these observations. Except in obvious target areas, surveillance will be most useful in forensic reconstruction, rather than in active incident prevention.

What remains of privacy protections often conflicts with security needs. A good example is the recent decision to scrap an important data-mining program at the Department of Homeland Security on the grounds that it might implicate the innocent in terrorism or other illegal activities. A more appropriate solution would have been to require that data used by the program be confirmed by at least two independent sources, as is routinely done in the intelligence community.

This is clearly one of the ten most important trends for antiterrorism. It may be one of the top five.

Expert Comments:

AYERS (10): Because of the success of ubiquitous surveillance in the U.K., it would appear that individuals in the U.S. will have to settle for what was previously considered to be the "Big Brother" approach. While this may generally keep people "honest," it might also encourage a collective sense of paranoia—people are, after all, actually being watched. It might additionally make a population which is already litigiously inclined even more determined and/or reckless in pursuit of monetary gain. While some individuals would simply use the system for their own agenda (absolutely anything could be offensive to someone), terrorists could exploit the tendency of others to "give in" when threatened with legal action. Furthermore, if terrorists could tie up specific surveillance procedures in litigation, disruption of terrorist operations would be difficult. It would therefore be beneficial to governing authorities who foresee the dying destiny of privacy in America, to fully consider the unintended consequences and take action to prevent terrorists from exploiting legal loopholes in their efforts to destroy us from within.

BRAY (4): Yes, and this loss of privacy has largely occurred without consideration of what will be lost if it does die (in fact, privacy has probably already died). Recent public debates have considered whether the U.S. federal government has the right to conduct electronic surveillance of its citizens, to include monitoring financial transactions and telephone conversations. Most of these debates seem to perceive that ensuring both privacy and protection is not possible—but such a belief is fallacious. Improving the ability of government as an information processing system to better aggregate, filter, act upon, and redirect information must not—and does not—require sacrificing the freedoms of individual citizens.

To prove that privacy and protection are equally obtainable, consider an example where public key encryption allows the masking of collected information from human eyes, but not from processing and linking to other sources of information by trusted information systems themselves. By use of encryption, this masking of collected information provides only "de-identified" information (with personal identifiers removed) to government workers (Straub and Collins, 1990; Rindfleisch, 1997). However, the trusted information systems themselves can access personal identifiers and link different sources of information.

Ideally, these trusted information systems would work non-stop to sort through and identify suspicious patterns of information. Examples of suspicious patterns include an individual living in a large city purchasing a large quantity of castor beans (which can be used to make ricin toxin) with no discernable legitimate purpose, or regular records of large bank deposits from an unclear source of questionable origin. If the patterns are extremely suspicious, the information systems can present the suspicious patterns (de-identified, with personal identifiers removed) to government workers. These workers then decide whether to convene an expedited court hearing to judge if the encrypted personal identifiers associated with the information should be unlocked. Lawyers for a defense—in the absence of the unknown individual(s)—and a prosecution, present opposing sides to the best of their ability. A federal judge decides whether the de-identified pattern of activities provides sufficient cause to lift the freedom of privacy for the collected information. Should the judge rule that the de-identified pattern of information is suspicious enough to merit unlocking the protected identities, an electronic key issued by the court will permit this action. Similar to issuing a warrant, such an approach maintains anonymity of collected information unless a court hearing finds probable cause and temporarily removes this freedom.

Achieving both privacy and protection offers several added benefits: bridging of different government cultures, encouraging collaborations, and increasing the likelihood of positive outcomes. Recall the example of detecting a bioterrorism agent—this situation requires collaboration between the public health and national security communities. Currently, however, collaborations between such communities are few, a result partially from different organizational cultures surrounding information exchange. Exchange of information between public health professionals is open and collegial, whereas the national security community emphasizes compartmentalization and security.

For public health, a central challenge involves linking multiple health records accurately to a common individual across all 50 states without access to a personal identifier. The privacy of individuals is a top priority for public health, specifically the protection of individual health information. The U.S. federal government is limited from collecting personal information as a result of the Health Insurance Portability & Accountability Act of 1996 (HIPAA). Identifying attributes that could be useful in linking different pieces of health information to a common individual—Social Security number, home address, or name—are not available by current law to federal agencies, including the U.S. Centers for Disease Control and Prevention. Health organizations must strip locally stored information of personal identifiers when sent to external partners outside of a state.

For national security, a central challenge involves maintaining the integrity of our national borders despite the sheer volume of traffic that comes in and out daily. Should national security efforts only monitor individual border crossings, they risk security that is either too loose at stopping illegitimate traffic or too restrictive at permitting legitimate traffic. Realistically, our national borders cannot be completely contained and still function. Instead, national security must strive to monitor activity both inside and outside of our borders, to detect threats before they arrive at our borders and catch any that manage to evade detection and enter the country.

Fortunately, the earlier example combining the use of public key encryption and the court system can also help solve these challenges for both public health and national security. By collecting information that is de-identified from human eyes, but not from automated processing by trusted information systems, the privacy of individuals can be maintained for routine government efforts. When a clear danger to either public health or national security presents itself, a court order can be sought to unlock any identities associated with the collected information. Hence, it is possible to meet the needs of both public health and national security without violating the privacy of law-abiding citizens.

CHOBAR: Americans will probably fight to keep their "civil liberties" within privacy, which could delay or significantly slow down the policing and finding of those involved in terrorism or terrorist plots.

COSTIGAN (8): Lack of interest in privacy will accelerate its decline. Younger people, raised in the information technology-driven society, will not learn the values of privacy. Hackers will keep the flame alive in the infotech world, creating more robust and secure spaces for private communications, and privacy advocates will do their best. Greater susceptibility to identity theft will make for new terrorist advantages. When people fail to recognize the need for privacy or expose their network of friends or business networks, they will be easier to exploit. In other countries, privacy is not considered ever to be of particular value.

JENKINS: Privacy will continue to be a political battleground as technology improves—more CCTV, smart cameras, face recognition, bulk detection of explosives, etc.

KADTKE: If global terrorist activities continue to increase, the response of nations (particularly in the West) will certainly increase as well. Increasing legal authority for monitoring, search, seizure, and prosecution may accelerate, and political and public support for such reaction will likely grow stronger as well. Information technology will be increasingly relied on for surveillance and tracking of both physical actors as well as cyber-actors. Unfortunately, these trends are already leading to serious degradations of personal privacy, as IT capabilities can already be used to mine for a variety of types of open information on personal activities, and their constraint under current law and regulation is often vague.

KAPINOS: Certainly, with enhanced capability for electronic surveillance across many venues, as well as improving data-mining tools, it is more important than ever that we develop a consensus on the rule sets to govern these capabilities. Laws, policies, and procedures must be established at all levels of government that define how we control, manage, and use the information that we can obtain. We must ensure the proper balance between the legitimate needs of the law enforcement and intelligence communities verses the Constitutional rights of our citizens.

KRIESBERG: Much discussion seems to pit security and freedom against each other as if they were in opposition, when that is not usually the case. Trying to maximize security by restricting freedom is often counterproductive. Enemies are created by overzealous imposition of restrictions. Useful ideas are lost. Resources are wasted in imposing non-essential limitations.

LaDUKE (9): Words spoken or transmitted will increasingly be the primary means of detection of hostile interests. But privacy intrusions in efforts to intercept those words are receiving increasing resistance in the U.S. A culture clash between tolerance and privacy intrusions is emerging, for example, the LAPD's "Muslim Mapping Plan." (http://www.latimes.com/news/local/la-me-muslim15nov15,0,6998542.story?coll=la-home-center)

MILLER: This may change, and one can certainly find evidence of push-back by elements on both the far right and the far left of the U.S. political spectrum. It is true that privacy loss tends to ratchet downward without meaningful upticks, but the excesses of the recent past may have created their own antivirus, if only temporarily. The efforts of terrorism should not be hampered unduly by privacy concerns. A claim that terrorism can be obliterated by sufficient abrogation of personal rights is surely unreal. And, it is difficult to argue that the state does not retain sufficient power to effectively pursue and negate the impact of terrorist violence directed at the civilian population—at least in the U.S.

NOLTE: See Don Kerr's remarks on this. (He is principal deputy DNI.) This is, it seems to me, a huge issue. If Kerr is right and we've lost privacy in the traditional sense, what new definition of privacy, if any, will publics insist on?

Osborne: Privacy will be redefined in an iterative process as transparency grows within law enforcement and in society. As the public debate around privacy issues grows due to increased use of cameras and other surveillance equipment in urban areas for crime detection/law enforcement, public use of small cameras, recorders, and at home surveillance systems will grow. Police activity will be tracked via GPS on vehicles and perhaps on officers. Videos of officers' interactions will be used for accountability and lawsuit protection. Police will become more accountable to citizenry as crime mapping on the Internet and other types of data are made available for analysis outside of the law enforcement environment, to be used by city planners and private security.

Steele: Challenges to information security are making levels of intelligence and military secrecy less possible. This will challenge target ascertainment.

Tan: The events of 9/11 have resulted in a massive assault on and erosion of civil liberties throughout the world. Lawyers and civil society activists have since then been engaged in an on-going debate over "security versus freedom"— this debate is important and must be encouraged. Governments and security services must be prepared to participate in it, with a view to negotiating with the rest of civil society where the boundaries and balance might lie. The failure to keep talking and keep negotiating means that we would have lost to the terrorists. Without doing too much, the terrorists have managed to erode some fundamental freedoms such as privacy. The security versus freedom (i.e., freedom from fear, right to privacy, etc.) is an important debate and civil society must agree to where that balance should lie. Without legitimacy, the cause is on the way to being lost.

Youngs: Privacy is a right that the public is still reluctant to give up, however, this will change in the event of another attack. If holy warriors wreck havoc in the United States by mass murder and assassination, then citizens will look to the government for protection. Hate crimes will increase against Muslims and more Americans will become armed. Several states have seen an increase in requests for carrying concealed weapons. If chaos prevails more citizens will take the law into their own hands.

ENERGY TRENDS

18. Despite efforts to develop alternative sources of energy, oil consumption is still rising rapidly.

- The world used only 57 million barrels of oil per day in 1973, when the first major price shock hit. By 2004, it was using 83 million barrels daily, according to the U.S. Energy Information Administration. Consumption is expected to reach 97 million barrels daily by 2015 and 118 million by 2030.

  – The United States alone consumes about 20.7 million barrels of oil per day. Nearly 60 percent of that is imported.

  – In 2005, the most recent data available, China consumed 6.534 million barrels of oil per day, making it the second-largest user of oil in the world. Its oil demand has grown by 7 percent per year, on average, since 1990. Most of China's imported oil (more than 3.1 million barrels a day) comes from the Middle East.

- However, oil's share of world energy consumption has begun to decline: It is expected to drop from 40 percent in 1999 to about 37 percent in 2020.

Assessment:

Nothing is likely to reverse this trend in the next 25 years.

Implications:

Oil prices now are high enough to provide an incentive to develop new fields, such as the Arctic National Wildlife Refuge and the deep fields under the Gulf of Mexico.

Environmentally sensitive areas will be developed using new drilling techniques, double-walled pipelines and other precautions, that make it possible to extract oil with less damage to the surroundings. But they will be developed.

Any prolonged rise of oil prices to triple digits will erode support for environmental protections in the United States, leading to widespread development of whatever energy sources are most readily available, regardless of the long-term consequences.

Implications for Terrorism:

The West will remain vulnerable to any instability in the Middle Eastern oil producing countries.

A primary goal of Muslim terrorists will be to interrupt the flow of oil to the United States.

Energy facilities also will make inviting targets for regional terrorist organizations with purely local goals. Attacks on Mexican natural gas pipelines by the tiny Popular Revolutionary Army are one such case.

Expert Comments:

CHOBAR: Disruption of any major oil production facilities (oil fields, oil platforms, rigs, or wells) might still have significant impact upon the economy, as well as the economy and economic growth of the United States.

COSTIGAN (1): Yes and it's not likely to decline. For the foreseeable future, the cheapest to pump oil will remain in the Middle East. Saudi Arabia will continue to have to balance its own more radical elements against the necessity of selling their only product: producing oil for the world's increasing consumption. While attacks against Americans and their allies will continue, terrorists will increasingly target what they perceive to be apostate leaders, aiming to kill off government targets instead of concentrating solely on the "consumers."

New oil targets will be in more pristine areas, like Alaska, Canada, the deep seas.

CZARNECKI: I take this to mean that efforts to curb energy demand and consumption are not working and will not work, specifically in this case with respect to oil. This again is non-uniform around the globe. The transitional economies, particularly India and China, represent the greatly increased demand for oil. The developed economies of Europe and North America are far more able, even if economically painful, to moderate oil demand. The trends affect terrorism in two ways. First, continued increased consumption means that countries where the oil exists will also continue to be troublesome neighbors, supporting terrorism due to religious and ideological reasons (e.g. Iran, Venezuela.) Second, the increased demand for oil also means greatly increased competition as the difference between supply and demand irreversibly increases (another "Gap" problem, again.) Competition can mean violence due to war, to subversive actions, and to criminal acts—all of which can include terrorism.

FORSTER: This is a strategic issue for counter-terrorism efforts. Maintenance of an oil-based economy forces the U.S. to accommodate repressive regimes rather than promote and pursue modernizing reforms. A significant reduction in the use for petroleum and natural gas, whether through the introduction of new energy sources or conservation, however, will not significantly alter the geopolitical dilemma the West faces in the Middle East in particular unless a new energy strategy is married with a nuclear non-proliferation strategy.

KADTKE: As the global demand for oil skyrockets due to the rapid development of new economies (China, India), the competition for petro-based energy will increasingly intensify. This will cause global stress at the nation-state level, including increasing flexing of economic muscle by Russia and Venezuela, as well as traditional Islamic nations. While not a first-order influence to terrorism, it can provide an influx of financial resources to radical and even unstable states.

MEILAHN: I'm not so sure that a primary goal of terrorists will be to interrupt the flow of oil to the U.S. Disruption of the market would send their financiers into bankruptcy, so it is contrary to their goals. On the other hand, as soon as the U.S. has enough alternative energy sources that it does not rely on the Middle East, U.S. interests will dictate that less attention will be given to those states. Thus, less U.S. presence will be there. Thus, Al Qaeda will no longer be able to use U.S. "occupation of Muslim lands" as an excuse to enact terror against U.S. targets. Smaller scale local terror nodes will likely target the infrastructure in order to meet their own goals—such as Shi'ia in Saudi attacking refineries. Al Qaeda may attack infrastructure targets to make a point that the "apostate" rulers should not be collaborating with the "infidel" U.S./West.

MILLER: Short of a catastrophic cut-off of middle-East oil, I don't see any moderation in the world's appetite for it. This overwhelming fact will continue to highlight terrorism for the U.S. and other developed nations. We cannot afford to assume that 99 percent of terrorism will continue forever to be local problems for local regimes.

SANDERS (6): See comments under "Complexity and the Future of Terrorism" in Appendix C.

TAN: Energy security is becoming a serious security issue. I disagree with the view that oil prices will be stable and that growing competition from other sources will limit the price of oil. The problem is not the shortage of oil but the scramble for oil, which is at the heart of great power rivalries now emerging between the U.S.A., Japan, and India on the one hand, and China on the other. Energy security is intimately linked with other security issues such as terrorism and maritime security due to its innate vulnerability—e.g., oil refineries, oil pipelines, power grids, nuclear plants, long and vulnerable sea lanes of security, port security, ship security, LNG tanker traffic, etc.—all vulnerable terrorist targets.

YOUNG: With respect to terror, increased consumption only plays into the hands of terrorists as the U.S. is the world's greatest oil consumer. Oil pipelines, shipping, and refineries in the Middle East remain vulnerable to terror attack and will continue to be an attractive target in the future as terrorists seek to create economic instability in the West.

---

19. CONTRARY TO POPULAR BELIEF, THE WORLD'S CONFIRMED OIL SUPPLY IS GROWING, NOT DECLINING.

• As a result of intensive exploration, the world's proven oil reserves climbed steadily since the 1980s and now hover at over 1.3 trillion barrels. Natural gas reserves stood at about 6.2 trillion cubic feet in 2007, about 1 percent more than a year earlier.

   – Recent discoveries of major oil fields in Canada, Brazil, and under the Gulf of Mexico have substantially increased the world's known oil reserves.

   – Claims that the world's oil reserves may be up to 20 percent smaller than previously believed are not credible, in part because they originate with an odd coalition of the American Petroleum Institute and alternative energy proponents—two groups with a vested interest in keeping oil prices high.

   – Exploitation of oil in Venezuela has barely begun. Reserves there may be even larger than those in Saudi Arabia, according to some estimates. However, it is more expensive to refine and use, because it contains much higher levels of sulfur than the Middle Eastern oil currently in production.

   – India also is believed to own substantial reserves of oil in deposits beneath the Indian Ocean.

• OPEC officials claim that the eleven member countries can provide for the world's energy needs for roughly the next 80 years.

   – OPEC supplies about 40 percent of the world's oil and holds 60 percent of the known oil available internationally.

   – Even 80 percent of OPEC's estimated supply would still be oil enough to supply the world for the next 64 years.

Assessment:

Talk of "peak oil," the suggestion that crude production has topped out, or soon will, is unjustified and, in FI's view, unjustifiable. Our best estimate is that the world has used about one-fourth of its recoverable oil, and almost certainly no more than one-third. This trend will remain intact until at least 2040.

Implications:

Higher oil prices should make it cost effective to develop new methods of recovering oil from old wells. Technologies already developed could add nearly 50 percent to the world's recoverable oil supply.

OPEC will continue to supply most of the oil used by the developed world. According to the U.S. Department of Energy, OPEC oil production will grow to about 57 million barrels of oil per day by 2020.

Russia and Kazakhstan will be major suppliers if the necessary pipelines can be completed and political uncertainties do not block investment by Western oil companies. Russia will grow into the world's second-largest oil producer by 2010.

Alternative energy sources face problems with economic viability. Barring substantial incentives, this will inhibit efforts to stem global warming for the foreseeable future.

A generalized war in the Middle East after the United States leaves Iraq could drastically reduce the region's oil output. This is unlikely, but the probable impact of such a conflict is so great that the possibility cannot be ignored.

The spread of fundamentalist Muslim regimes with a grudge against the West also could keep OPEC oil out of the American market.

If the United States loses access to Middle Eastern oil, it will buy even more from Canada and Venezuela, tap the Arctic National Wildlife Reserve, and develop the deepwater fields under the Gulf of Mexico much faster than expected.

In a prolonged energy emergency, America also would be likely to develop its vast reserves of oil shale, which have long been economically viable at crude prices over $40 per barrel. New technology reportedly makes it profitable at any price over $17 per barrel. With enough shale oil to supply its own needs for 300 years, the United States could become one of the world's largest petroleum exporters.

Developing shale would devastate the environment, but with crude oil prices in triple digits during a Mid-East war, the environment would be considered expendable.

Implications for Terrorism:

Broader development of global energy resources could partially insulate the West from the effects of attacks on their energy supplies.

However, development of American shale resources would deprive the Middle Eastern oil states of their "lock" on the world's energy markets and reduce the value of their only significant resource. This would trigger a wave of resentment among Muslim extremists and could unleash a wave of terrorism more destructive than anything yet seen.

Expert Comments:

MILLER: This does not for a minute reduce our dependency on oil. This is not comforting. On the contrary, oil dependency tends to make us hypersensitive to disruptions and violence in parts of the world that we would otherwise probably prefer to ignore.

20. WHEN NOT PERTURBED BY GREATER-THAN-NORMAL POLITICAL OR ECONOMIC INSTABILITY, OIL PRICES WILL AVERAGE AROUND $65 PER BARREL.

- The International Energy Agency's *World Energy Outlook 2007* concurs.

- Prices approaching $100 per barrel in the fall of 2007 are an aberration caused by a global shortage of refinery capacity and by fears of instability triggered by the Iraq war.

  - New energy demand from the fast-growing economies of China and India has raised the floor that until 2004 supported oil in the $25 per barrel range.

  - The "risk premium" built into the price of oil is estimated at $10 to $15 per barrel.

- Yet in the long run other factors will tend to depress the price of oil toward its former levels.

  - New refineries in Saudi Arabia and other countries scheduled to come on line by 2010 will ease the tight supply-demand balance for oil.

  - As seen in Trend 19, new oil supplies are being found or developed in many parts of the world.

  - The twenty most-industrialized countries all have at least three-month supplies of oil in tankers and underground storage. Most have another three months' worth in "strategic reserves." In times of high oil prices, customer nations can afford to stop buying until the costs come down.

  - OPEC has stated that it prefers to see the price of oil in the neighborhood of $45 per barrel.

Assessment:

Given the condition of the American dollar, it might be better to denominate this trend in euros. Aside from that, the long-term trend is toward stability in energy prices.

Implications:

Barring an American invasion of Iran, any excursions beyond $100 per barrel will be extremely brief. Given continued concerns about instability in the Middle East, oil prices will slowly decline to $60 or so per barrel.

In response to high (by American standards) gas prices, the U.S. Government probably will boost domestic oil production and refining to increase the reserve of gasoline and heating oil. This stockpile would be ready for immediate use in case of future price hikes. This will make it easier to negotiate with OPEC.

A key step in controlling oil prices, and an indicator of Washington's serious about doing so, would be development by the government of at least four new refineries around the country, probably for lease to commercial producers. We rate the odds at no more than 50:50.

The United States almost certainly will drill for oil in the Arctic National Wildlife Reserve, though efforts will be made to minimize environmental damage, for example, drilling will take place only in the winter, when the tundra is rock hard.

By 2020, the new fields under the Gulf of Mexico will come online, putting even more pressure on oil prices.

Implications for Terrorism:

Depriving the United States and its allies of Middle Eastern oil will be a major goal of terrorist strategy.

Pipelines from Russia and the "Stans" will be particularly inviting targets for Muslim terrorists.

Expert Comments:

MILLER: My years on the fringes of the oil business have convinced me that the price of crude is not nearly as important as its volatility.

YOUNG: High oil prices create terror 'enablers,' that is, create economic windfalls that enable states such as Iran to proceed with its nuclear ambitions. Iran is also a known financial supporter of Hizballah and Hamas. Only with high oil prices could Iran continue this type of support. Other states such as Saudi Arabia can continue to utilize their oil wealth to build mosques and proselytize radical Islam in religious madrassas. Many of these religious madrassas are located in Pakistan where terrorists are recruited by a variety of terror organizations and will continue to exist as long as they are funded with petrodollars.

21. GROWING COMPETITION FROM OTHER ENERGY SOURCES ALSO WILL HELP TO LIMIT THE PRICE OF OIL.

- Nuclear power is growing rapidly.

  - Nuclear plants supply about 15 percent Russian electricity. By 2020, Russia will consume 129 billion kWh of nuclear energy per year. Plans call for construction of twenty-six more nuclear plants by 2030, when 25 percent or more of the nation's electricity will be nuclear.

  - In early 2004, China had only nine operating nuclear power plants. It plans to build thirty more by 2020, bringing nuclear energy consumption from 16 billion kWh in 2000 to 142 billion kWh.

  - By 2020, Canada will use 118 billion kWh.

  - Even the United States is weighing the construction of new reactors.

- Renewable sources accounted for about 14 percent of the world's energy in 2005.

  - However, more than half of the world's renewable energy came from hydroelectric dams. Hydroelectric power generation has been declining since its peak of 727.62 billion kWh in 1996.

  - Worldwide wind-power generating capacity grew by 30 percent annually in the decade ending in 2005, to a total of 59,000 MW, according to the Earth Policy Institute and the Worldwatch Institute. This is a twelve-fold increase in ten years.

  - Photovoltaic solar energy production has been growing at a steady 25 percent per year since 1980. Commercial solar cells are now cheap enough to compete with other power sources, especially in sunny regions.

- Natural gas burns cleanly, and there is enough of it available to supply the world's total energy demand for the next 200 years. Consumption of natural gas is growing by 3.3 percent annually, compared with 1.8 percent for oil.

- Although most of the world's scientists gave up on cold fusion long ago, the U.S. Navy has continued work on the process. Its researchers have announced development of a reproducible cold fusion system that consistently releases more energy than it consumes.

- According to the U.S. Department of Energy's Energy Information Agency, shifting 20 percent of America's energy supply to renewable resources by 2020 would have almost no impact on the total cost of power. At present, less than 5 percent of the energy used in the United States comes from renewable resources.

Assessment:

This trend will remain in effect for at least 30 years

Implications:

Though oil will remain the world's most important energy resource for years to come, two or three decades forward it should be less of a choke point in the global economy.

Solar, geothermal, wind, and wave energy will ease power problems where these resources are most readily available, though they will supply only a very small fraction of the world's energy in the foreseeable future.

Declining reliance on oil eventually could help to reduce air and water pollution, at least in the developed world. By 2060, a costly but pollution-free hydrogen economy may at last become practical.

Fusion power remains a distant hope.

Cold fusion also remains a long shot for practical power, but FI believes it can no longer be discounted. If the Navy's reports of success prove correct, power plants based on the process could begin to come on line by 2030.

Implications for Terrorism:

Alternative energy will reduce the vulnerability of terrorist target nations to oil price shocks, but only to an extremely limited degree.

In the event that cold fusion proves to be a useful energy source—as U.S. Navy experiments seem to indicate is at least possible—it could prove as destabilizing as shale oil, though probably after a longer period of infrastructure development.

Expert Comments:

COSTIGAN (2): Yes, but not by much in the near term. Further, new sources of energy production and storage will increase the number of targets for terrorist attacks. New nuclear power plants, hydrogen fuel pumping stations, liquid natural gas storage and pipelines, smaller local power plants, etc., will fast become attractive targets for terrorists or for one-off discontents looking to make a newsworthy mess. Industrial targets will also proliferate. Companies will sprout to help harden targets, but decentralization will be hard to achieve.

MEILAHN: See Trend 18.

STEELE: As the developed world shifts to renewable and sustainable energy, the transitional period from dependence on oil consumption to new energy forms creates a window that increases the urgency of terrorist targeting capitalizing on the window of dependency.

YOUNG: Reducing the price of oil resulting from competition from other energy sources will help reduce the aforementioned financial windfall from high oil prices and thus reduce the capacity to support terror. Reducing the price of oil thus becomes a tactic in the war against terror.

ENVIRONMENTAL TRENDS

22. PEOPLE AROUND THE WORLD ARE BECOMING INCREASINGLY SENSITIVE TO ENVIRONMENTAL ISSUES AS THE CONSEQUENCES OF NEGLECT, INDIFFERENCE, AND IGNORANCE BECOME EVER MORE APPARENT.

- The World Health Organization (WHO) estimates that 3 million people die each year from the effects of air pollution, about 5 percent of the total deaths.

  - In the United States, an estimated 64,000 people a year die of cardiopulmonary disease caused by breathing particulates. A 2004 report for the U.S. Environmental Protection Administration estimated that pollution by American power plants causes 23,600 needless deaths per year.

  - In sub-Saharan Africa, the toll is between 300,000 and 500,000 deaths per year.

  - Pollution-related respiratory diseases kill about 1.4 million people yearly in China and Southeast Asia.

  - None of India's 23 million-plus cities meets WHO air quality standards.

  - In developing countries, indoor air pollution is an even bigger problem. Indoor smoke from burning fuels such as dung and wood—which more than half the world's population relies on for cooking and other basic energy needs—creates particulates that penetrate deeply into the lungs. An estimated 1.6 million people a year die from indoor air pollution, according to the WHO.

- Contaminated water is implicated in 80 percent of the world's health problems, according to WHO.

  - An estimated 40,000 people around the world die each day of diseases directly caused by contaminated water, more than 14 million per year.

  - In India, an estimated 300 million people lack access to safe drinking water, due to widespread pollution of rivers and ground water.

  - The European Parliament estimates that 70 percent of the Continent's drinking water contains dangerous concentrations of nitrate pollution.

  - In the United States, there is growing concern that pollutants such as perchlorate, the gasoline additive MTBE, and even the chlorine used to kill water-borne pathogens may represent significant health concerns.

- Though some debate remains about the cause, the fact of global warming has become undeniable. At Palmer Station on Anvers Island, Antarctica, the average annual temperature has risen by 3 to 4 degrees since the 1940s, and by an amazing 7 to 9 degrees in June—early winter in that hemisphere.

- Pew Research Center reports that its 2007 Global Attitudes Project survey of 46 countries found much more concern for the environment than in the 2002 survey.

  - In the United States, the number citing environmental problems as the top global threat rose from 23 percent to 37 percent.

- In India, the number went from 32 percent to 49 percent; in another survey of Indian concerns in the late 1990s, the environment had come in dead last.

- In both Japan and China, 70 percent of respondents said environmental problems were the greatest global threat to the world.

• Many governments are taking more active measures to protect the environment.

- After years of ineffective gestures, Costa Rica has incorporated about 25 percent of its land into protected areas, such as national parks.

- Cambodia has protected a million-acre forest.

- Gabon has set aside 10 percent of its land for parks.

- Liberia is protecting 155,000 acres of forest in an effort to safeguard endangered western chimpanzees.

- In 1999, Brazil raised the maximum fine for illegal logging.

- In an effort to promote cleaner energy technologies and to slow global warming, most European nations now tax carbon emissions or fossil fuels. In Germany, a carbon tax raises the cost of gasoline by nearly 11 cents per gallon.

- Antipollution legislation in Europe could reduce premature deaths by 80,000 between 2000 and 2020, according to the World Health Organization. In Germany alone, 17,000 premature deaths would be avoided.

- Anticipating a three-foot rise in sea levels, the Netherlands is spending $1 billion to build new dikes.

Assessment:

A solid majority of voters throughout the developed world, and even some in the developing lands, now recognize the need to clean up the environment, and especially to control greenhouse warming. They will keep this trend intact for at least the next 30 years.

Implications:

Throughout most of the world, polluters and private beneficiaries of public assets will increasingly confront restrictive regulations designed to serve the interests of the community at large.

CO_2 will remain a problem for many years to come. If air pollution were halted instantly, it would take an estimated 200 years for carbon dioxide and other greenhouse gases to return to pre-industrial levels.

Impurities in water will become an even greater problem as the population of the developed countries ages and becomes more susceptible to infectious diseases.

Recent analyses say there is a 90 percent chance that the planet's average annual temperature will rise between 3 and 9 degrees Centigrade over the next century. This will cause severe dislocations both for plant and animal populations and for many human activities.

Environmental policies will provoke a political backlash wherever they conflict with entrenched interests, as they have long done in the American West.

Implications for Terrorism:

There is at least a possibility that the industrialized countries could be the focus of terrorism inspired by resentment in developing lands that receive their garbage and recyclables. We do not view this as a significant threat for the near to medium-term future.

Expert Comments:

ANONYMOUS (10): As global warming becomes a dominant international issue, "eco-terrorism" could evolve from an occasional nuisance to a major threat. This could take the form either of attacks against infrastructure (power grids) seen as contributing to the problem, or individually targeted attacks against presumed guilty parties in the anarcho-syndicalist tradition. U.S. political and business leaders could be prime targets, given our prominent role in generating greenhouse gases.

COSTIGAN (3): Yes, and for good reason: Earth is all we have. Nevertheless, environmental issues will also become another rallying cry and source of propaganda for terrorists. Some Islamists have made the claim that had Islam been the dominant force in the industrial/post-industrial period the environment would not have been so maltreated. As this is a hypothetical, the evidence that Islam would have been a better caretaker is not to be found. However, many religions (including communism, if you are willing to call it a religion) hold the maintenance of the environment to be one of the key tasks for humans, so there is nothing unique about the claim. And look at how badly communist countries treated the environment. That said, cleaning up the environment, making strides in conservation, etc., will be critical in its own right and, as a minor side benefit, will reduce the ability of extremists to take this line of propaganda.

Additionally, and maybe proportionately to our increased concern, as the environment comes to be a more important part of our everyday thinking it may become a direct target. The sinking of an oil tanker in any number of locations could cause an Exxon Valdez-like amount of damage, along with the concomitant media frenzy, damage to the company, etc., etc. Such an attack could be seen as a double victory, hitting both the apostate/heretics (the sellers) and the criminal governments (the buyers). Environmental terrorists would not be likely to take this approach, as doing direct damage to the environment is unacceptable—unless it could be pinned on someone/something else; i.e., they mount the attack but attempt to convince the world that it was corporate greed or inept or venal politicians that are responsible.

CZARNECKI: Global warming continues to increase with concomitant climate effects. This comment does not place any "point of origin" for the warming. It simply is a scientific fact and extrapolated trend into the future. From current climate models it appears that the effects of warming are likely to be most impacting in the areas that can least adapt to the warming, that is the developing world. Water and food will become scarcer from time to time as the global agricultural economy adjusts/adapts to the changing weather. However, there will be "slack-less" times when agricultural production falls behind demand. Coupled with the growing gap in wealth and income between the rich and the poor, both nationally and internationally, this will drive more people to desperate action, including violence on a societal scale.

MILLER: Interesting trend with no clear impact on terrorism. I could see this going either way. Since these issues tend to cut across national boundaries, they could serve to bind people together even more. On the other hand, this could also become another source of irritation and worse between people in different parts of the globe.

SNYDER (5): Given its current trajectories, global climate change will continue to disproportionately disadvantage North Africa, Asia Minor, the Middle East, and the Sub-Continent, raising temperatures and reducing rainfall, causing food production to decrease, conflicts over water to grow, and increasing levels of socioeconomic distress.

Tightening world supplies of commodity crops due to droughts, water shortages, soil degradation, and the conversion of arable land to the production of bio-fuels will lead terrorists to target bulk crops. Exotic insects, plant pests, mold spores, and plant disease can be easily smuggled into the U.S. and released onto farmland. While having relatively modest immediate impacts, such agro-terrorism would have substantial cumulative effects.

YOUNG: As the world becomes more sensitive to environmental issues, the *raison d'être* for environmental or eco-terrorists is decreased. Perhaps this is the one issue that can actually cause a reduction in terrorism in the short term.

---

23. WATER SHORTAGES WILL BE A GROWING PROBLEM FOR MUCH OF THE WORLD.

- In many regions, they are severe already.

  - The northern half of China, home to perhaps half a billion people, already is short of water. The water table under Beijing has fallen nearly 200 feet since 1965.

  - Australia's Murray-Darling river system, which supplies water for 40 percent of the country's crops and 80 percent of its irrigation, no longer carries enough water to reach the sea without constant dredging. Salinity in the Murray is rising so quickly that the water is expected to be undrinkable in 20 years.

- There is worse to come. According to U.N. studies, at least 3.5 billion people will run short of water by 2040, almost ten times as many as in 1995.

  - Ten years later, fully two-thirds of the world's population could be living in regions with chronic, widespread shortages of water.

  - One-third of the population of Africa and most of the major cities in the developing world will face water shortages, according to the United Nations.

  - Many climatologists believe that global warming will make drought in the United States much more frequent—even the norm—west of the Mississippi River.

- Water usage is causing other problems as well. For example, irrigation water evaporates, leaving minerals in the soil.

  - By 2020, 30 percent of the world's arable land will be salty; by 2050, 50 percent.

  - Salinization already is cutting crop yields in India, Pakistan, Egypt, Mexico, Australia, and parts of the United States.

Assessment:

This trend will remain with us for the very long term.

Implications:

Providing adequate supplies of potable water will be a growing challenge for developing and developed countries alike.

Such problems as periodic famine and desertification can be expected to grow more frequent and severe in coming decades.

In many lands, including parts of the United States, growing water shortages may inhibit economic growth and force large-scale migration out of afflicted areas.

Climate change is expected to reduce the flow of Australia's parched Murray River by a further 5 percent in 20 years and 15 percent in 50 years.

Water wars, predicted for more than a decade, are a threat in places like the Kashmir: much of Pakistan's water comes from areas of Kashmir now controlled by India.

Other present and future water conflicts involve Turkey, Syria, and Iraq over the Tigris and Euphrates; Israel, Jordan, Syria, and Palestine over water from the Jordan River and the aquifers under the Golan Heights; India and Bangladesh, over the Ganges and Brahmaputra; China, Indochina, and Thailand, over the Mekong; Kyrghyzstan, Tajikistan, and Uzbekistan over the Oxus and Jaxartes rivers; and Ethiopia, Sudan, and at least six East African countries, including Egypt, over the Nile.

In the United States, repair of decayed water systems is likely to be a major priority for older cities such as New York, Boston, and Atlanta. Cost estimates for necessary replacement and repair of water mains range up to $1 trillion.

Implications for Terrorism:

Terrorist incidents could be a component of future resource conflicts. These are unlikely to strike directly at the developed lands. However, Western industrial facilities in the affected countries could draw attention as high-value, high-visibility targets whose destruction would cause both embarrassment and economic hardship for the local government.

There is at least a possibility that water shortages could help to inspire terrorism by providing one more cause for the sense of unfairness that contributes to extremism.

Expert Comments:

AYERS (4): We have only just begun to fight over water. Furthermore, with water becoming increasingly valuable, and since it is an absolute necessity for the continuation of life on the planet, it follows that terrorists will increasingly see water as an exploitable resource for terrorist operations. One of the best ways for extremists to win the world for Islam, for instance, is to control water resources—water will be provided only after conversion. Alternatively, water will not be on a theologically motivated terrorist's "untouchable" list, since martyrdom is so often related to religious extremism. Therefore, sabotage of varying degrees may be lurking in the future of water supply safety.

CHOBAR (6): Our water supplies in the United States, and many other nations, are extremely vulnerable. The poisoning of water, using undetectable chemicals, is a major policing problem, for which most of our water supplies, aquifers, lakes, and rivers are wide open to potential calamities which will kill many more people than terrorists flying airplanes into the Twin Towers.

COSTIGAN (9): Climate cycles will intensify droughts, and environmental immigration will be on the increase. Reduced water supplies, like those seen currently in the southern United States, could become terrorist magnets: attacking Lake Lanier at its weakened state could create intense pressure (fear, movement of peoples, etc). Extremists will seek an advantage from world-wide suffering.

CZARNECKI: This trend is a function of global warming for the most part. It is also enhanced by Trend 2. Humans absolutely need clean water to live; clean water is becoming scarcer throughout the world. The growing gap between the rich and the poor comes into play because the rich nations/societies/groups will be able to use their wealth to obtain clean water. The poor have only their labor and, with Trend 5, that labor no longer has the value it once had. Increased violence, including terrorism, results.

FORSTER: By 2025, it has been predicted that 250 million people in Africa will be threatened with water shortages. In 2007, Georgia experienced intense droughts, as Atlanta has only an 80-day supply of water if weather patterns do not change. The shortages of water will increase the likelihood of inter- and intra-state conflict contributing to an increase in failing states and economic dislocation. This socioeconomic environment will breed increased militancy and potential extremism.

MILLER: This is a well-kept secret, but the problems in Bangladesh (flooding) and Africa (drought) underscore the critical nature of Mother Nature. Ironically, this may actually serve to moderate terrorism. People who are swimming or desiccated may not have time to engage in terrorism conducted for "mere" political gain.

YOUNG: Water issues in the Middle East are a part of the peace process, but are not usually susceptible to terrorist events.

---

24. RECYCLING HAS DELAYED THE "GARBAGE GLUT" THAT THREATENED TO OVERFLOW THE WORLD'S LANDFILLS, BUT THE PROBLEM CONTINUES TO GROW.

- Americans now produce about 4.5 pounds of trash per person per day, twice as much as they threw away a generation ago. In 2005, they sent about 245 million tons of "municipal solid waste" to landfills. Seventy percent of U.S. landfills will be full by 2025, according to the EPA.

- Japan expects to run out of space for industrial waste as soon as 2008 and for municipal solid waste by 2015.

- In London and the surrounding region, landfills will run out of room by 2012.

- In some other regions, simply collecting the trash is a problem. Brazil produces an estimated 240,000 tons of garbage daily, but only 70 percent reaches landfills. The rest, 72,000 tons per day, accumulates in city streets, where it helps to spread disease.

- Recycling has proved to be an effective alternative to dumping.

    – Some 37 percent of London's municipal waste is recycled, with a target of 45 percent by 2020.

    – Seattle, with one of the most effective recycling programs in the United States, recycles about half of its solid waste.

    – As of 2005, Germany recycled 60 percent of its municipal solid waste, 65 percent of manufacturing waste, 80 percent of packaging, and 87 percent of construction waste, according to the Environment, Nature Conservation, and Nuclear Safety. Largely as a result, the number of landfills for domestic waste has been reduced from about 50,000 in the 1970s to just 160.

Assessment:

The challenge of dealing with garbage will grow for so long as the world's middle classes continue to expand or until technology finds ways to recycle virtually all of the materials used in manufacturing and packaging. This trend will remain intact through at least 2050.

Implications:

Recycling and waste-to-energy plants are a viable alternative to simply dumping garbage.

This trend will push the development of so-called life-cycle design, which builds convenient recyclability into new products from their inception.

Expect a wave of new regulations, recycling, waste-to-energy projects, and waste management programs in the United States and other countries in an effort to stem the tide of trash. In the United States, it will of course begin in California, a jurisdiction often cited by policy forecasters as a bellwether of change.

State and local governments will tighten existing regulations and raise disposal prices in Pennsylvania, South Carolina, Louisiana, and other places that accept much of the trash from major garbage producers such as New York.

Trash producers in the developed world will ship much more of their debris to repositories in developing countries. This will inspire protests in the receiving lands.

Beyond 2025 or so, the developing countries will close their repositories to foreign waste, forcing producers to develop more waste-to-energy and recycling technologies. Ultimately, it may even be necessary to exhume buried trash for recycling to make more room in closed dump sites for material that cannot be reused.

Waste-to-energy programs will make only a small contribution to the world's growing need for power.

Implications for Terrorism:

See Trend 22.

Expert Comments:

ROBERTS: In discussing this trend, you cite "industrial waste" and "manufacturing waste." There can be some nasty substances (mostly chemical, but sometimes radiological)—possibly nastier than most people know but which some malicious people are sure to be aware of. Signs of black markets in toxic waste, in terms of disposal, have already arisen—notwithstanding the Basel Convention (Basel Convention on the Control of Transboundary Movements of Hazardous Wastes and their Disposal http://www.basel.int/.) Illicit, unsanctioned, or unpoliced disposal sites for toxic waste could provide villains with sources 'off the radar screen' of many intelligence and security agencies.

25. Preference for industrial development over environmental concerns is fading very slowly in much of the developing world.

- The Pew study cited in Trend 22 found that less than one-fourth of respondents in any African country rated environmental problems as the world's most important threat.

  - In Ethiopia, where desertification is at its worst and drought is a constant threat, only 7 percent did so.

- Beijing has made repairing the environment a national priority. Yet 70 percent of the energy used in China comes from coal-burning power plants, few of them equipped with pollution controls.

  - The country intends to build over five hundred more coal-fired plants in the next ten years.

  - Scientists estimate that by 2025 China will emit more carbon dioxide and sulfur dioxide than the United States, Japan, and Canada combined.

Assessment:

View this as a counter-trend to Trend 22. It will remain largely intact until the poor of India and China complete their transition into the middle class, around 2040.

Implications:

Broad regions of the planet will be subject to pollution, deforestation, and other environmental ills in the coming decades.

Acid rain like that afflicting the United States and Canada will appear wherever designers of new power plants and factories neglect emission controls.

In India, an area the size of the United States is covered by a haze of sulfates and other chemicals associated with acid rain. Look for this problem to appear in most other industrializing countries.

Diseases related to air and water pollution will spread dramatically in the years ahead. Already, chronic obstructive pulmonary disease is five times more common in China than in the United States. As citizens of the developing countries grow to expect modern health care, this will create a growing burden on their economies.

This is just a taste of future problems, and perhaps not the most troublesome. Even the U.S. Government now admits that global warming is a result of human activities that produce greenhouse gases. It now seems that China and India soon will produce even more of them than the major industrialized nations. Helping the developing lands to raise their standards of living without creating wholesale pollution will require much more aid and diplomacy than the developed world has ever been willing to give this cause.

Implications for Terrorism:

See Trend 22.

Expert Comments:

MILLER: For the moment, this is definitely true. Not much to do with terrorism, though.

ROBERTS: Your set of trends on the environment (and ecology) may be among the most crucial. On Trend 22, I agree with Czarnecki and Snyder that climatic change will be a great destabilizer. Similarly, on Trend 23, Forster pegs shortages of water, some of which will [be] caused or aggravated by climatic change, will drive conflict. The knock-on/domino/ripple effects of environmental degradation and disruption, especially from climatic change, will destabilize failing states. Climatic change will have a pervasive impact: disruption of agriculture, destruction of infrastructure, engender socio-economic chaos in fragile societies, lead to mass migration, see consequent aggravation of ethno-cultural hostilities, and generally wreak havoc among weak states.

26. CONCERN OVER SPECIES EXTINCTION AND LOSS OF BIODIVERSITY IS GROWING QUICKLY.

- An estimated 50,000 species disappear each year, up to 1,000 times the natural rate of extinction, according to the United Nations Environmental Program. By 2100, as many as half of all species could disappear.

  - Eleven percent of birds, 25 percent of mammals, and 20 percent to 30 percent of all plants are estimated to be nearing extinction.

  - Some 16,118 species are now listed as threatened (7,925 animal species and 8,393 plant and lichen species), according to the 2006 Red List of the International Union for Conservation of Nature and Natural Resources. This is an increase of nearly 2,700 in four years. The real list is likely much larger, as the group has evaluated only 40,000 of the 1.5 million species on its list.

  - Amphibian populations are in decline throughout the world, for reasons that remain poorly understood.

- Coral reefs throughout the world are dying rapidly.

  - Caribbean reefs have lost 80 percent of their coral cover in the past three decades.

  - In Indonesia, home to one-eighth of the world's coral reefs, more than 70 percent of the reefs are dead or dying.

  - Most scientists believe that climate change is largely responsible for killing coral. Other suspected culprits are over-fishing and pollution.

- Just twenty-five so-called "hot spots" covering 11 percent of the world's surface have lost 70 percent of their original vegetation. These hot spots are home to 1.2 billion people, or one-fifth of the world's population.

- What is left in its natural state, about 2 percent of the planet's surface, is home to 44 percent of all plant species and 35 percent of all vertebrates other than fish.

- The chief cause for species loss is the destruction of natural habitats by logging, agriculture, and urbanization.

– Some 30 million acres of rainforest are destroyed each year. More than half the world's rainforests are already gone. At current rates, the rest could disappear in the next 40 years.

- Though commercial fishing is not known to have exterminated any species—largely because the last few members of a species are too costly to catch—it is turning out to be one more important cause of species depletion. Stocks of cod, tuna, swordfish, marlin, and sharks are down 90 percent or more since modern industrialized fishing began 40 years ago.

Assessment:

This trend has at least three decades to run.

Implications:

Saving any significant fraction of the world's endangered species will require much more effort and expense than many governments find acceptable. For species such as corals, if the loss is attributable largely to climate change, it may not be possible.

Species loss has a powerful negative impact on human well-being. Half of all drugs used in medicine are derived from natural sources, including fifty-five of the top one hundred drugs prescribed in the United States. About 40 percent of all pharmaceuticals are derived from the sap of vascular plants. So far, only 2 percent of the 300,000 known sap-containing plants have been assayed for useful drugs. Most of the species lost in the years ahead will disappear before they can be tested.

The Indonesian economy loses an estimated $500,000 to $800,000 annually per square mile of dead or damaged reef.

Australia may lose even more as degradation of the Great Barrier Reef continues. The U.N. Intergovernmental Panel on Climate Change predicts that the Reef will be "functionally extinct" by 2030.

Diverse ecosystems absorb more carbon dioxide than those with fewer species. Loss of biodiversity thus is a potential cause of global warming.

Implications for Terrorism:

We see no obvious implications for terrorism.

Expert Comments:

No comments were received for this trend.

27. URBANIZATION, ARGUABLY THE WORLD'S OLDEST TREND, CONTINUES RAPIDLY.

- Forty-eight percent of the world's population currently lives in cities, according to the Population Reference Bureau's 2006 *World Population Data Sheet.* By 2030, that figure will grow to 60 percent, as some 2.1 billion people are added to the world's cities.

- More than three-fourths of the population in developed countries live in cities. In North America, urbanization is the highest, at 79 percent. But cities are growing fastest in the developing world.

- The big are getting bigger. In 1950, there were just eight megacities, with populations exceeding 5 million, in the world. By 2015, there will be fifty-nine megacities, forty-eight of them in less developed countries. Of these, twenty-three will have populations over 10 million, all but four in the developing lands.

- Natural increase now accounts for more than half of population increase in the cities; at most, little more than one-third of urban growth results from migration.

• Up to 1 billion city dwellers lack adequate shelter, clean water, toilets, or electricity. The United Nations estimates that these problems cause 10 million needless deaths annually.

• Urbanization has significant environmental consequences.

- Fuels burned in cities account for 75 percent of global carbon emissions from human activity, according to the Worldwatch Institute.

- NASA scientists point out that urbanization also tends to put buildings and blacktop on the most fertile land, eliminating significant quantities of carbon-absorbing plants.

- Urbanization also deprives surrounding areas of water: Instead of sinking into the ground, rain is collected, piped to the city, used, treated as gray water, and then discarded into the ocean. In some regions, such as near Atlanta, water levels in local aquifers are declining rapidly because the water that once replenished them now is lost.

• The United States is the one major exception to the global urbanization trend. This automobile-reliant society built one of the best highway systems in the world and has relatively little mass transit, so more Americans live in the suburbs than in the cities. This could only occur where there are large swaths of land with low population density.

Assessment:

After surviving for some 3,500 years, this trend is unlikely to disappear in the next 50.

Implications:

Cities' contribution to global warming can only increase in the years ahead.

As the world's supply of potable water declines, people are concentrating in those areas where it is hardest to obtain and is used least efficiently. This trend will aggravate water problems for so long as it continues.

Many more people will die due to shortages of shelter, water, and sanitation. Epidemics will become still more common as overcrowding spreads HIV and other communicable diseases more rapidly.

Since urban growth is now due more to natural increase than to migration, programs designed to encourage rural populations to remain in the countryside may be misplaced. Education and family planning seem more likely to rein in the growth of cities.

Implications for Terrorism:

This is a top-ten trend.

Concentrating the poor and powerless in cities produces conditions ideal for the spread of petty crime, violence, and the kind of religious extremism that lends itself to terror-prone political ideologies. It also provides easy targets for terrorism in some ethnic and sectarian conflicts.

Expert Comments:

ANONYMOUS (6): Third world megacities provide a cauldron in which criminal, radical, and pathologically violent elements can easily blend. Moreover, some are or will become effective "ungoverned territories" as police/domestic intelligence lack the resources to exercise surveillance and control in sprawling slums. This provides an especially fertile environment for the growth of terrorist groups and for unfettered plotting, with easy access to technology, communications, and transportation.

ARMSTRONG: See earlier comments in Trend 1 on local vs. global/U.S.

BRAY (5): Yes, urbanization creates problems both socially and environmentally, but also in terms of urban infrastructure. Specifically, for the government services that try and provide urban stability—and their need to balance protection and privacy of their citizens. For urban governments to achieve both privacy and protection, the ability to authenticate and exchange information securely across multiple departments and agencies is essential to prevent unintentional sharing of government information with incorrect or unidentified third parties (U.S. GAO, 2001, 2003a). If government workers are to collaborate frequently across departments and agencies, they need to locate and validate the identity of each other before they can confidentially share collected information (U.S. GAO, 2006b). This process requires a single security "trust broker" to provide common authentication across all government workers and databases. Such a single authenticating trust broker, when combined with database encryption for all government technology assets (to include files located on laptops), could help to prevent data leak concerns associated with an event similar to a recent laptop theft at the U.S. Department of Veterans Affairs. The stolen government laptop contained the unencrypted personal records of 26.5 million individuals (*New York Times*, 2006d).

Equally, for workers and databases to exchange information successfully, they need to "speak" a similar language. Unfortunately, proprietary databases built by one government agency often cannot share information with other departments and agencies. A common, flexible language for the electronic subcomponents of our system of government: where none currently exists: will address this problem (U.S. GAO, 2002, 2003c, 2004a). Creating a single "big picture" across government requires the ability to query across multiple databases simultaneously. A panel of CIA experts recently echoed the need for better cross-government collaborations: internal fragmentation hurts the intelligence efforts of the national security community (Kerr et al., 2006; U.S. GAO, 2006c). For government as an information processing system, both workers and databases are the important nodes that must frequently interact and exchange information.

CZARNECKI: Humankind still has not come to terms with organizing itself in socially constructive, densely populated cities. Call this trend the catalyst or reactor vessel for the other baseline trends. Driven by resource scarcity and/or perceived wealth (relative) from urban jobs, humans flock to cities, particularly in those places that can least afford to adapt to urbanization. Once again, desperation sets in, coupled with the studied sociological perverse effects of crowded environments with unhealthy social structures. Look to Karachi, Pakistan for the future according to this trend.

JENKINS: Judging by Rio de Janeiro, Sao Paulo, Mexico City, Lagos, Johannesburg, Mumbai, megacities border on ungovernability. Policing has not kept up with growth. The danger is that of creating neo-Medieval societies with people of means residing, working, shopping, and dining behind protected perimeters, dangerous no-man's lands in between, and no-go zones for police. Threatened people are inclined to spend money on private security, not police. This is an important policy issue for financially strapped local governments: public order or private security?

KADTKE: Within a very few decades, nearly half the world's population will reside in urban areas, and the greatest growth will occur in some of the poorest areas. These areas have unique characteristics and exhibit many special problems, including resource requirements, pollution density, and social stresses caused by high population densities. They are also clear breeding grounds for extreme political and terrorist movements, due to the readiness of resources, and they present enormous problems to policing and maintaining of civil order.

MILLER: Now, this is a problem that impacts terrorism, as France and other European countries are discovering. The growing numbers of disaffected will only increase the size of the fertile ground of terrorism recruits.

OSBORNE: As communities are faced with increasingly limited resources to meet taxpayers' needs, the one-person and small police departments will be incorporated into other entities. Regional police and other modes of policing, including privatization will emerge. Data gathering requirements for intelligence-led policing may require a system wherein commanders and analysts are regionalized while ground troop officers are localized.

SMYRE (5): With more large cities in the world, and more people packed in less space, there will be greater loss of hope in times of economic and social problems (lack of food due to extreme oil shocks), potentially leading to multiple reasons for different kinds of terrorism.

SNYDER (2): The urbanized share of the world's population will continue to grow rapidly, rising from 50 percent today to 60 percent by 2030. The fastest growing cities lie in Africa, the Middle East, South Asia, and Latin America, where 25 percent to 90 percent of the urban population ALREADY live in mega-slums in which there are no basic utilities and essentially NO effective police presence. This is an invitation for political unrest and violence.

YOUNG: With respect to terror, urbanization can create the seeds for social discontent and possible urban warfare and terror acts. Conversely, if individuals/immigrants are properly assimilated within the host society and jobs are created, urbanization can act as a terror deterrent.

TECHNOLOGY TRENDS

28. TECHNOLOGY INCREASINGLY DOMINATES BOTH THE ECONOMY AND SOCIETY.

- New technologies are surpassing the previous state of the art in all fields, and technological obsolescence is accelerating.

- For most users, computers have become part of the environment rather than just tools used for specific tasks.

  – With wireless modems, portable computers give us access to networked data wherever we go.

  – Internet-equipped cell phones are even more convenient for access to e-mail and some Websites.

- Robots are taking over more and more jobs that are routine, remote, or risky, such as repairing undersea cables and nuclear power stations.

  – Flexible, general-service personal robots will appear in the home by 2015, expanding on the capabilities of devices such as robotic vacuum cleaners and lawn mowers.

- By 2015, artificial intelligence (AI), data mining, and virtual reality will help most companies and government agencies to assimilate data and solve problems beyond the range of today's computers.

  – AI applications include robotics, machine vision, voice recognition, speech synthesis, electronic data processing, health and human services, administration, and airline pilot assistance.

- Superconductors operating at economically viable temperatures will be in commercial use soon after 2015.

Assessment:

Technologically related changes in society and business seen over the last 20 years are just the beginning of a trend that will accelerate at least through this century.

Implications:

New technologies should continue to improve the efficiency of many industries, helping to keep costs under control.

However, this increased productivity has retarded United States job creation since at least 2002. Other developed countries are likely to feel the same effect in the future.

Technology made international outsourcing possible. It will continue to promote outsourcing to the benefit of the recipient countries, but to cause painful job losses in the donor lands.

New technologies often require a higher level of education and training to use them effectively. They also provide many new opportunities to create businesses and jobs.

Automation will continue to cut the cost of many services and products, making it possible to reduce prices while still improving profits. This will be critical to business survival as the Internet continues to push the price of many products to the commodity level.

New technology also will make it easier for industry to minimize and capture its effluent. This will be a crucial ability in the environmentally conscious future.

In 1999, a team at the technology organization Battelle compiled a list of the ten most strategic technological trends for the next 20 years. The list is available at the Battelle website at http://www.battelle.org/SPOTLIGHT/ tech_forecast/technology2020.aspx. Key technologies for 2020, as forecast by Battelle:

- Gene-based medical care, from custom-tailored pharmaceuticals to cloned organs for transplantation

- High-powered energy packages such as advanced batteries, cheap fuel cells, and micro-generators

- "Green integrated technology" to eliminate manufacturing waste and make products completely recyclable

- Omnipresent computing with computers built into consumer products, clothing, and even implanted under the skin

- Nanomachines measured in atoms rather than millimeters that do everything from heating and cleaning our homes to curing cancer

- Personalized public transportation that integrates out cars into a coordinated transport network, automatically picking the fastest routes and bypassing traffic jams

- Designer foods and crops genetically engineered to resist disease and pests and be highly nutritious

- Intelligent goods and appliances such as telephones with built-in directories and food packaging that tells your stove how to cook the contents

- Worldwide inexpensive and safe water from advanced filtering, desalination, and perhaps even extraction from the air

- Super senses that use implants to give us better hearing, long-distance vision, or the ability to see in the dark

Implications for Terrorism:

This is a top-ten trend.

Networks of video cameras are just the first of many high-tech tools that will affect antiterrorist operations in the years ahead.

To prevent or interrupt terrorist attacks, nanotech sensors capable of detecting explosives, chemical, and biological weapons will be scattered around prime targets, such as major public gatherings, relaying the location of any possible threat to the local command center. This is a likely prospect for 2015 and beyond.

Intelligence analysts, already overwhelmed by the amount of data collected each day, will face a growing torrent of data in the years ahead. As surveillance spreads through society, this will be a problem for police agencies as well. Until automated systems become available to help monitor incoming data, much of the information collected by cameras and other tools will be used more to provide evidence for prosecutions than to prevent or interrupt terrorist actions.

To assist them, engineers will develop automated systems to help "mesh" information from incompatible data stores, recognize patterns in the data, develop rigorous hypotheses, perform collaborative analyses, and "capture" the skills of the most capable analysts so that others can benefit from them, even when the analysts themselves are not available. Eventually, these systems will spread from the intelligence community to law enforcement. These techniques may offer the best chance of giving security agencies a clear advantage over their adversaries.

The recent decision by an American court to block data mining by the Department of Homeland Security is a significant loss to security efforts in this country. While similar military projects continue, the DHS shares data with the regional Fusion Centers responsible for much of the work carried out at the local level. Loss of this resource will make their efforts notably less effective.

Expert Comments:

ANONYMOUS (7): This will continue to provide almost endless possibilities for those with even modest technological skills to disrupt the integrated workings of the economy and society. Given the fact that engineers and technologists are often attracted to terrorist causes (e.g., the 9/11 plotters) it is only a matter of time before existing technology is once again turned against society in a major way. Industry and governments will need to work together to find palliative strategies (switching to less toxic chemicals, moving LNG terminals to less populated areas) but this will be neither cheap nor easy.

ARMSTRONG: The increasing availability of information has significant consequences on peace and conflict and the utility of terrorism. The direct kinetic effects of bullets, bombs, and terrorism in general are secondary to their influence on the public opinion of foes, allies, and neutrals. Global information and transportation systems create two-way access to dynamic and global Diasporas based on "imagined communities" that are subjected to campaigns of strategic influence by the enemy while the United States sits idly by. Because the asymmetry in information operations decreases the fungibility of hard power assets, we must look at the biggest value of the "D" in WMD not as destruction but as disruption through the multiplicative effect of perceptions driven by the act, not the immediate effect of the act. We must look at technology not only as a tactical tool, but as one of operational and strategic consequence. The enemy does.

AYERS (5): a) Virtual worlds (e.g., Second Life), which are providing new opportunities for individual and commercial growth, can be used by terrorists to further their efforts in perpetrating kinetic and non-kinetic attacks. They supply extremists with flexible, and perhaps safer, venues for training *jihadis* ideologically, methodologically, and sociologically without requiring physical presence or large amounts of physical space. They may also, in the near future, provide terrorists with new ways of performing intelligence collection, information operations, and information warfare. If we are to credibly counteract the potential for terrorists to utilize virtual worlds for nefarious purposes, the intelligence community, law enforcement entities, and policy makers need to begin preparing for this eventuality sooner, rather than later.

b) Learning agents coupled with robotics will not only transform the manner in which intelligence is obtained and processed—they will transform the way in which intelligence data is viewed and acted upon by collectors, analysts, law enforcement practitioners, managers, and decision makers. Increasingly, all will be able to verbally question systems that seem much more like cognitive assistants (or super-intelligent coworkers) than the static technology we are now used to. Output will be visual (similar to our reporting systems of today) and/or auditory. These robotically supported cognitive assistants will be linked to databases worldwide as well as other learning agents of varying types and will be able to dynamically process monumental amounts of information while considering data that might normally be weeded out or inaccessible to humans or manually driven systems (e.g., those engaged in the current processes of research, analysis, and reporting.) While not all intelligence questions will be answerable instantaneously by the robotic/cognitive agents, time that humans would normally spend sifting through a substantial number of reports could be spent dissecting questions that need more attention, and reviewing agent responses. Intelligence reporting as it exists currently will increasingly become obsolete. Human expertise can be kept indefinitely, and detailed information about thinking processes could be made immediately available to those who question research methodology. (This comment is a projection based on research performed by George Mason University Learning Agent Center personnel.) Unfortunately, the period between the attainment of "massive systemic overload" and the achievement of dependable capabilities developed to alleviate overload (such as the aforementioned robotically-supported cognitive assistants) will be extremely difficult, if not chaotic. It is unlikely that significant progress will be realized without having to go through a great deal of anguish in the meantime.

BRAY (1): Recall the major events of the last five years—Inadequate response to Hurricane Katrina in 2005, faulty intelligence prior to the second Iraqi war in 2003, incorrect estimates of the Al-Qaeda threat prior to the 9/11 attacks. These failures all occurred because our system of government could not appropriately link the knowledge it had across multiple departments to take action. Repeat investigations by the U.S. Government Accountability Office all report the same theme: More than sufficient information existed to mitigate these events, but the information was in a highly distributed and fragmented form across multiple departments and the White House.

Granted, the role of government is a large and onerous one. No other system exists with such a broad scope of duties to serve and protect us as citizens. For every government failure, multiple successes occur without making headlines. When our system of government works well, we all take it for granted. Government agencies confront a difficult task of determining truth from fiction, with limited (or potentially biased) sources of knowledge available.

I can attest to these difficulties. Starting the in autumn of 2000, I accepted a role with the Bioterrorism Preparedness and Response Program at the Centers for Disease Control and Prevention (CDC)—first as a fellow, later as IT Chief of the Bioterrorism Program. At 9am on the morning of 11 September 2001, I was to give a presentation to various government officials on how improvements in the information technology infrastructure of public health laboratories could aid national response to a bioterrorism event. The meeting never started. Instead, members of my program at the CDC were sent to an off-site command area when American Airlines Flight 11 hit the World Trade Center at 8:46am.

The events that followed—to include the anthrax events of 2001, West Nile Virus, Severe Acute Respiratory Syndrome, monkeypox, and other disease outbreaks—all demonstrated to me that our government faces significant obstacles in effectively "connecting the dots" of knowledge held in the minds of numerous individuals working for different organizational units. Not only is the challenge to discern truth from fiction, but also to put all the pieces of knowledge together to form a complete picture. In this age of knowledge-overload, no one individual harbors sufficient knowledge to either mitigate negative outcomes or capitalize on positive opportunities. Knowledge exchanges in these government agencies must transcend physical group proximity, social networks, and the institutions themselves.

There is a significant correlation between globalization efforts and increasing knowledge velocity, volume, volatility, and veracity concerns. Human societies, economies, and civil infrastructures are increasingly interdependent and complex. Instead of attempting the traditional "top-down" approach to management, my research espouses a "bottom-up" approach to cultivating individual insights. Recall the events of 9/11 and Hurricane Katrina: no one individual harbored sufficient knowledge to mitigate these events. Such realities will occur with increasing frequency for employees of either government agencies or private entities. To assemble the entire puzzle, knowledge exchanges must occur among multiple individuals in different organizational units and institutions without prompting from the "top", but instead must be motivated at the grassroots by collaboration-fostering incentives, values, and trust-relationships; such an idea embodies innovative "knowledge ecosystems."

BRUH: Two can play the game. I believe that while new technology will be essential to effective law enforcement it will be a mixed blessing, and not just because of frauds and other crimes perpetrated through the Internet. More and more individual criminals, criminal organizations, and governments engaged in criminality will be using technology to commit serious crime in the U.S. and elsewhere. Some such crimes will occur in and or originate from the U.S., and even more will be initiated elsewhere. The technology will include the use of sophisticated cameras, electronic and wireless listening devices, and weapons, among a host of other technologies. Greed will still be at the root of most crime, but terrorism will be the world's greatest threat for as far as anyone can now see due to the many ways that large numbers of humans can be destroyed rather quickly by many who want to do such a thing.

CHOBAR (4): Just like it is said, "As soon as the U.S. releases new currencies, the counterfeiters already are equal to the task of printing money," sophisticated technology enables terrorists and terrorism to be ahead of policing agencies. Money often is no stumbling block. Thus, with wealthy individuals supporting terrorism, the very latest in technology can almost instantaneously be in the hands of terrorists. This can cover every new technological device from A to Z; satellite cell phones to ground-to-air missiles, to laser technology, to the most hideous war weapons—capable of killing hundreds and thousands of people at one time.

COSTIGAN (4): Yes, and with far-ranging negative and positive consequences. If terrorist attacks continue in the United States, technology may be sought out as the first resort to discover terrorists. False-positives will also increase, government will continue to lose legitimacy, and privacy will continue to wane. Initially costs of systems will be borne primarily by the government, while private industry attempts to continue to maximize the bottom line. Security for corporations will continue to be dominated by profit margins, and so high-tech solutions will not be preferred options. However, failing government response, corporations may decide to build private militaries and intelligence networks to protect themselves and their investments.

CZARNECKI: What this really means is that information increasingly dominates. Information can be compiled through computing and/or genetics, at least as far as technology forecasting can see. Who will benefit? The rich? At who's expense, since information, like energy, can neither be created nor destroyed, just converted? The poor? Information-related technologies expand to suppress the violent inklings of the poor; Orwell's *1984* gets an updating in the name of security and public safety. Because of this, Trend 28 decreases the likelihood of terrorism—but at the cost of individual privacy and civil rights.

FRASER: For many years, law enforcement intelligence units have compiled intelligence based on information supplied by informants or through other human contacts. Many of these units have been extremely unwilling to share this information with other units—either within or outside their agency—because they fear that if action is taken—arrests are made or criminal/terrorist rings are broken up—their sources/informants will be compromised. The tendency has been to wait for the perfect set of circumstances to get the largest possible haul so as to get the maximum benefit from the informant. The new technology offers the potential to push intelligence units toward a bias for action since intelligence information will come form a wide variety of sources many of which are not individual informants. Action can be taken much sooner without worrying about blowing an informant.

However, care must be taken not to stop gathering human intelligence. Relying too much on these new diverse automated sources can lead to too much information without context and/or human cross-checking. By combining human sources with data mining, expert systems and artificial intelligence perhaps we can avoid making the sort of intelligence mistakes that led our leaders to believe that Iraq's WMDs were an immediate threat to the U.S.

JENKINS: See Trend 5.

LANOTTE: "[T]o assist them, engineers will develop automated systems to help "mesh" information from incompatible data stores, recognize patterns in the data, develop rigorous hypotheses, perform collaborative analyses, and "capture" the skills of the most capable analysts so that others can benefit from them, even when the analysts themselves are not available." This is indeed a lofty goal. I can only assume that, along with this prediction, true artificial intelligence (AI) technology is imbedded in the prediction. Along with the introduction and use of AI in criminal cases, will be the requirement to make the evidence admissible in court.

Nozawa: In the United States fundamental scientific advances have been few since 1992. Administration policy put advanced scientific projects on hold, and agencies such as DARPA [Defense Advanced Research Projects Agency] and AF Lab resorted to developing widgets. New discoveries were ignored. DARPA's attempt to regroup under the present Administration and "reach for the far shore" appears to have failed. The situation is unchanged today.

The United States is far behind Japan in the development of robots using advanced multiple-valued logic. The U.S. wasted its time in internecine wars arguing about whether fuzzy logic and other non-probabilistic logics were real or not. During the same period, China surpassed Japan and developed the largest cadre of fuzzy logicians.

Artificial intelligence as defined in the 1980s was dead by 1991. It had been built around a collapsed objective scientific philosophy. Only robotics and vision survived and continued. DARPA in 2007 is unable to make real headway since no new fundamental knowledge has been discovered by DARPA to overcome the disaster of the 1980s. Scientific semeiotics provides the answers needed, but DARPA and others have lacked the talent necessary to recognize the value of Scientific Semeiotic…they don't know that they don't know.

Airline pilots assistance and similar systems lack systems design methodologies to develop the envisioned technologies. Again, scientific semeiotic provides the necessary system design processes to develop these advanced systems.

Technologically related changes have been on hold for most of the last twenty years. The end of Cold War, the peace dividend, and the artificial stoppage of scientific advancement has resulted in the downward trend with nothing to stop it unless a fundamental change in scientific philosophy is made.

If the terrorists (jihadist) see what is developing in systems design and intelligence analysis, then they will merely need to be patient and let us destroy ourselves through neglect, incompetence and the absence of critical thinking.

Osborne: There are not enough trained, skilled, and knowledgeable law enforcers who can tackle problems based in current technology—identity theft, white collar crimes, and cybercrime. Emerging technologies are likely to bring further challenges, which justice and security agencies will [be] ill-equipped to face. However, sometime in the next 20 years, more sophisticated technologies will become much easier to use with relatively little training. These tools will be widely adopted and will transform intelligence and policing.

Snyder (7): IT applications will continue to eliminate mountains of paperwork—and paperworkers—de-staffing back-office operations and curtailing commodity white-collar employment in the industrialized world.

Steele: The reliance of microchip technology in about everything would render major systems inoperable if coordinated EMP [electromagnetic pulse] bombs were detonated in a variety of critical locations, such as air traffic control centers. EMP bombs over grid-locked highways might be followed by explosives, gas, or anthrax.

Tan: Technological change and innovation is something that will increasingly dominate society but this very change brings challenges. Technology promises to unleash new means of dealing with the security and terrorism challenges we face, but the danger in building systems—for instance, in data mining, etc.—is that we can be driven too much by technology, neglecting the fact that no one can replace excellent intelligence analysts who have the in-depth training and deep knowledge to be able to make sense of the vast amounts of information and intelligence that is coming through. Ultimately, technology provides the tools for counter-terrorism, but this fixation with technology unfortunately often comes at the expense of developing good human analysis and judgment. These ultimately cannot be replaced by technology.

Young: If certain parts of certain societies continue to believe they are disenfranchised by globalization as represented by technological advances, terrorism will continue to plague the world.

29. Research and development play a growing role in the world economy.

- Total U.S. outlays on R&D have grown steadily in the past three decades.

    – In 2006, the United States spent about $330 billion on R&D.

- China has taken second place in the world's R&D spending, with a budget estimate at $136 billion in 2006, up from $60 billion in 2001.

    – Still more spending may be hidden in military budgets.

    – China says it will raise its R&D spending from about 1.23 percent of GDP in 2004 to 2.5 percent in 2020.

- R&D outlays in Japan have risen almost continuously, to nearly 3 percent of GDP. In 2006, Japan spent about $130 billion on R&D.

- R&D spending in the European Union (EU-15) amounted to $230 billion in 2006, about 1.9 percent of GDP.

    – The European Commission has set a goal of raising R&D spending to 3 percent of GDP by 2010.

- In Russia, R&D funding is roughly 1.5 percent of GDP, up from just 0.7 percent in 1997. This amounted to about $26.25 billion in 2006.

    – The Russian government funds around 60 percent of research in the country. About 44 percent of Russia's R&D budget goes to defense research, 10 percent to space.

    – These figures do not include whatever clandestine military research escapes notice.

- Corporate R&D in the United States has shifted in the post-September 11 period, with less emphasis on pharmaceuticals and computer-related fields and more focus on biotechnology, nanotechnology, and security technologies.

- Western corporations are outsourcing a growing fraction of their R&D to foreign contractors, just as they do other functions.

    – Much of this work goes to India, some to Russia and Eastern Europe, but the growth area is China.

Assessment:

This trend is stabilizing as developed nations, particularly the United States, devote more of their resources to less productive activities. We believe this is a temporary phenomenon. The trend will regain momentum in the years ahead. It will not fall off this list before the middle of this century.

Implications:

This is a significant factor in the acceleration of technological change.

The demand for scientists, engineers, and technicians will continue to grow, particularly in fields where research promises an immediate business payoff.

Low-wage countries such as China once took only low-wage jobs from advanced industrialized countries such as the United States. Today higher-paid jobs in science, technology, and the professions also are at risk.

Countries like India, China, and Russia once suffered a brain drain as those with high-tech skills emigrated to high-demand, high-wage destinations. Today, many students and professionals spend time in the West to learn cutting-edge skills, and then return to their native lands to work, start companies, and teach. This promotes the growth of some developing countries while reducing the competitive advantages of the developed world.

Implications for Terrorism:

A host of new high-tech tools will become available for antiterrorist activities in the years ahead. They will require more training for effective use and may even require tighter recruitment standards to ensure that new intelligence, security, and law enforcement personnel will be able to adapt to fast-changing techniques and demands.

Expert Comments:

FORSTER: Research and development of new technologies will increase the ability to prevent and protect society against terrorist attacks. Intelligence and law enforcement will improve their ability to identify threats, predict actions, and intervene. Additionally, new research and development will improve the ability to mitigate the effects of terrorist actions and maintain continuity of operations. However, as new capabilities are disseminated throughout society, terrorist groups will inevitably adapt them to meet their needs. Thus, this trend, like many, is a double-edged sword.

NOZAWA: A long term "Manhattan Project" [is required] to build capability in scientific semeiotics. The knowledge exists, only the will is missing. It's all in our native language. Unlike the Manhattan Project no massive investment in hardware is needed. It's all mind building. It's knowledge warfare.

30. THE UNITED STATES IS CEDING ITS SCIENTIFIC AND TECHNICAL LEADERSHIP TO OTHER COUNTRIES.

- "The scientific and technical building blocks of our economic leadership are eroding at a time when many other nations are gathering strength," the National Academy of Sciences warns. Although many people assume that the United States will always be a world leader in science and technology, this may not continue to be the case inasmuch as great minds and ideas exist throughout the world. We fear the abruptness with which a lead in S&T can be lost—and the difficulty of recovering a lead once lost, if indeed it can be regained at all."

- Although R&D spending is growing in raw-dollar terms, when measured as a percentage of the total federal budget or as a fraction of the U.S. GDP, research funding has been shrinking for some 15 years. In 2005, the United States spent about 2.68 percent of its GDP on R&D, down from 2.76 percent in 2001.

  – Washington has often reduced the post-inflation buying power of its R&D funding request. In the FY 2007 budget, for the first time, it cut R&D funds in absolute dollars as well. The 2007 funding request for R&D totaled about $137 billion, down about 1 percent from FY 2006.

– Some areas were harder hit. The National Science Foundation lost 3.2 percent of its previous budget; the National Institute of Science and Technology lost 6 percent. Some programs funded by the Federal Energy Efficiency and Renewable Energy Office lost 18 percent.

• Military research now absorbs much of the money that once supported basic science.

– Since 2000, U.S. federal spending on defense research has risen an average of 7.4 percent per year, compared with only 4.5 percent for civilian research.

– In 2006, 59 percent of U.S. federal research funding went to defense projects.

– Of that, an estimated 40 percent went to "earmarks," congressional pet projects often of doubtful value.

– The DARPA has been legendary for its support of "blue sky" research that led to dramatic technical advances, including the creation of the Internet. Today it focuses increasingly on immediate military needs and low-risk development efforts.

• Washington's neglect of basic science is being felt in many ways.

– Only half of American patents are granted to Americans, a number that has been declining for decades.

– Only 29 percent of the research papers published in the prestigious *Physical Review* in 2003 were by American authors, down from 61 percent in 1983.

• More than half of American scientists and engineers are nearing retirement. At the rate American students are entering these fields, the retirees cannot be replaced except by recruiting foreign scientists.

– Between 25 percent and 30 percent of high school graduates who enter college plan to major in science or engineering. Fewer than half of them receive a degree in those fields.

– The number of U.S. bachelor's degrees awarded in engineering in 2005 was nearly 15 percent below the peak 20 years earlier. The United States needs 114,000 engineering graduates each year, according to the Department of Labor. According to most reports, it graduates about 65,000.

– According to the National Academy of Engineering, the United States produces only about 7 percent of the world's engineers.

– Only 6 percent of American undergraduates are engineering majors. In Europe, the number is 12 percent; in China, it is 40 percent.

– Of the doctoral degrees in science awarded by American universities, about 30 percent go to foreign students. In engineering, it is 60 percent.

• By inhibiting stem-cell research, cloning, and other specialties the United States has made itself less attractive to cutting-edge biomedical scientists.

– The United Kingdom is capitalizing on this to become the world's leader in stem-cell research. In the process, it is reversing the brain drain that once brought top British scientists to the United States,

More than seventy leading American biomedical researchers have moved to the U.K., along with many less-noted colleagues.

– Latin America also has been receiving scientific emigrés from the U.S.

• Since post-9/11 immigration restrictions were enacted, the number of foreign students taking the Graduate Record Exam has declined sharply.

– Applications were off by 50 percent from China, 37 percent from India, 15 percent from South Korea, and 43 percent from Taiwan as of 2004. Though recovering slowly, their numbers remain depressed.

– Instead of building relationships in the United States—professional loyalties that could contribute to American S&T—these missing students will form their attachments to U.S. competitors.

– This is significant. About 25 percent of America's science and engineering workforce are immigrants, including nearly half of those with doctoral degrees. During the 15 years ending in 2007, one-third of the American scientists receiving Nobel Prizes were foreign-born.

• According to Purdue president Martin Jischke, by 2010 more than 90 percent of all scientists and engineers in the world will live in Asia.

Assessment:

This trend emerged from a wide variety of ill-conceived political decisions made over the last 30 years. It will take a generation to reverse.

Implications:

If this trend is not reversed, it will begin to undermine the U.S. economy and shift both economic and political power to other lands. According to some estimates, about half of the improvement in the American standard of living is directly attributable to research and development carried out by scientists and engineers.

The Bureau of Labor Statistics predicts that the number of job openings in science and engineering will grow by 47 percent in the five years ending 2010—three times as fast as non-technical fields. The United States will not produce nearly enough home-grown technical specialists to fill them.

Demand to import foreign scientists and engineers on H-1B visas also will continue to grow.

Publicity about the H1-B program, and about the offshoring of R&D to company divisions and consulting labs in Asia, in turn, will discourage American students from entering technical fields. This has already been blamed for shrinking student rolls in computer science.

In 2005, China for the first time exported more IT and communications goods ($180 million) than the United States ($145 million.) Its lead has grown each year since then.

Implications for Terrorism:

This is a top-ten trend.

The growing sophistication of scientists and engineers in the developing world threatens to put chemical, biological, and nuclear weapons in the hands of international terrorist organizations. The success of A.Q. Khan in creating Pakistan's nuclear program and spreading his knowledge to the Middle East is likely to be just the first of what could be many such examples. This will make intelligence and security duties much more difficult to carry out successfully.

Expert Comments:

ANONYMOUS (9): This exacerbates the effects of rapid technological advance because it diminishes the capabilities of the leading counter-terrorism power to monitor the emergence of new technologies that could be put to terrorist use or diversions of existing technologies. To keep tabs on technological threats, new global or multilateral scientific and technological monitoring mechanisms will be needed, although concerns about safeguarding intellectual property will complicate such efforts.

ARMSTRONG: The U.S. is not ceding its leadership. In fact, S&T is one of the few areas where the U.S. retains global respect, even in the Muslim countries with extremely poor (and violent) views of America. While many look at S&T as almost a liability, that we're dependent on it and that we're not developing enough talent, the rest of the world is mimicking our skills and building on it because of the value they see in it. I have hosted two discussion panels on using S&T as diplomacy for DHS science and technology conferences. The key take-away has been the value of enhancing S&T relationships for long-term benefit. Working with foreign scientists, as well as their communities, either here or abroad, not only taps into and develops additional research and development capacity, it also promotes changes in commercial, academic, infrastructure, and legal systems that form the foundation of democratic institutions, a potential win-win for people and societies and S&T. A promising reality is polling showing American S&T continues to be admired by countries that are increasingly opposed to American politics. The real risk is not empowerment of other countries (see earlier comments on technology and globalization), but on outsourcing, which is a different strategic threat than terrorism, although it increases our liability as disruption on our periphery or in countries beyond our control will have implications for the United States.

CHOBAR (5): I worked for a huge global corporation before returning to education. I watched as this company brought in new employees to various U.S. divisions, from every nation on the planet, to train them in the latest communication, transportation, power generation, water processing, aviation, electrical distribution, security, and water desalination. Policing of people's backgrounds was seldom done. These people went back to their home countries with huge 6" spiral bound notebooks, as well as hundreds of CDs and DVDs of product information. We hand [over] this phenomenal scientific and technical information under the umbrella of being "corporate employees." However, in the hands of terrorists or terrorism supporters, this same scientific and technical leadership is used against us and other nations of the world.

COSTIGAN (5): Fine educations are now available elsewhere, perhaps closer to home, and the response to pre-9/11 immigration policy lead to fewer foreign students in U.S. universities, making them a harder sell. Vigorous attempts by government, and perhaps just the passing of time, have lead to a recent rebound of foreign enrollment after the 9/11 slowdown. Needless to say, universities are a primary engine for the U.S. S&T and the economy. Thus it is critical that foreign students, with their leads in S&T, seek their education in the U.S. Perhaps just as important as the economic factors, when fewer students come to the United States, the U.S. also loses the opportunity to influence future worldwide corporate and governmental leadership. While high technology may assist in capturing terrorists or reducing the need for interests in terrorism-prone areas, friendly governments and organizations are key to continued strength.

NOZAWA: In the long run, we can recapture the S&T leadership since we still own the knowledge. We have a head start in winning the knowledge war. Charles Sanders Peirce did all the homework and tradeoff analyses and gave us the answers on a golden platter. For the moment, we see neither the knowledge nor the golden platter.

SANDERS (7): See comments under "Complexity and the Future of Terrorism" in Appendix C.

SNYDER (3): Growing shortages in our domestic supply of STEM (Scientists, Technicians, Engineers, and Mathematicians) recruits will make the U.S. increasingly dependent on imported high-skill labor, 25 percent to 30 percent of whom have come from Muslim countries in recent years.

Note that U.S. employers and business lobbies are urgently seeking to double or triple the H-1B visa cap from its current limit of 65,000 per year. Imported personnel could be placed in the U.S. as "sleepers"—for which we are already screening applicants—or could subsequently be suborned into collaborating with terrorists by threats to family members back home. Conversely, Islamists may inveigh against Muslims who work for Americans as traitors, in an attempt to deprive the U.S. of critically needed skills.

31. TRANSPORTATION TECHNOLOGY AND PRACTICE ARE IMPROVING RAPIDLY.

- The newest generation of aircraft, such as the Boeing 787 and future Airbus A350 XWB, are using lightweight materials and more efficient engines to cut fuel costs, stretch ranges, and increase cargo capacity.

  - In the United States, two companies have even announced plans to build supersonic business jets and have them in the air by 2013 or so. One has already taken deposits for several dozen aircraft.

- The airline industry is developing technical advances such as improved satellite navigation and communications, runway collision avoidance systems, and safer seat designs.

  - The Enhanced Ground Proximity Warning System (EWGPS) compares an aircraft's GPS location with digital topographic maps to warn when a plane is in danger of flying into terrain. No plane equipped with it has ever had this kind of crash.

  - These improvements will also allow planes to fly closer together, increasing the carrying capacity of air routes.

- Rail travel is getting faster. The new TGV Est line, which runs 300 km (180 miles) from Paris to Frankfurt, operates at 320 kph (198.8 mph) inside France, compared with 300 kph on other parts of the TGV system.

- Advances in automobile technology, such as road-condition sensors, continuously variable transmissions, automated traffic management systems, night-vision systems, and smart seats that tailor airbag inflation to the passenger's weight, are reaching the marketplace.

- The first commercial hybrid gas-electric cars are available already, with more scheduled for future model years.

Assessment:

These advances will continue at least through mid-century.

Implications:

One of the fastest-growing transport industries is trucking, thanks to the expanded use of just-in-time inventory management and Internet-based companies that rely on trucks to deliver their products. This field will grow more efficient as GPS-based truck tracking, RFID-based cargo management, more efficient engines, and other new technologies spread through the industry.

To reduce the number and severity of traffic accidents, trucks on the most heavily used highways will be exiled to car-free lanes, and the separation will be enforced.

New hybrid car models will begin to gain significant market share from traditional gas guzzlers between 2010 and 2015.

Following European practice, even "legacy" air carriers in the United States will begin to replace the spokes of their existing hub-and-spokes system with high-speed trains for journeys of 100 to 150 miles.

By 2015, improved technologies and concerns about the long-term cost of energy will lead even the rail-resistant United States to begin modernizing its train system.

New aircraft navigation and safety technologies will reduce the number and severity of crashes.

By 2010, smart-car technologies will begin to reduce deaths due to auto accidents in Europe and, a few years later, the United States.

Cities increasingly will struggle to reduce auto congestion by limiting the use of private automobiles, as in Munich, Vienna, and Mexico City; by taxing auto use in congested areas, as in London; or by encouraging the development and use of mass transit, as in Copenhagen and Curitiba, Brazil.

Technology may offer other alternatives. One proposal is "dual-mode transportation," in which private cars would be used normally on short hauls but would run on automated guideways for long-distance travel.

Implications for Terrorism:

The continuing growth of international travel, internal rail networks, and feeder airlines will make it easier to establish and propagate a bioweapon-induced epidemic through the target countries.

In the long run, automated transport systems could become a new target for sophisticated terrorists. The toll in lives and economic impact from a successful attack on a high-speed rail system or an automated highway could be significant.

Expert Comments:

AYERS (7): "The enemy of the enemy is my friend." There will be ever-increasing cooperation and capabilities between various criminal elements (drug cartels, ID theft rings, and black-marketers), dissidents, anarchists, terrorists, and rogue elements of power within the governments of nation-states. With global communications, war planning on a global scale—from coalitions of terrorist and criminal groups to coalitions of states (and maybe a combination of all three) is not only possible, but probable. Instantaneous communications make simultaneous operations an easy task (as seen with the attacks of 9/11). Conversely, the massive amounts of and differing modes of communications, combined with antiquated hierarchical structures within Western governments, will make the West more vulnerable, unless or until a method of instantaneous and ubiquitous information gathering and threat warning can be achieved. In the meantime, psychological "blowback," in the form of technology abandonment by the many, could become an issue. Communications might become more difficult because of the overwhelming nature of such, thus limiting the adoption of new technology (or the use of high-tech communications in general). Threat information might therefore ultimately be unattainable or stalled in the process of distribution.

CHOBAR: Because of the speed these advances provide, it also makes policing harder and therefore can enable terrorism to happen much more quickly.

YOUNG: Technological advances have been a boon to counterterrorism activities. A whole new industry has been created with respect to Homeland Security, and technological advances should progress as the terrorists seek to counteract the new technologies meant to discover and defeat them.

YOUNGS: Our country's public mass transit systems are each unique, open, dynamic, and inherently vulnerable to terrorist attacks. As terrorism appears to be increasing against transit systems, the transit sector continues to focus on policing, new technology, environmental design, and public outreach as means to enhance security while maintaining the precipitous balance between security and public convenience. It is the continued cooperation, communication and collaboration between the governmental and non-governmental regulatory bodies that will make the various transit systems continue to succeed and progress as funding allows.

---

32. THE PACE OF TECHNOLOGICAL CHANGE ACCELERATES WITH EACH NEW GENERATION OF DISCOVERIES AND APPLICATIONS.

- In fast-moving engineering disciplines, half of the cutting-edge knowledge learned by college students in their freshman year is obsolete by the time they graduate.

- The design and marketing cycle—idea, invention, innovation, imitation—is shrinking steadily. As late as the 1940s, the product cycle stretched to 30 or 40 years. Today, it seldom lasts 30 or 40 weeks.

  – Almost any new consumer product can be exactly duplicated by Chinese factories and sold on e-Bay within a week after it is introduced.

- Some 80 percent of the scientists, engineers, technicians, and physicians who ever lived are alive today—and exchanging ideas real time on the Internet.

Assessment:

This trend will continue for many years. However, we may grow less able to perceive it.

Implications:

Subjectively, change soon will move so rapidly that we can no longer recognize its acceleration, save as an abstract concept.

All the technical knowledge we work with today will represent only 1 percent of the knowledge that will be available in 2050.

Industries will face much tighter competition based on new technologies. Those who adopt state-of-the-art methods first will prosper. Those who ignore them will eventually fail.

Products must capture their market quickly, before the competition can copy them.

Brand names associated with quality are becoming even more important in this highly competitive environment.

Lifelong learning is a necessity for anyone who works in a technical field—and for growing numbers who do not.

In what passes for the long run—a generation or two—the development of true artificial intelligence is likely to reduce human beings to managers. Rather than making new discoveries and creating new products, we will struggle to understand and guide the flow of novelties delivered by creations we cannot really keep up with.

Implications for Terrorism:

This is one area in which antiterrorist forces have a clear advantage. Technologically sophisticated and backed by government budgets, intelligence and security services will be able to adopt useful innovations much faster than terrorist organizations such as Al Qaeda. This improves their chances of monitoring or disrupting terrorist communications, financing, and operations.

Expert Comments:

ANONYMOUS (8): This trend will have both positive and negative effects. On the one hand, accelerating progress in information and surveillance technologies could provide counter-terrorist authorities with unprecedented capabilities to monitor potential threats. But on the other hand, dramatic advances in bio and nanotechnologies, among others, will offer small groups and individuals continually evolving (and hard to detect/defend against) opportunities (manufactured viruses, nanobots) to cause massive casualties and physical damage.

BRAY (9): See Trend 5.

BRUH: While clearly there are departments and agencies that are short of funds and, therefore, cannot take advantage of technological improvements in a timely fashion, I believe that another concern is more important. Few organizations, in government or in the private world, have not wasted vast amounts of funds trying to adopt new technologies. This occurs either because the projects are not well thought out or through selecting managers that are either not sufficiently knowledgeable or capable of driving a program to its successful completion. Moreover, organizations often select contractors that are incapable or inappropriate for the tasks. With funding always being of concern to security and law enforcement organizations, they must strive to do better in this regard. It requires the continuing personal involvement and leadership of the head of every organization.

JENKINS: See Trend 5.

KRIESBERG: Yes technological changes will continue to accelerate. That is unsettling, opening new opportunities and new problems. There are more and better ways to monitor and to evade monitoring.

The implications for countering terror depend on the social sensibility and policy about the ability to use the new technologies.

LADUKE (2): Scientific and technical knowledge is social collateral for destructive force and is being manipulated by a global stage of "actors." (See comments [in Trend 8] on global economy growing more integrated.) This coupled with a power struggle between corporate/institutional interests and national defense interests (see comments on diversity [in

Trend 7]) is creating a substantial threat to U.S. interests. The rise of nanotechnology could give individuals and small groups new forms of less controllable and less detectable mass destruction by 2020.

MILLER: Technology will no doubt impact tremendously both the practice of terrorist violence and the conduct of counter-terrorism. As it has in the past, the struggle between the two forces will be carried out at least in part using the latest technology. It would seem that either side can concede victory to the other by relying on traditional implements and ignoring technology advances. Otherwise, this front in the "war" will most likely continue as an active area of ebb and flow, with neither side prevailing. Terrorists will continue to invent new ways and means of violence, and the state will continue to invest in research and development.

YOUNG: This concept was well proven in Iraq with the improvement in insurgent tactics but also in the technological advances in IEDs. At the beginning of the war, IEDs were relatively crude but became more sophisticated in design and triggering devices as the war progressed. Moreover, the advent of EFPs became the ultimate IED in destructive power. As a result, better, more complete armor was devised by the U.S. to counteract technological advances by the insurgents.

33. IMPORTANT MEDICAL ADVANCES WILL CONTINUE TO APPEAR ALMOST DAILY.

- Genetic research has accelerated advances in medicine and in the growth of medical knowledge. Early results include possible cures for hemophilia, cystic fibrosis, familial hypercholesterolemia, a number of cancers, and AIDS. Eventually, some 4,000 hereditary disorders may be prevented or cured through genetic intervention.

    - At Sangamo Biosciences, in California, researchers have experimented with rewriting the patient's own DNA, rather than replacing it, to correct hereditary errors. The technique may lead to practical therapies sooner than conventional gene splicing.

    - Also in the works: gene-based diagnostic tests that may identify cancer early and tell which drugs are most likely to benefit individual patients with heart disease, cancer, and other ills.

- A process called RNA interference, which deactivates individual genes, is quickly revealing the genes' functions.

    - It also may be used to disable disease-causing genes, perhaps making it possible to cure cancer, viral ills, and some hereditary disorders.

    - One potential cure for HIV/AIDS is expected to be ready for human testing by 2010.

- In research performed outside the United States, stem cells promise to repair damaged brains and other organs. Embryonic stem cells have already been found to repair damaged heart muscle.

- Growing knowledge of biochemistry, aided by advanced computer modeling, has made it possible to design drugs that fit specific receptors in the cell.

    - Drugs created through this technology often are much more effective than natural derivatives and have fewer side effects.

    - Nearly four hundred anticancer compounds are being tested in people, almost all of them "designer drugs." In 1995, only ten anticancer drugs were being tested, all either natural products or derivatives of existing drugs.

- Other transplanted tissues come from cloning and related technologies used to grow stem cells.

  – Radical new treatments for diabetes, Parkinson's disease, perhaps Alzheimer's, and many other disorders are expected to arrive within the next five to ten years.

  – Scientists at Wistar Institute, in Philadelphia, have found a strain of mice that can regrow severed limbs and damaged organs, including heart muscle. Liver cells injected into other mice enable the recipients to regenerate for at least six months.

- Brown fat, found in many animals and in human babies, is converted almost immediately to body heat; it does not cause obesity. White fat goes straight to the waist and other bulging body parts. Scientists at Boston's Dana-Farber Cancer Institute have found the gene controlling brown fat production, perhaps opening the way to end the epidemic of obesity.

- Surgeons working via the Internet can now operate on patients in remote areas, using experimental robot manipulators to handle their instruments.

  – Nanotechnology research is beginning to produce medically useful products, such as nanoparticles that can carry medication into the cell. Much more complicated devices for both diagnosis and treatment are in the concept stage.

  – Scientists are beginning to understand the fundamental processes of aging, bringing the possibility of averting the diseases of old age, and perhaps of aging itself.

Assessment:

The flow of new medical advances will not slow in the next 40 years, and probably not in the next 75.

Implications:

In the next ten years, we expect to see more and better bionic limbs, hearts, and other organs; drugs that prevent disease rather than merely treating symptoms; and body monitors that warn of impending trouble. These all will reduce hospital stays.

Outside the United States, transplants of brain cells, nerve tissue, and stem cells to aid victims of retardation, head trauma, and other neurological disorders will enter clinical use by 2012. Laboratory-grown bone, muscle, and blood cells also will be employed in transplants.

Expect also the first broadly effective treatments for viral diseases, experimental regeneration of lost or damaged human tissues, and effective ways to prevent and correct obesity.

By 2025, the first nanotechnology-based medical therapies should reach clinical use. Microscopic machines will monitor our internal processes, remove cholesterol plaques from artery walls, and destroy cancer cells before they have a chance to form a tumor.

Forecasting International believes that cloning and related methods will be accepted for the treatment of disease, though not to produce identical human beings.

Even without dramatic advances in life extension, Baby Boomers are likely to live much longer, and in better health, than anyone now expects. However, this trend could be sidetracked by the current epidemic of obesity, which threatens to raise rates of hypertension, diabetes, heart disease, and arthritis among Boomers if a cure is not found quickly enough.

However, a significant extension of healthy, vigorous life—to around 115 or 120 years as a first step—now seems more likely than no extension at all.

High development and production costs for designer pharmaceuticals, computerized monitors, and artificial organs will continue to push up the cost of health care far more rapidly than the general inflation rate. Much of these expenses will be passed on to Medicare and other third-party payers.

Severe personnel shortages can be expected in high-tech medical specialties, in addition to the continuing deficit of nurses.

A growing movement to remove barriers to stem-cell research in the United States could speed progress in this critical field. This could be expected to produce new treatments for neurological disorders such as Parkinson's and Alzheimer's disease and many other illnesses now incurable or untreatable. It also would recover one aspect of America's lost lead in science.

Implications for Terrorism:

New drugs and medical technologies are improving health and extending lives throughout the developed world—though not as effectively in the United States as in some other countries. This is likely to serve as one more "proof" of the perceived injustice that inspires terrorism in some developing lands.

In addition, even within the wealthy industrial countries, advanced medical technologies tend to be most readily available to the rich and may be almost inaccessible to the poor and socially dispossessed. While not in itself inspiring terrorism, this could easily contribute to political unrest in many Western countries. In this way, it could both make it harder to gain public cooperation for security measures and serve as one more justification for those already inclined to violence.

Expert Comments:

SMYRE (6): The ability to utilize medical advances in low cost ways in developing countries will provide the opportunity for those in poverty to improve their health. If this occurs in connection to increased economic opportunities, the pool of young people without hope from which terrorists recruit, should decline.

YOUNG: Again, with war come advances in every aspect of the conflict, including medicine. Many soldiers survive today because of technological medical advances, both during the battle and during recovery. Prosthetics and other recuperative techniques will continue to evolve.

34. THE INTERNET CONTINUES TO GROW, BUT AT A SLOWER PACE.

- In mid-2007, Internet users numbered about 1.173 billion, up just less than one-fourth in three years.

• Most growth of the Internet population is now taking place outside the United States, which is home to only 19 percent of Internet users.

  – U.S. Internet users now account for about 75 percent of the American population, a figure that has only crept higher for several years.

  – In mid-2007, the most recent available data showed 162 million Internet users in China (12.3 percent of the population), 42 million in India (3.7 percent), and 86.3 million in Japan (67.1 percent.)

  – Internet penetration is lagging badly in Africa, where only 3.6 percent of the population is online. Most Internet users are in the North African countries or in the republic of South Africa. In between, Internet connections are scarce.

• When it comes to percentage of broadband users, the United States ranks only 15th among the developed lands and 24th over all. About 47 percent of American Internet users have broadband service, compared with 90 percent in South Korea.

  – Americans also get poorer service, paying about $35 per month for download speeds of 1.5mbps and only 256kbps upload speeds. Japanese Internet users pay about the same for 50mbps service.

• In mid-2007, there were 2.66 billion IP addresses on the Internet. Of these, nearly 1.4 billion were in the United States, 251 million in the U.K., 154 million in Japan, and 116 million in China.

• E-commerce is still growing, but not as quickly as it once did.

  – In the United States, total retail sales in the first quarter of 2007 came in at about $999.5 billion, Internet retail sales at $31.5 billion, just 3.2 percent of the total and growing by only 0.1 percent of the total for the last three quarters.

  – Total Internet sales are expected to reach $116 billion for the year.

  – Sales growth, as much as 25 percent per year in 2004, is expected to slow to 9 percent annually by 2010.

• Not long ago, the Internet was predominately English-speaking. In mid-2007, English and "Chinese" (we assume this combines mainland Mandarin, Taiwanese Mandarin, and Cantonese) were tied at 31.7 percent of Internet users.

  – More than 5 percent of Netizens spoke Spanish, Japanese, German, or French.

Assessment:

This trend will continue until essentially no one in the world lacks easy access to the Internet, about 30 years by our best estimate.

Implications:

Americans will continue to dominate the Internet so long as they produce a substantial majority of Web pages—but that is not likely to be very long.

Analysts believe that Internet growth will not accelerate again until broadband service becomes less expensive and more widely available. This is a matter of government policy as much as of technology or basic costs.

Demands that the United States relinquish control of the Internet to an international body can only gain broader support and grow more emphatic as Americans make up a smaller part of the Internet population.

B2B sales on the Internet are dramatically reducing business expenses throughout the Internet-connected world, while giving suppliers access to customers they could never have reached by traditional means.

The Internet has made it much easier and cheaper to set up a profitable business. An online marketing site can be set up with just a few minutes' work at a cost of much less than $100. This is fostering a new generation of entrepreneurs.

Internet-based outsourcing to other countries has only just begun. Growth in this field will accelerate again as overseas service firms polish their English, French, and German and find even more business functions they can take on.

Cultural, political, and social isolation has become almost impossible for countries interested in economic development. Even China's attempts to filter the Internet and shield its population from outside influences have been undermined by hackers elsewhere, who provide ways to penetrate the barriers.

Implications for Terrorism:

This is a top-ten trend.

The Internet will remain a primary tool for the management of terrorist operations, particularly as encryption becomes ever more difficult to break. In addition, Internet-based crime may serve as a funding source for some terrorist organizations. In compensation, the growing availability of large quantities of public records and other information over the Internet should bring new opportunities for investigation and interdiction of terrorist activities.

Expert Comments:

ARMSTRONG: See earlier comments on technology in Trend 28.

AYERS: There is a growing interest among social scientists in the way Internet usage is changing socialization. Rather than being a tool for encouraging harmony and peaceful coexistence through increased communication, it seems that the lack of accountability behind the communication has resulted in aggressive displays of decidedly antisocial behavior. The fringes of society can locate the "like-minded" so easily that they rarely have to deal with "polar opposites" unless they seek out opportunities to do so. Those who are of a mindset to probe for differing points of view may simply be trolling for potential targets (such as blogs or chat rooms) within which to engage in deception, inject argumentation, create disruption, generate conflict, and project power in ways that were inconceivable prior to the advent of the Internet. Considering recent news reports detailing abuse and other types of violence documented by the perpetrators themselves in film and text with the specific intention of placing the evidence in "e-space," it would appear that "e-inspired" vilification and assault is on the rise. As aggressively anti-social behavior becomes "the norm" on the Internet, it is also becoming more evident in the physical world. As individuals adopt the role of agitator (whether in "e-space" or physical space) more will follow, if only out of a need for self-defense. This willful polarization of society only serves to enhance terrorist objectives. A population with large and increasing numbers of "sociopaths online" is a target-rich environment for recruitment by terrorists. If Western teens can be coerced into beating up other teens or innocent strangers for a few seconds of "fame," what else might they be capable of?

BRAY (7): Depends on what you mean by the Internet. If by "World Wide Web" yes, it is slowing down and in fact the World Wide Web is ready to die and be replaced with a newer generation concept yet unknown. The Internet itself (as infrastructure) will always exist, but in several areas (VoIP, video) the Internet has experienced dramatic, accelerating growth as more Internet users employ such technologies. So it's difficult to say generically that the Internet is growing/ slowing, but you need to consider specific technologies and why specific technologies might be slowing to make way for something newer.

CHOBAR (2): There is no way local or national policing can monitor all the Internet activity, or if policing does occur it is difficult to do well. Thus, the Internet has given terrorists a "silent," speedy, and effective method for high-speed communication and dissemination of information. This information can provide instant information from the location of troops to the actual providing of classes on building newer, more sophisticated weapons of destruction.

COSTIGAN (6): Many governments will attempt to slow the growth of the Internet or, more precisely, to decrease their population's ability to inform themselves in a direct effort to control information flow. In the face of renewed terrorist attacks, even democrat governments may seek ways to reduce information flow. For example, instead of letting the world know which group perpetrated an attack, in an effort to not boost the stature of one terrorist group a government might say it was any number of terrorist groups, but the effect will be the same: reduced information. Additionally, for terrorists, temporary defacement will remain the most likely outcome of "web attacks," but they will continue to exploit weaknesses in Internet-connected systems, potentially using the Internet to mount lightweight attacks against certain systems (supervisory control and data acquisition [SCADA] networks etc.) if the effort is manageable, cheap and, ideally, an insider is available. Were they to succeed, the damage could be considerable, but it will likely be hit or miss and the overriding question is whether they believe their time would be better spent elsewhere. Importantly, the Internet's value as the cheapest and best communications and propaganda delivery method will override any attempt to fundamentally "crash the system."

KADTKE: With the increasing spread of cyberspace, we are currently witnessing a host of new social networking capabilities and online virtual communities. We have recently seen the first cyberspace enabled-political debate, and governmental as well as private sector organizations are holding meetings and doing business in Second Life and similar virtual worlds. Sociologists observe that many users of these communities relate more closely to the virtual environment than their real lives. Are we trending toward a time when much of the world's population relates more closely to virtual online communities of interest, rather than their traditional physical social organizations or even their nation? What will be the effects as these virtual communities seek to exert political power locally and globally?

MILLER: Conducting counter-terrorism in cyberspace is clearly one of the critical battlefronts. This will increase in activity and importance.

NOLTE: The Internet will remain a source of friction in civil liberties discussions in the U.S. (and elsewhere), as we attempt to rebalance the security/privacy understanding in a very different environment. This clearly impacts the domestic security effort and may have effects internationally as well.

SMYRE (7): This is a two-edged sword related to terrorism. If the increase in the use of the Internet can bring more in poverty to be able to take care of themselves, the cause of terrorism should be reduced. On the other hand, the more on the Internet spreading knowledge of how to make bombs and how to network with other terrorists, the great the level of terrorism that could result.

SNYDER (4): At current growth rates, rising volumes of video-graphic materials transmitted via the Web are now expected to saturate the Internet's carrying capacity by 2010 to 2012, making the entire network increasingly vulnerable to hacker attack and "cybertage."

The IT press reflects a widespread professional consensus that the hacker community has long had the capacity to compromise the Internet, and there is open debate over why no serious attack on the Net has been launched since 2002. One speculative conclusion to this debate has been that the Internet is so vital to the terrorist community's capacity to organize, recruit, and operate that there is a tacit agreement NOT to shut it down.

YOUNG: Most people recognize that without the Internet, the terrorist would be without one of his most valuable tools. The Internet is used for recruiting, fund raising, communication, financial transfers, training, and proselytizing. It has become so valuable that most if not all terror groups have their own websites recognizing that they must keep in the public forefront in order to remain relevant. While the Internet may grow at a slower pace in the future, terrorists will continue to rely on its existence for their existence.

YOUNGS: Whether growing or slowing, the Internet is one of law enforcement's most valuable tools, just as it is a critical, viable tool for terrorists.

---

35. ADVANCED COMMUNICATIONS TECHNOLOGIES ARE CHANGING THE WAY WE WORK AND LIVE.

- The Internet is as much a communications medium as it is an information resource.

- Telecommuting is growing rapidly, thanks largely to e-mail and other high-tech forms of communication. About 80 percent of companies worldwide now have employees who work at home, up from 54 percent in 2003. The number of telecommuters in the United States reached an estimated 20 million in 2006.

  - AT&T says that 90 percent of its employees do some work away from the office, while 41 percent work at home one or two days per week. This saves the company a reported $180 million a year.

  - However, Millennials already have abandoned e-mail for most purposes other than communicating with "clueless" parents and grandparents. Most have adopted instant messaging and social-network Websites to communicate with their peers.

- "Podcasting"—recording college lectures, news stories, business reports, and the like for playback on the Apple iPod—allows users to listen at their convenience.

- Better communications is a major goal of many government agencies, particularly in law enforcement and disaster services, which need to coordinate the activities of many different agencies under emergency conditions.

- So-called "Web 2.0" services are building communities nearly as complex and involving as those existing wholly in the real world.

  - Second Life is a 3-D virtual world entirely built and owned by its residents. Launched in 2003, by May 2007 it had 6.8 million residents, 1.75 million of whom had logged on in the previous two months. Here in the real world, designers earn substantial incomes creating fashions and other paraphernalia for Second Life characters. One resident was banned when his character raped another "avatar" in virtual reality.

  - MySpace and Facebook have a total of more than 180 million members who form communities of friends, most of whom have never met except on the Internet.

  - A number of people have taken to wearing a small Web camera, either recording their entire lives or broadcasting them over the Internet.

Assessment:

Again, this trend has only just begun.

Implications:

E-mail promised to speed business. Instead, it absorbs more time than busy executives can afford to lose. Expect the nascent reaction against e-mail to grow as many people eliminate mailing lists, demand precise e-communications rather than open-ended conversation, and schedule only brief periods for dealing with mail.

Instant messaging is likely to be even more destructive of time for the under-thirty set.

However, e-mail is a major contributor to globalization and outsourcing, because it eliminates many of the obstacles of doing business across long distances and many time zones.

Unfortunately, e-mail and other modern communications techniques also have made possible a variety of crimes, from online fraud to some forms of identity theft.

They also make it virtually impossible to retract ill-considered statements or embarrassing online activities. Once something exists on the Internet, it is all but immortal and nearly impossible to hide.

Implications for Terrorism:

This is a top-ten trend.

See Trend 34.

Expert Comments:

Armstrong: See earlier comments on technology in Trend 28.

Ayers (8): "The enemy of the enemy is my friend." There will be ever-increasing communication and cooperation between various criminal elements (drug cartels, ID theft rings, and black-marketers), dissidents, anarchists, terrorists, and rogue elements operating from within the governments of nation-states. With global communications, war planning on a global scale—by coalitions of terrorist and criminal groups as well as coalitions of states—is not only possible, but probable. Instantaneous communications make simultaneous operations an easy task (as seen with the attacks of 9/11). Conversely, the massive amounts and differing modes of communications, combined with antiquated hierarchical structures within Western governments, will make the West more vulnerable, unless or until a method of instantaneous and ubiquitous information gathering and threat warning can be achieved. In the meantime, psychological "blowback," in the form of technology abandonment by the many, could become an issue. Communications might become more difficult because of the overwhelming nature of such, thus limiting the adoption of new technology (or the use of high-tech communications in general). Threat information might therefore ultimately be unattainable or stalled in the process of distribution.

Bray (8): See Trend 5.

Costigan (7): Of course, but there may be a backlash. Trust is easiest to establish in direct meetings. Banks and financial services companies will attempt to develop better technical systems for trust, but costs will be passed on to the consumer. With continued clever schemes by criminals, establishing a trusted (electronic) connection with your bank will become more difficult still, perhaps even too cumbersome for many. Will that lead to a desire to bank and shop locally? Despite terrorists using communications technologies much in the same ways as other groups, they will continue primary recruiting in trusted spaces—face to face, group to group, with online outreach being a method of last resort. Terrorists and other criminal elements will exploit communications technologies for spreading fear, psychological warfare, making and moving money, planning and research, performing operational assessments, recruiting and encouraging sympathy, and maybe—a low probability—for destruction.

KRIESBERG: Advanced communication technologies will foster diffusion of ideas and awareness of circumstances of others. Diaspora communities will flourish. There are more risks of intense conflicts as cultural differences have more chances to produce clashes.

But it can also generate more appreciation of diversity.

Attention to the implications of these developments is vitally important.

LaDUKE (8): Ubiquitous publication of news will increase publicity and will continue to increase the "instantaneous" stakes of changes in global public sentiment. U.S. weakness in managing with public sentiment is helping fuel sponsorship and recruitment for terrorism, which is being used as a tool to dissuade U.S. interests.

The military is waging war with what Barnett calls a "leviathan force," and he contends that the military needs a network of "system administrators" (http://www.ted.com/index.php/talks/view/id/33) to manage humanitarian aid and public sentiment.

Communications in the military tactical sense is not designed to support the kind of culturally sensitive communications that need to occur to change public sentiment in cultures that are very foreign to our own. Essentially, the discipline of public relations needs to increase dramatically within the military and the defense department and globally thread the needle between silence and propaganda.

SANDERS (8): See comments under "Complexity and the Future of Terrorism" in Appendix C.

STEELE: Harnessing the "Medici Effect" [Johansson, Frans, *Medici Effect: What Elephants and Epidemics Can Teach Us About Innovation* Cambridge: Harvard Business School Press, 2006] Proactively searching for the interaction effects and using multivariate thinking in the interaction of Proteus "planes of influence" might increase potential target awareness. The world as a complex cross-impact matrix, not just wildcard thinking.

TAN: This trend also facilitates the spread of radical Islamist and indeed any type of millenarian/apocalyptic ideology in this post-modernist age. It creates a virtual world where these ideologies take root and grow, affecting the real world through its ability to self-radicalize individuals, link up cells, develop terrorist ideas and plans, and help organize actual attacks. The most insidious is the ability to enable a worldwide network of jihadists to emerge and develop. How do you better contain this trend?

YOUNG: There is hardly any terrorist who is not familiar with the common cell phone or satellite phone. As encryption becomes more in the public domain, terrorist communications will become more difficult to intercept.

www.ingramcontent.com/pod-product-compliance
Lightning Source LLC
Chambersburg PA
CBHW081828280526
45789CB00007B/2379